BLOOD, SWEAT, LEATHER & TEARS

by Johna Johnson

BLOOD, SWEAT, LEATHER AND TEARS
by
Johna Johnson

An Old Dogs Publishing Paperback.
First published in Great Britain in 2022 by Old Dog Publishing
5 Hogshill Lane, Cobham KT11 2AG
1st Edition 2022
Copyright © 2022 Johna Johnson

CREDITS
Cover illustrator: www.pippip.net

EDITORIAL
Craig Brackenridge

INSTAGRAM AND ALL ROUND GOOD GUY
Steve Piper

For Olly & Alfie P IOW

You CAN teach an old dog new tricks

Danny DC   PjH

KP • Pappy • JP
Danny Decourtelle • Eddie Marsan • Mick Lynes • Dom Whellams
Callum Sammon and Jodie Richardson • Helen Edwards • Mark Rocky Lowther
Lee Bowen • RTMP • Steve Pullen
Garry Bushell - Bushell is the best-dressed man in town
(you can say that again, the scruffy sod!)

Dave Barbe Drummer of
Adam and The Ants 1977 -1979

Johna has put together a painstaking log of a magical time we all shared. Going back through those dates and events, brought back some great memories, triumphs and disasters. Of course, my experience differed in as much as I was playing, but it was made the more special because of the lads and lassies that followed us.
I always felt, more than playing for the band, I was playing for the fans (some of who are good friends to this day), because in a way, I was one.

An absolute honour, ladies and gentlemen.

Dave Barbe Drummer of Adam and the Ants 1977 -79

Adam and the Ants: Introduction

I want to dedicate this book to all the Ants crew and The Bradford punks and all the punks I met around the country in those heady days of punk rock 1977 onwards. I would gladly live those days again but do more of it

I specially want to dedicate the book the people who are no longer with us. Ants Crew: John Vick, Gary O'Connell, Mathew Ashman, Mark 'Kid' Ryan, Grahame Stevens, Brendan [Mel] Mellon, Graham Harris, Dillon aka 'the Hoss', Erica Howlett, Paul 'Pony' Kirby, Garry Orange, Metin, Jerry Lamont and Womble.

Bradford Punks who are no longer with us : Big Alex Simpson, Karen Barnes, Little Louise Duckworth, John Jankowicz, John Tilliard, Dave Wilcox [The Negatives], Johnny Bee, Eddie Reidy and Dino Christo, Big Jane English, Steve Hussein, Ashton Filby, Simon Pollard [Wrist Action] Harvey Mitchell, Andrew Firth, Alan Price [Tallulah], Gary [Elvis] Normington.

The rest of the Ants crew: Martin Pope, Duncan Grieg, Jon Srobat, Fiona Cartledge, Boxhead, Kevin Tredrea, Mark Townsend, Kevin McGovern, Mark Harding, Mark Hutchings, Chuck Grinder, Jon 'Chukka' Webb, Steve Shaw, Paul 'Pony' Kirby, Justin Semmens, Robbo Johnson, Paul Wannless, Fiona Cartledge, Garry Orange, Dave Patten, Ian Rouault, Mick Mercer, Tony D, Jane Suck, Jerry Lamont, Stevie Parker, Paul Delaney, Cetin, Metin, Joe Kollar, Huw Griffiths, Godfrey, Dean Parkinson, Dave Holloway, Clapham Sarah Downer, Nicky Stephenson. Mannie Zerafa ,Bradley Hall, Tom Vague, Kevin [Crazy K] Langton, Terry Smith, Daniel [Spud] Graham, Kevin Addison, Frenchy Groder, Fergus Crockford, Russell RJ Jones, Ady Gunn, Paola Mazzanti, Clanger, Robert Raymond [aka Longfellow] and anyone who's names I've forgotten.

A special mention to Duncan Grieg, Martin Pope, Pete Vague, Robert Raymond aka Longfellow, Rosie Mellows, 'Boxhead' David Ager, Robbo, Paolo Mazzanti in Milan, Marco 'Frenchy' Groder, Val Brogden, Tom Vague and Kevin Tredrea for help from their memory banks, and the rest of the Ants crew. I want to also thank Julia and Brian Collier, Simon Atherley, Steve O'-Conner and the creative writing group, Mike O'Leary, etc, also Marcus from Unity/GCL for his support in the early days, Stef Morrel, Jayne Kennedy, Rowena Harding, Jessica Johnson, Vince Luttman for helping to edit the book and encouragement.

Thanks to Table Talk Facebook group. If anyone wants to read more about the time Adam and the Ants played in Italy in October 1978 then you can get Paolo's excellent book 'Whip Avant-garde' which he sells on eBay.
Also thanks to Jo Gahan for use of the Adam Pic from Chelmsford, Gino Silano for the inspiration for the book title.

An Introduction
By Johnny Bivouac Guitarist of
Adam and the Ants 1977 -78

Glam has lost its lustre, prog rock is disappearing up its own backside and disco rules the mainstream. There's something called pub rock which has a certain back to basics charm, but seems to consist of bands made up of older, long haired, bearded men in denim. Bolan and Bowie they are not. In our outpost of north London, rumours filter through of something called 'punk' but we only get it second hand initially via the NME and Sounds. The Melody Maker isn't interested at this stage and The Sun peddles the predictable black bin liner/safety pins/outrage angle. Then, one day at Mark 'The Kid' Ryan's house, we listen to 'Anarchy In The UK' and our world changes forever. Cut to a few months later and I'm onstage at the legendary Marquee club in Soho playing guitar with Adam and the Ants. The crowd is going absolutely apeshit.

The band is on fire. Adam is a fantastic performer and has the crowd in the palm of his hand. If I was there now, I'd pinch myself but at the time I was just floating along with an air of slight disbelief and not really taking it in. Johna's recounting in (chapter four?) of this book of the Ants Marquee residency gigs is the best description I've ever read of it and brought it all back to me. He captures the joy, the madness, the violence and the sheer ecstasy of the whole event, a coming together of a young tribe who had found a voice at last. It could be a dangerous time – violence was never far away and menace hung in the air between the various factions – Teddy Boys, Soul Boys, Greasers, Skinheads, even the hippies sneered at punks – but also a time of freedom of expression in all manner of forms that would change the world forever. The barricades had been smashed open. Johna captures that time evocatively and in a very personal way in this book. It took me back. What a time to be alive. *

Johnny Bivouac (aka John Beckett) played guitar for Adam and the Ants between 1977 and 1978. He went on to have a successful career in music and film and is now mainly working as a composer and music supervisor for film and TV, but still rocks out on occasion..

An Introduction
By Popey Original Ant kid 1977-80.

Who could have possibly known as I approached the Marquee club on that cold October evening in 1977 with my old school friends Jon and Dunc; that by 9.30 that night our life's Journey and focus would dramatically change course.

We had intended to check out The Buzzcocks but with the club only half full, The support band The Ants took to the stage bringing a huge personality and atmosphere. They looked amazing, Adam, especially with all the make-up and leather.

After a few songs, the backstage door at the rear of the stage opened and the Punk icon Jordan appeared, The woman who everybody was terrified of when they visited Seditionaries.

She strode to the mike and screamed one song "Lou" then departed- It was proper theatre.

The music was so powerful, fast, dangerous and intoxicating,

Adam's movements were so aggressive and athletic. The set concluded with Adam smashing his guitar to bits as the band left the stage, a discarded piece of which I kept for years. During the performance most of the audience in the hall was pretty unresponsive there was just one individual throwing himself around at the front - that was Justin- I was keen to join him and in a month Jon, Dunc and I were back at the Ants at the Marquee, down the front throwing ourselves about. I had already seen plenty of punk bands by this time but The Ants were different. I had found my band.

We made it our business to try to get to as many Ants shows as possible over the next three years. So Dunc Jon and I, The three musketeers and Fiona Cartledge started travelling to gigs outside London using the National Express coaches to get to Bristol, Nottingham, Manchester and Brighton among others. Four punk school kids in homemade clothes arriving into hostile territories covered in Jordan make-up and getting a mixed reaction - bad and extremely bad. We were not deterred.

We had stolen some fencing clobber from school and sprayed the band's name and our favourite songs like Fat Fun, Hampstead, Send a Letter to Jordan and Puerto Rican on the padded jackets and trousers. These songs remained all-time favourites of mine - We even gave Jordan a fencing mask but I'm not sure she could get all her hair inside it.

All the Ants imagery, badges, flyers It felt we had our own scene within a scene, Applying Jordan style make-up in the Northern Line tube windows once it went underground after East Finchley, making clothes, I remember the first time I was staying away from my family home, punk is in its infancy, the adventurous 14-year-old, hanging with friends, being independent, using squats in Belsize Park and Leicester Square and throwing in the odd cameo appearance at school.

Within months there were other regular fans, bitten by the same bug as me gradually joining us, travelling nationally from city to city loving the music and the exhilaration and danger of the gigs. After a fairly short time, there were loads of us- the tide had turned- we could hold our ground on our travels and in London, The locals no longer bullied us. We were untouchable, a hundred strong.

Those Early times were just the best.The band were so accessible to us from the start, within a few gigs we had become firm friends. We were always on the guest list. I ended up weight training with Dave Barbe at his home and we all hung out with Matthew Ashman for frames of snooker and for parties at his flats. Adam was always a bit more aloof but always spoke about us the ant fans warmly. From the start, the originally terrifying Jordan looked after us- made sure we were safe. In late 1977 the band and road crew even gave us a lift back to London after their first Brighton show was cancelled.

With such happiness and camaraderie what could go wrong?

Well, nothing lasts forever- Jordan left, Adam became very popular in the underground scene. We found ourselves fighting off hundreds of middle of the road fans trying desperately to preserve our smaller niche scene.

It was an unwinnable battle - besides Adam, was thrown out of his own band and had his eyes on a different future. In 1980 The Dandy Highwayman was being created. It was over. The Invasion tour followed where early ant fans Martian Dance fittingly supported the band they had followed loyally.

The Ants. It was the final hurrah. Adam's people advised Adam to distance himself from us and the trouble that seemed to follow the band around. Many of us were already queuing to get tattoos covered up and to look to pastures new.

I
KINGS OF THE WILDFRONTIER:
UNPLUG THE JUKEBOX

'A new Royal Family
A wild nobility
We are the family

I feel beneath the white
There is a redskin suffering
From centuries of taming

No method in our madness
Just pride about our manner
Antpeople are the warriors
Antmusic is the banner!'

I'm sitting on my settee at home, wondering what has happened to my life. I'm thinking to myself: 'It's been a really bad time of late. I've lost my job, my girlfriend's left me - even my trusty pet dog Herbert has left me. He was last seen heading towards the countryside with a huge bone in his mouth. Maybe he had had enough of all of the arguments with Sammy?' I continue wondering: 'How could this happen to me? I listened to all of the right people. The people who told me to keep doing the right things and everything would turn out alright.' Well, I'm sitting here and know that everything is far from alright. I'm drinking a can of medication Stella Artois, wallowing in my self-pity and trying to think of a time that was as bad as this. After some reflection, I can't think of a worse time in my life. I'm left feeling fatigued and worn out just by thinking about it all. I reach simultaneously for the remote and turn on the TV.

Perhaps through miraculously bad timing - it's right there in front of me; the answer to my question. There's a man dancing around on a TV music programme, dressed up as a dandy highwayman. It's Adam and the Bloody Worth-

Its? - as I ended up calling them after they went pop. As I watch him gyrating on the TV, something still looks familiar. It's the dance moves I think; as every so often he twitches or jerks a leg that same way, the very same way that I'd seen a thousand and one times before, all those times I'd been crammed into a tight, sweaty club, watching him and admiring his posture, pose and gyrations.

Suddenly, the pain, anguish and anger of those times all comes flooding back to me. Oh, the indignities I've suffered at the hands of that band. The band I once loved, who have since become known to the whole world. A band that were so special, so unique, so… Now, it's just pain. I start to recall the lovely ladies I'd met in the bars after Monsieur Ant's transformation had taken place. We'd always get along famously until the conversation moved onto music. I recall a conversation I once had with a lady in a bar.

She'd asked me: "So who's your favourite band then?"

"Adam and the Ants," I'd replied, followed closely by, "But not that Adam and the Ants, not the one in the charts." I'd start to back track in an embarrassing attempt to explain myself. "Well, technically it is that band, but a different, better version; the original version were a band that looked cool as fuck, a band who sung about sex, Futurism, the day they met God, about…"

"Oh, I really like Adam and the Ants as well," she exclaimed.

"Well, yes," I continued, "But you don't like the real Adam and the Ants, and you don't know the real Adam and the Ants. You couldn't understand. It's different."

I remember feeling all that frustration swelling up inside again, trying to explain what seemed like an almighty chasm: the difference between the two bands. They, the original Ants, were a punk band, not a 'Top of the Flops' band, not something to be spat from the lips of Jimmy Savile or Noel fucking Edmonds. "The only thing that connects both of the bands is Adam", I continued in my effort to explain: "You see, the real Adam and the Ants are now called Bow-wow-wow, and instead of Adam they've got a pretty young female vocalist called Annabella Lwin…" As I continued my sermon I began to lose the will to live, and whatever attraction my new acquaintance possessed had suddenly disappeared. I already sensed that things were going nowhere - she looked increasingly fidgety, perhaps even a little bored, and with each sentence I spoke, I felt the hole that my words were digging was becoming deeper and deeper. It seemed as though what had begun 5, 10, 15 minutes, or even an hour before, was drawing to a close. Damn,

I had such great plans, I thought. Things hadn't even developed beyond a chat in a bar. Come to think of it, I didn't even know her name. Yet there I was getting all cosy, thinking, albeit for a few seconds, that I might have pulled here… damn this conversation, and any thoughts I'd had of hooking up with this girl. There's nothing like getting ahead of yourself is there?

"Look," I'd said. "Adam and the Ants are my band not yours. How many times did you see them?" Before the lady had even had time to reply, but knowing full well she probably hadn't even seen them play live, I said, "Well… I've seen them so many times I can't even remember how many, 50, 60, 70 - possibly a hundred, who knows? We, the Ants crew, hitched all over the country just to watch them. We starved. We slept in ditches. We crashed in motorway services' cafes. We got attacked everywhere we went. All of this and much more, just to watch the band we loved. Would you do that for Adam and the Ants?" Again, I left no space for a reply. "Exactly, you see. This was our band, and we've put the hours of dedica-tion in to prove it." The girl yawned, finished her drink, and went off to dance to Depeche Mode or the Human League or Howard bloody Jones. So that was that; another failed attempt. Adam and the Bloody Worth-Its? put me through so much pain and now they were ruining my sex life. That's what you get for loyalty. My memory fast tracks forwards, and I'm still sitting here on the settee, reflecting upon that encounter. A chance encounter, all those years ago. I say all those years ago but it was only three - but it feels like a lifetime now. I could just imagine (as it seemed I'd done a million times since then) arguing about which version of Adam and the Ants was best. I'll bet she had secret pictures of Adam on her toilet wall. There were plenty of other embarrassing moments, like the times I played football and everybody could see the Ants tattoos on my legs, which made them laugh and jeer. The opposition fans would start wolf whistling at me every time I got into a dangerous position to score, in the hope that this would put me off. They would shout insults or start singing 'Stand and Deliver' or one of the other pop songs.

They'd shout, "Oi, mate! What does 'Ant music for a future age' mean? Are you an alien or something?" But if I did score, oh, how I would proudly shout: "1-0 to the real Adam and the Ants."

These memories also brought back to me the time that I was locked up in a de-tention centre. I had written to Adam, as I did on a regular basis, to keep up to date with upcoming gigs and record releases. Back then, Adam was always good at communicating with his fans. Even though he himself didn't have a pot to piss in, he would always find the time, paper, and the cost of a stamp and envelope to write back. Anyhow, I was sat in the dining hall of the detention centre and the screw who was handing out the mail stood over me and bawled in his loudest voice, "Johnstone, you have a letter from someone called Timmy and the Termites!" Everyone in the hall laughed. I wasn't laughing though. I fucking hated it. That was my band, you bar steward.

So exactly why, then, did Adam ask Malcolm McLaren for career advice? As far as I was concerned, he didn't need McLaren's advice. He had it all already. Adam wrote great songs; his band looked great, they made great records, the band's artwork and imagery were superb. And as for his lyrics? Wow, those lyrics were an education in themselves. I'd certainly never heard of Friedrich Nietzsche, or Filippo Marinetti or Alan Jones before Adam started singing about them. As far as I was concerned, following the Ants was very educational. In fact, the whole punk movement was educational for me. I came across a lot of subject matter that wasn't covered in our school curriculum which was a lot more informative and interesting plus it was an exciting way to educate yourself. There was no motivation needed .You could call it life skills, I guess. Best of all though, and perhaps the most overlooked, was the dedicated and hardcore following the band had. So you see, for me at least, Adam already had it all. And then, to make matters worse, McLaren charged him £2,000, apparently.

Cut back to the present again and I'm still watching the TV. It's halfway through the video. I can't relate to what I'm seeing. It's over-the-top pop. It's boring and meaningless. How do you go from hardcore punk to hardcore pop? They were two extremes. Incensed and trembling with rage, I get up and put my foot through the TV. I sit down again and feel even worse. 'Well, that achieved a lot,' I tell myself morosely and if that's not bad enough, I'm nearly at the end of my can of medication. I feel an almost urgent need for another one, so I get up and go to the fridge. Inside are stashed about half a dozen cans. I grab one and slam the fridge door behind me as I turn away. I return to my seat, twist open the ring pull on the can of golden nectar and proceed to drink it. It goes down like a dream. I lie slowly back, begin to bask in the warm radiance of alcohol and my mind wanders again.

This time it's back to Sunday 9th of November 1980 and the pain I'd felt. That was the date of my last ever Ants gig, besides the gig at Hull. I don't count that gig because I never went in, luckily for me. I went to Hull with 40 other people in an articulated lorry owned by New Model Army. We got there and I was the only one who'd been able to get on the guest list as all the tickets had sold out so we all went back home again. I was glad of this because someone had set fire to part of the venue in an attempt to get in and my name had been put forward as the culprit. Luckily I had forty witnesses after the police asked to speak to me. Anyway, the day of the final Ants gig had been a rubbish day from the start. The Soldier Ants (what some of the hardcore fans called ourselves now - although not everyone liked the name) had landed in Liverpool from various parts of the country for the start of the new 'Kings of the Wild Frontier' tour. It was a promotion for the new album which went under the same name. None of us had heard the album yet, and I was presuming that the three new tracks which Adam sang on the 'Invasion' tour: 'Kings of the Wild Frontier' (the title track); 'Killer in the Home' and 'Ants Invasion' - which were all decent songs - were all going to be on the new album, so we were slightly optimistic it was going to be a decent album.

We arrived at the station, where we were met by two old Ants stalwarts and ex-Ants roadies: Robbo and Boxhead. Boxhead had perhaps the finest quiff in all of Liverpool, his home town. Robbo was as hard as nails, a notorious northerner, and again he was someone who'd been around the Ants since the start. Those two funny buggers were always a joy to be around. They escorted us to the venue, which was a massive old theatre at the end of a crumbling street. Firstly, we went to make sure that we were on the guest list as had been promised. We asked the lady in the booth if she had the guest list:

"Yep," she replied, and asked for our names. "Err… it's Johnny, OC, Mel and Brinsley", I replied. Yep, it was all confirmed. We were all on the list. Great! Falcon Stuart, the old X-Ray Spex and now the new Ants manager, had fulfilled his promise and put us on the list. But, as we soon discovered, although he had put us on the list, we'd been bundled up to the top floor of this massive theatre. The support band started up and we couldn't see a blooming thing. We spent most of their set trying to figure out ways of getting past the bouncers to go down to the ground floor. Anyhow, eventually we did it, by hook or by crook. We did so by climbing down one by one. I got down one of the floors by the stairs and then ended up dangling by my hands and dropping from the first floor balcony to the ground floor. I remember thinking, it's a good job they had the sense to take at least a few of the ground floor seats out. Bloody good job that; otherwise, instead of that great Merseyside tradition of 'never walking alone', I would be never walking again.

So, while a few of us literally did dangle our way down, a few more blagged their way downstairs by stealing or borrowing band members' or roadies' passes and then returning to use the same passes again to take another two or three more people down. We also used this same trick with the passes to get people in who we knew who didn't have a ticket. After all, a guest list can only be so long. Anyhow, apart from this small space that I and a few others had dropped into, when we looked around at ground floor level, it was an all seated venue. It was so different from the places I'd seen the band perform on so many occasions - spit-and-sawdust pub back rooms, places where they didn't even sell tickets, they just took yer money on the door. So, with all these seats, there would definitely be no dancing tonight.

As the auditorium started filling up, we gradually became aware of the audience who were filing in. The audience seemed to comprise largely of 15-year-old schoolgirls with white stripes across their noses, which may be all well and good if that's your thing - but it certainly wasn't ours! And all those kids were all dressed like bloomin' Adam clones. This wasn't, or at least hadn't been such a bad thing because Adam was stylish, and we'd all taken fashion tips off him in the past, but no one had ever gone to a gig dressed as Adam. And it wasn't so much about the age of the audience - Dunc and Popey and some of the others were only 13 when they started following the Ants - it was about people with a different mindset and attitude to ours.

These people weren't like us on any level. They represented the norm, the status quo or whatever you want to call it. We were trying to break out of this and create something different, so to find ourselves, after all the dedication and loyalty, back in an environment we were trying to break away from was an anathema to me. It was awful and it just didn't look or feel right anymore. To make matters worse, the tour hadn't even started yet. This was the first date! It just felt like we were no longer needed. Suddenly we, his old and dedicated fan base, were now surplus to requirements.

When the gig started, the whole tone of the event had changed. As expected, 'Kings of the Wild Frontier', 'Killer in the Home' and 'Ants Invasion' were included. Some of the new songs we were hearing for the first time sounded like an 'Ant invasion of the American wild west'. There was definitely a western theme going on, but the new songs didn't have an edge to them - they sounded too jolly, even poppy, or sounded like they belonged in a musical: 'Feed Me to the Lions', complete with interwoven 'Lawrence of Arabia' theme, 'Jolly Roger'… 'Human Beings'… 'Los Rancheros'… I'm all for evolving or moving forward but in my opinion the new songs are not as good as the songs they are replacing. Adam has clearly changed direction musically and his new songs are probably more accessible to the wider public. After what McLaren did maybe Adam sees it as a contest to be more successful, which means you have to compete in the charts. So that's where he is heading?

I was feeling out of place in this gig. We were outnumbered by the White Stripers (which we decided to call the band's new fans) and I think I truly, finally realized it was all over when Adam suddenly stopped the gig halfway through a song in order to berate the band. He said: "Come on, we're professional now. You can do better than that." As if the band hadn't been professional for at least the past year previous. The band are good. They can all play; particularly Marco on guitar - so there was no need for that. It didn't bother me if people made mistakes and I don't like perfection anyway. It seemed inhuman to be perfect. It wasn't what punk was about. It was about having a go. That seemed more human to me, and more unifying, because perfection doesn't exist. I think I will always remember that moment in my head as the final moment of my life following Adam and the Ants. It felt like the ultimate insult to us; admonishing his band to 'do better' for the benefit of a largely pop-orientated 12 to 15-year-old audience. The evidence was right in front of our eyes. Adam had deserted us. If ever it were needed, this was our cue to leave the gig. We, the old fans, turned, looked at one another and almost en-masse walked towards the exit. We would never return.

Outside of the venue we met a then unknown young musician called Ian Astbury, who relocated himself to Bradford a couple of weeks later where he joined a local band called Violation.

Violation were a Bradford Punk that started around late 78/early 79 .Original Members were Aki Newaz , Mick " Oxfam Harry Brady . Mick Isles and Barry Jepson. I think Aki's introduction to working with bands was maybe when His Brother Rab ,Me and Tim Calvey formed a punk band in 78 called Plastic Bucket and the Abortions.

We were doing it because we noticed bands got more attention from female punks, and we wanted to be more popular with the ladies . Firstly we had shirts

made with Plastic Bucket and the Abortions wrote on the back .That was my con-
tribution to the band . but it had the opposite effect We got no ladies interested
in us and often a negative snarl from some . We some how managed to do some
rehearsals which was I think down to Aki .He got the instruments and rehearsal
place which was a church near his parents shop . We had a couple of rehearsals
and gave it up as a bad job . Aki seems to think we played a gig but I can't remember it .I'm not saying we influenced Aki in any way because we would have
been the first band at that time ,but Aki went on to put together a proper band
with proper musicians and we were yesterdays Chip paper.

I think Violation played about 10 gigs in and around Bradford .West Yorkshire
with OC taking over from Mick Brady halfway through the year and then he decided to call it a day .Then Ian Astbury came and joined them and changed their
name to Southern Death Cult .

When Ian joined they changed their name to Southern Death Cult. After leaving the theatre, we all retired to a bar across the road - there must have been about
50 of us altogether, from London and its surrounding areas, along with Middlesbrough, Bradford, Bournemouth, Liverpool, Newcastle, Birmingham and all over
the UK.

As we reflected upon the pantomime we had just witnessed, the scene began to
resemble a funeral, as we all knew we would never see the Ants again. We started
to get drunk. We were pissed off about the Ants; pissed off about all that time in-
vested in our band, a band that we all assumed would always be there for us, in
much the same way that we had been there for them. It felt like four years' wasted
time. Time and time again we had shown loyalty. We had been loyal, so why
wasn't the loyalty being repaid? Now a lot of little things began to fall into place
and make sense. Adam had been keeping his distance from us since the 'Invasion'
tour. He had been a bit aloof but, in hindsight, if I'm honest with myself, it was
already over long before then, way back on the New Years Eve of 1979. We'd
thought it was a joke, a piss-take, when Adam got the band to do a cover of the
Village People's 'YMCA' and yet in reality he was sealing the deal with that song,
'kissing goodbye to us', the original Ant fans. Coming to think about it, Dave
Barbe had told us two years' previously, backstage after a gig somewhere, that
Adam wanted to be famous, so we had been forewarned. We'd chosen not to listen, and now it had become a reality.

The pub we were getting drunk in was starting to bear a not uncanny resemblance to the last days in the Berlin bunker. The ladies' toilets were full of male Soldier Ants, lines of coke, speed, beer and of course the beautiful Ant ladies with their long green trench coats, suspenders, sexy lingerie and little else. One girl didn't even wear the lingerie; she said she "liked to be accessible at a moment's notice." Some Soldier Ants also wore Seditionaries' bondage trousers, which had a continuous zip running from the fly front to the small of the back, apparently designed specifically for accessible sexual encounters. I'm sitting at the bar and in the mirror behind the bar I see a girl in the background who looks like Simone. I look round in disbelief, thinking to myself: "It can't be Simone." I stare at the girl but after closer inspection I realise it's not Simone…well it can't be, can it; Simone's dead. But this girl is a dead ringer for her. The girl glances over, notices I'm staring, and turns away.

Ah yes, the lovely Simone. Oh how I miss her, with her platinum blonde spiky hair and her Kabuki make-up (modelled on the Kabuki stage make up that Adam wore Kabuki make up til April 79). I remembered the time when I was fortunate enough to spend a passionate night with her in a sex club off Tottenham Court Road after the Rock Garden gig. Sadly, that was to be a one-off incident, despite however much I would have liked to have continued that relationship. But Simone didn't really do boyfriends, she simply took what she needed when she needed it. Simone was the Ant girl that every Soldier Ant desired, but Simone played it careful. She could afford to pick and choose. It was always Simone's shout, and on that one occasion, from that point of view, I was very lucky indeed. Well, we all deserve a break once or twice in our lives, don't we? I'm sure others have had the privilege as well but if they have they haven't mentioned it, which seems to differ with other conquests. Oh well.

So, as the night wore on, there were people in the bogs shagging for all their worth, as though they were never going to see each other again. I thought - maybe we wouldn't? Who knew?

I heard Johnny Aggro shout "Bend over," and then the sound of a single slap.

I asked "Who you in there with Johnny boy?"

A silence followed, and then, a "Fuck off, you nosey bar steward." I walked out of the bogs and back into the bar.

I noticed Brinsley was being his usual self, going around winding people up saying, "I haven't seen you since Chester." It was some vague reference he had cribbed from a porno magazine about a travelling salesman having sex with suburban housewives. He was always topical. There was a large, local, body builder guy standing at the bar, with his very attractive girlfriend. Popey, Dangerous D (or just Dunc, depending on the mood), Johnny Aggro, Passive Pete and I were all stood salivating, looking on (so, as it turned out was every other bloke in the pub save for those already busy elsewhere). All the girls, it seemed, were starting to feel a bit insecure, glaring menacingly at the beautiful woman, and mumbling things along the lines of "what's she got I haven't?" Their comments were seemingly falling on deaf ears. En masse, all the girls suddenly headed for the door, shouting expletives loudly as they left.

Brinsley, always the 'erudite cheeky charmer', walked across to a vase resting on the side of the bar. He picked out some plastic flowers and proceeded towards where the body builder bloke and his stunning lady friend were standing. He wore a grin like Alice's Cheshire cat on his little face, knowing all the pub's male eyes were fixed admiringly upon the body builder's lady friend. Suddenly, Brinsley squeezed in between Body Builder and his lady friend and handed the lady the plastic flowers, saying in a child-like voice, "These are for you." The lady smiled at Brinsley and Brinsley basked in his consummate moment of glory. Body Builder looked embarrassed and didn't know what to do. Brinsley was so small in stature that had Mr. Muscle the body builder punched him, it would have made him look like a bully. And then, if Body Builder had resorted to violence, it would have been a very big mistake, because make no mistake, there were enough Soldier Ants in the bar - and trust me they could handle themselves. The poor bloke wouldn't have stood a chance.

Mr. Muscle recognized he was in a total no-win situation, his muscles seemingly sagging as his chest deflated, and rapidly decided to remove himself and his lady friend from the bar. As the couple made a less-than-strategic withdrawal, they left to a chorus of baying wolf whistles and heckling shouts of "Leave your lass here mate, we'll look after her!" As the evening wore on, we ended up getting totally pissed and chanting old Ants' songs: "10, 9, 8, 7, 6, 5, 4, 3, 2, 1, at the Screen on the Green now." Everyone charged into each other like the mock fighting at the gigs; 'Fall In'. This is one of the Ants' oldest and liveliest tracks. If there was ever going to be trouble then this song would usually kick it off. But then, it wasn't the only one; far from it. There was 'Kick' and 'Red Scab' among others. Maybe it was the intensity or the frantic pace of the songs that sent people over the top? It's been said in the past that some people used to turn up at Ants gigs just to watch the crowd and observe the violent dancing. And yes, those early shows were violent on occasion, but it looked like people were having nervous breakdowns and rolling about on the floor in an epileptic fit.

As the evening drew to its ultimate and final end everyone was feeling quite depressed again, even with the drink, and believe me, plenty was consumed. Confusion reigned, as people wondered about the future of the Ants. The new single 'Ant Music' was playing on the jukebox, but appeared to be stuck. "Unplug the jukebox and do us all a favour", sung Adam on the jukebox repeatedly. Ironic? Yep, but also ultimately uncalled for. It was both grating and annoying to us old fans, and it just made us miss our band even more. And still Adam continued to bleat out the repeated hook, "Unplug the jukebox and do us all a favour, that music's lost its taste so try another flavour", which prophecy looked like leaving us with no choice. And so, as if by some magic, a strange, albeit some might say predictable quirk of fate, Popey did exactly that. He walked over, picked the jukebox up, unplugging it in the process and did us all the very considerable favour of launching it out through the pub doorway and into the bloody street. A mighty roar went up from the Ant people as we celebrated. Whilst still basking in the euphoria of the moment, the final bell sounded for closing time. We said our last goodbyes and vowed to stay in touch. There were genuine tears of sadness that night. We had been through a lot together; the battles of Birmingham, of Middlesbrough, of Huddersfield, of Salisbury and High Wycombe to name just a few, and of course the various encounters whenever the Ants played on the London circuit, which seemed to consist of nothing but fighting right-wing fascist skinheads.

All these years later, I wonder what everyone is doing now. I just can't get their faces out of my mind. In those final moments before I drift off into my lager induced coma. Suddenly I'm standing outside the 'Man in the Moon' pub, bang next to the old punk meeting place the Beaufort Market on the King's Road. Someone hands me a flyer; it reads: '11th, 18th and 25th May 1977. Live at the Man in the Moon pub, Kings Road, SW3 X-Ray Spex supported by the Ants.' This was the gig where I was to meet my mate Sunni from Bradford. He'd come down to see X-Ray Spex play and I'd said I would meet him afterwards.

II
ANARCHY IN THE UK

'Right now, ha, ha, ha, ha, ha,
I am an anti-Christ
I am an anarchist
Don't know what I want
But I know how to get it
I want to destroy the passerby
'Cause I want to be anarchy
No dogsbody'

After I'd seen some footage of the Pistols wearing these fantastic-looking clothes I thought I would like to wear some, so I tried to find out where to buy them. It turns out the shop was run by the Sex Pistols' manager Malcolm McLaren and his girlfriend, Vivienne Westwood. I had to look for images of the band, going through music magazines and fanzines to find the information we needed, so it meant reading all the Sex Pistols interviews again for clues. Eventually we found all the information we needed: Seditionaries, 430 King's Road, Chelsea, SW3. That's where it was and that's where I was heading as soon as I was able.

Finally everything was sorted with work. I had taken two days holiday and had saved up about £150 for the journey. I gathered that the clothes from Seditionaries were more expensive than your normal clothes, and I hoped to see a couple of punk bands while I was there too. I was wondering what would be the best form of travel. I had been thinking of hitching but then it was my first trip to London and I might get lost. Not only that but I would have to carry lots of stuff back with me, hopefully, so I decided to go by coach. When I got home from work on the Tuesday night I had a bath, and sorted out what I might need for two days in London. I was so excited and I went to bed early so I would have plenty of sleep. The next day I actually woke up before the alarm clock went off at 8am. I jumped straight out of bed, put on my best punk attire which consisted of a nice charity shop jacket, a home-made spray painted T-shirt with zips, and some trousers which had come with a home-made bondage kit, bought from X Clothes in Leeds.

X Clothes sold these T-shirts with blood spattered limbs and old boots like car crash victims, which were awful. I never bought one - they seemed like a cheap shock tactic. But they did sell these home-made bondage kits which consisted of a few straps and buckles that you sewed onto your clothes any way you liked. Quite a few of us bought these. One of the reasons for buying clothes in London was because charity shops were becoming so expensive to buy from now; all the punks were shopping there so they took advantage and started putting up their prices so we couldn't afford to shop there much now. I thought I might as well have a look down in London, particularly at Seditionaries. I grabbed my bag and was straight out of the door on my way to the coach station. The coach was due to leave at 8.45. I arrived with 10 minutes to spare, so I grabbed a paper and some food for the journey. I was so excited I wished I could just beam myself down to London Star Trek style, so that I could just crack on with absorbing punk culture. The coach arrived on time and I boarded. It was quite packed, but I managed to get a corner seat at the back and, armed with my cassette player, I sat down to relax for my four hour journey.

That journey seemed to take forever and we stopped at Leicester Forest Services. We stretched our legs and boarded the bus again for the final part of the journey. After a further two hours we arrived at Brent Cross. Then we were heading into London - I could feel it. London was massive in comparison to Bradford or Leeds - you could see all these big buildings. It just felt bigger. As the coach headed deeper into London, there was such a contrast between the housing on the outskirts - seemingly typical suburbia, just like we might find in the more exclusive parts of Bradford - except here it was row after row after row of semi-detached housing in leafy suburbs. As we grew nearer, though, the landscape seemed to gradually change, until it appeared darker and more menacing. Boarded-up houses seemed commonplace back then. Crumbling, high rise flats were everywhere; it started to feel almost claustrophobic. All the buildings looked taller than anywhere else I'd ever seen, giving the effect of shutting the sky out.

Suddenly, as we were going down this long road, I spotted a large council house which had 'ANARCHY IN THE UK' painted roughly in massive letters, right across the front. It looked amazing, especially to a young scrote like me from the north of England. I was on such a high after seeing that house that the hairs on the back of my neck were standing to attention. I was quite impatient, wondering what and who I might see and meet. When you're young with little life experience, you dream big - no silly dreams. You dream that maybe the Sex Pistols will be sitting in Seditionaries. Anyway, I'm daydreaming, thinking soon I will get to see the King's Road for the first time. It will be full of punks, all of them just like me. I can visit BOY, I can visit the Beaufort Market; I can go to see bands at the Roxy Club, the Vortex, the Red Cow, the Nashville. I can visit the Portobello Road, go to Rough Trade Records; have a drink in the Roebuck alongside Johnny, Joe and Sid. I re-awoke and continued to drink in the scenery of this my first trip to the capital. To be truthful, though, this wasn't my first visit. A year before I'd been down to watch Leeds play at Arsenal and at Spurs, but this was different - those times I had travelled by van with a bunch of fanatical Leeds fans and we saw very little of London. This time it was different. This time I was alone. This time I would see the city and visit the places I knew only as words, as names I had read about in the pages of music magazines and fanzines. Anytime soon I could be in those pictures myself.

30 minutes after driving past Brent Cross I could see the vastness that is London - which seemed never ending. Suddenly the coach is pulling into Victoria. I hurry down the aisle to get off first and land on both feet. I take a deep breath; I don't know why but my first thought was that the air wasn't as fresh as Yorkshire air, less pollution up north I guess. I run out of the station, I haven't a clue where I'm going. I approach an old lady and ask, "Do you know which way it is to the King's Road, please?" There's no eye contact, no acknowledgement. She's not even seen me. In fact, her eyes look lifeless. There is nothing to suggest she is alive other than that her legs are moving. As I quickly survey the situation before me, people just seem to be moving at a rapid pace. I'm not sure whether the people are rushing to or from a situation, but everyone seems as though they have just taken a line or two of sulphate. They look like robots on speed. Zoom one way, zoom the next. Life seems incredibly fast. Anyhow, the old lady doesn't reply, and to be honest I feel I'm in too much shock to pursue the matter further. She scuttles off at what seems -

to me - like a frantic pace for a dainty old dear.

After about ten minutes of being ignored I decide to be proactive. I go into a ticket office and ask how to get to the King's Road. Some chirpy old cockney guy with a smile on his face replies, "Now then young 'un, you turn left at the end of the road, then walk along there 'til you get to Victoria Station."

"I thought this is Victoria Station?" I reply.

"Well, yes, it is… but this is Victoria Coach Station. You need Victoria railway, tube and bus station." Tubes? What's a tube? I have never heard of the tube but I don't want to seem thick so I say nothing. He continues, "When you get down there, the buses are outside the station, or if you decide to take a tube then go into the train station and look for a sign."

"What sort of a sign?"

"It will be a circular sign with a red band through its centre with Victoria Station written on it", my new found friend says. Thanking him, I set off from the coach station, turn left, and after about 200 yards I see Victoria Station on the right hand side. As I'm walking towards it I'm thinking what the hell is a tube and how does it function? It sounds a bit space age to me and a bit claustrophobic. Yep, now I see the buses.

When I arrive at the bus terminus I catch a conductor getting off his bus and ask him, "Which way to the King's Road, mate?" I'm now about to receive a lesson in how difficult and complicated it is to travel round the maze that is London if you're not familiar with it.

"Whereabouts on the King's Road?" he asks.

"Seditionaries clothes shop?"

"What's that?" he asks.

"A shop," I say.

"The King's Road is full of shops, mate. Which end of the King's Road is it?"

"Ummmm… I don't know", I reply. I'm thinking to myself: this could be a long day.

"Well, the King's Road is about two miles long," he tells me.

"OK," I say, not knowing what else I could say. I just want to get to the King's Road and I'll find it somehow.

"Well, you can get the number 11 bus; it goes all the way down to Fulham Town Hall or you can get the blah blah blah bus and get off at Sloane Square and walk down the King's Road or it may be quicker by tube to Sloane Square. It's one stop from Victoria." There are so many variables - how do people find anything in this place? Do they have to learn all this at school or college? I decide to get on the number 11 bus, as it has just pulled in in front of me. I run up the stairs and sit on the back seat. A conductor comes to me.

"King's Road, please."

"Whereabouts?" he asks.

"Seditionaries."

"Where?" The conductor says, none the wiser as to my request.

"It's a big punk clothes shop on the King's Road."

"Oh, errr, right. There's a few of them", he says. I give him a £1 note, he gives me a ticket and some change. We're off. I'm so excited; I can't wait to get there. As soon as we set off we're stuck in traffic for what seems like a lifetime. Good job it's early afternoon or I may miss the shop being open. Anyway, the bus is creeping slowly along, funeral style - which is making me anxious. I can't wait to see the King's Road and every time the bus turns onto a new street I'm thinking is this it? My eyes are glued to the windows looking for signs of punk life.

We go round a sudden sharp bend and turn into a square with tall buildings all around, and then I see some punks come out of a tube station. They've come out of the station and are walking the same way as this bus. Yippee! As we continue to slowly crawl down what I'm now assuming is the King's Road, I see more and more punks, then further down the road, even more punks. They are everywhere now. Bugger it; I'm getting off the bus! What was great about London buses was there were no doors; you could jump on and off wherever you liked. I run down the stairs and jump off the bus to meet my new punk friends. I can't describe the feeling going through me at that moment. There were only a few punks in Bradford so to see so many together is unbelievable. I'm rushing all over the street trying to process the experience. I'm now walking down the King's Road and I see the sign on the wall. I'm really here. I walk past a pub called the Chelsea Potter. It's got benches outside. It's a lovely day so the pub is busy. I keep walking. Next I come across the shop BOY, on the left hand

side of the road a few yards on. I have a quick look around, but don't see much I like. I ask where Seditionaries is, which doesn't go down too well with the middle-aged man behind the counter but one of the punk assistants takes me outside and points me in the right direction. "Keep going down the road 'til you get to the World's End. You'll know when you are there, the road bends around the corner a bit then the shop is just on the right hand side."

I set off walking at speed. After about 10-15 minutes I walk past Robot, a shoe shop that sells brothel creepers and all sorts of retro 1950s footwear. I carry on, then I look up - across the road is the Roebuck pub. I carry on; I can call in there for a beer or three later, I think. Suddenly I've reached the bend in the road and I can see another pub called the Man in the Moon. I cross the road and walk round the corner. Seditionaries is immediately there. Finally I've arrived, and there are lots of punks outside. There is a black guy by the door who seemed to be some kind of security guard. Once inside it wasn't that big; there were mirrors at the back where the counter was, and the side walls were sort of tiled with a picture of what looked like a bombed out Dresden. At the back was an entire wall covered by an upside down photo of Piccadilly Circus. On another wall were hung some boots and more shoes were on a couple of shelves, beneath which lay the rubble of Dresden. Down the middle of the shop was a long, thin rail upon which hung all of the clothes they sold. These clothes looked good. Totally barmy. I'd never seen stuff like this before, except of course in pictures of the Sex Pistols, who wore this stuff all the time.

I turn round to see the sales girl (I know her name is Jordan from the Pistols' publicity stuff). This woman has more style in her handbag than any other woman on the planet. She is like no other woman alive, and she's very attractive with large breasts. I look at her face and she has some kind of Mondrian face painting going on. She looks fantastic. I'd imagined from her pictures that she may be aggressive, but to my surprise she is very friendly. I ask her if I can try things on. "Yes, of course", she replies. Now, as barmy as the clothes were, even more crazy was the price of them. T-shirts were about £5, which was a lot of money - you could buy a pair of Wrangler jeans for about £2. The plain knee-strapped trousers called bondage trousers were £30, but the tartan or leather or cord ones were £35. The boots I think were the same; £35. These were prices to make a simple northern lad gag. To put this into some kind of perspective, my weekly wage was £35, which was about the national average - not the wage of an apprentice or youngster - so these clothes really did cost a lot. Anyhow, having done my homework beforehand, I'd seen something I really, really wanted and remembered its name; an anarchy shirt.

I ask the assistant Jordan if they have any.

"No" is the reply. "There was only a small amount of those, and they sold out as quickly as they were made."

"Oh, OK then." So my shopping trip continues; I'm looking around the shop.

Suddenly Jordan says "You're from up north. Whereabouts?"

"Bradford", I tell her. "It's next to Leeds." Everyone knows where Leeds is or they've at least heard of it, mainly because of the football team, but less people seem to have heard of Bradford. Anyway, Jordan continues to chat.

"I know where Bradford is. I have relatives in Yorkshire. What brings you down to London?" I explain that I want to check out the London punk scene. I'm going to meet my mate Sunni at the Man in the Moon pub later to see a band called X-Ray Spex.

"Oh", she says. "That's just round the corner this side of the road on the left. I'll be there later to see a friend's band that is having their first official gig. They are called the Ants."

"I will try to catch them," I say but I'm not really taking it in. After awhile I opt for a pair of bondage trousers which have straps across the legs and a muslin with 'Destroy' printed on it,

alongside an upside down picture of Jesus on the cross and a large swastika, and a couple of T-shirts and some other bits and bobs. All this comes to about £51. I look in my pockets. I have £50 in notes but no change. I don't really want to break into another £20. So I keep looking at my money and dithering. Jordan asks what's wrong. I tell her I only have £50 and she seems to feel sorry for me.

Then she says, "I'll let you off the £1." I'm as happy as Larry now. Now although I had saved my money for this trip, I had already decided that I didn't want to spend all of it in there, as I was hoping to see a bit of London first. I thought I could always call back again, since it wasn't that far away from Victoria Coach Station. So I said goodbye to Jordan and walked towards the door. As I did so, I suddenly saw some punks nick a handful of T-shirts as quick as you like, then walk out right behind the black security guy. However much I liked the Seditionaries clothes, the prices were definitely well at odds with the punk ideal of DIY but they were well made. These young punks definitely had the right idea. Expect the unexpected and demand the impossible, I thought.

So I'm stood outside Seditionaries on the King's Road, in my new clobber, and I'm clutching a small brown paper parcel, containing the clothes I've come down in. I don't really know what to do next. Suddenly someone thrusts a flyer into my hand announcing: 'Tonight the 11th of May at the Man in the Moon pub X-Ray Spex plus support The Ants.' I remember that that's the gig Sunni is going to and Jordan had said the pub was just round the corner when she'd mentioned the support band, The Ants. I walked back around the corner to see if I could see anything happening - and there it was, the Man in the Moon. It was late afternoon by then, and there was no one at the venue as yet, just a couple of people having a pint. I asked at the bar what time people would start setting up for the gig; they told me it would be around 6.30 or 7pm-ish. I had about two hours to kill. I didn't have anywhere to stay, so I asked again behind the bar where could I find a B&B or a cheap hotel. The lady told me that the nearest place would be around Pimlico or Victoria Station way. I thanked her and walked out of the pub, there was a bus stop nearby with a bus just pulling in. I ran for it, jumped on, went upstairs and sat at the back. The clippie (it was a woman this time) asked where I was going? I just paid her the 10p or whatever it had been I'd paid coming from Victoria. What I didn't know was there were hundreds of buses in London, and they didn't all necessary go back to where you'd got on at Victoria. I never thought to check where the bus was going. Big mistake.

Before I knew it the bus had entered Sloane Square and had turned north towards Knightsbridge. After it went a bit further I could feel the anxiety swelling inside. I knew it, I was lost. I quickly ran down the stairs and explained to the clippie. She said, "Get off at the next stop, there's a tube station round the corner, or you can get …" Then she started with the variables again, "bus this, change at that, get this bus then that bus, blah blah blah." I got off the bus, went over to the other side of the road - and then suddenly realized I had started to feel proper hungry. So I asked a passerby where the nearest food joint was. They pointed me in the direction of a Donner kebab place two streets away. 'Kebab? What's that when it's at home?' I wondered as I set off walking down this road. I turned left, then right. As I was going along my way I was looking at my reflection in the shop windows, wearing my new Seditionaries clothes. I felt great, special, like a real punk now, you know all those silly adolescent thoughts you have when you're young and full of yourself. Suddenly I came across the food place; the menu was massive. I asked what a kebab was, as I had never heard of one. I was 10 when I had my first curry at a neighbours house, so I wouldn't have called myself a connoisseur of exotic food. The guy behind the counter explained.

"Kebab is bits of lamb meat with garlic sauce and salad, all wrapped up in a pitta bread." "Yeah, I'll try that", I said. When it arrived, it was massive, hot and greasy - and it tasted like heaven. Why don't they sell these in Bradford? I asked myself. Anyhow, it took me ages to eat it. The grease was running all over my fingers and I licked 'em clean. It was the best thing I had ever eaten in my life up to that point. Yep, I told myself, I would have to have another of those before I left London.

So there I am, walking back down the road after eating my new favourite food, when I hear a loud commotion behind me. "Oi! You!" "It's one of those dirty punk bastards!" One of them shouted to the others. Then it was a collective shout, "Get him!" I was looking around wondering who they were referring to, when, alarmingly, like a flash, it dawned on me… shit, it's me! I looked round and saw a group of about thirty Teds running towards me. Within a split second I have to risk assess this situation before these Teds are on me. One of them is pulling out what looks like an axe. I'm not about to ask if it is real. My risk assessment comes to an abrupt conclusion and I'm on my toes.

I have no idea where I'm going; down roads that all look the same, tall building after tall building, seemingly endless rows of them. After three streets I've managed to stay quite a way in front, but I'm getting tired. I look back towards those hate filled faces that are still trying to press as hard as they can. They are shouting all sorts of threats about what they are going to do to me when they catch up, which doesn't sound like a fun proposition. I'm struggling now. I pass the next sharp corner, spot a short wall and leap over it, only to find it's one hell of a drop at the other side. I slide down an embankment. I can see that there's a window fast approaching. I don't really want to crash through someone's window so I'm frantically trying to stop, but whatever it is I'm sliding down, it's a bit wet. And then of course, I'm thinking of my new Seditionaries clothes, I don't want to ruin them on their first outing. I'm also trying to cling to the bags for all my life's worth. Then, just as it seems like I'm going to smash through it, the window suddenly opens, and I slide straight through, nearly kicking a little old lady in the face. But I manage to end up with my legs on each of her shoulders, much to her shock. "Sorry, love," I say.

She looks totally shell shocked as she helps me untangle myself from her person and I pick myself up. Quickly I remember about the Teds. I look out of the window but I can't see them. Hopefully they've gone.

"Where am I?" I ask.

"You're in a brothel, dearie," she replies.

"Oh! Right. Ummmmm… yeah… OK then," comes my slow, unsteady reply. Next thing I do is check my new clothes for rips or tears. Luckily there is just a damp patch on my trousers. Just then a door opens, revealing a beautiful lady dressed in a catsuit in the act of whipping some guy who was down on the floor, clad only in a nappy. They both turn round to glare at my unwanted intrusion. "Evening all", I say in my best 'Dixon of Dock Green' voice. The door is kicked shut again.

"Fancy a cup of tea, love?" says the old lady.

"Yes, please, " I reply. So I'm sitting there drinking my tea and the old lady is chatting away.

"You from up north, dearie?" she asks. "Whereabouts?"

"Bradford," I tell her.

"Is that near Leeds? What's it like?"

"Well, it's like a smaller version of London", I say, totally lying as I barely knew anything about London, except that there are loads of people from all over the world living there. So in that respect I suppose I wasn't lying after all, because it was like Bradford in that way.

"Oh, right. In all my years I've never been out of London, except during the war when we were shipped out to the countryside to live on a farm", she says. I felt quite sad for her. Although London is a big metropolis it does people a great deal of good to get out of their own neighbourhood and see a bit of life and learn about other people. It's the essence of life for me; it broadens our minds to other possibilities in life. Having said that, my own parents hadn't travelled much in their lives. It costs money, so poor, working class families didn't travel much. The only people I knew who travelled regularly were football fans and lorry drivers. Hopefully things were starting to change

now. I certainly wanted to get out and see the world. I'm still quite dazed, I think. A couple of other scantily clad ladies drift past.

"Who's your friend, Gladys?" one asks, and they smile. I smile back.

"It's not what I would have imagined", I say to Gladys.

"They're good girls really," Gladys replies and then explains how most of the girls' clients are rich, well-to-do businessmen or judges; lawyers, politicians, establishment types. That's typical, I thought. It's OK for them to do what they like, but they don't like it when we want to do it. I remembered thinking that when I first left school, considering what I wanted to be I had always fancied being a man of leisure, like the toffs, living off the sweat and toil of others, contributing nothing and taking all. In reality I could never do that, my conscience would never allow it. My philosophy was 'Do what you like as long as you harm no one.' I suppose all I ever wanted was to just have fun with my life. I was sick of reading about other people's experiences, other people's lives. I wanted to experience everything for myself, not to spend my time reading about other people.

Anyway, there I am reflecting and chatting with this old bird, when I suddenly remember the gig. "What time is it?" I ask.

"It's 7.45", Gladys replies.

"Oh, really? Err, right. I had better be off," I say, while asking myself where did the time go?

"Where you going, dearie?" asks Gladys.

"I'm off to see a couple of bands in a pub at the bottom of the King's Road. They're called X-Ray Spex and the Ants. I also said I would meet a friend from Bradford there."

"Sounds more like an optician watching a flea circus than a concert," Gladys replied and followed her attempt at humour with some words of advice about transport and telling me that the buses were quite frequent on the main road back up the King's Road.

I thanked Gladys for the help and set off. After ten minutes I'm at the bus stop looking at the timetables. I have my clothes in my back pack now so it should be easier. After another 15 minutes a bus arrives, with all the destinations on the front. I see King's Road is signed and stick my hand out; it stops and I climb aboard. I pay the clippie then this time sits downstairs. I mention to the conductor, "I want the Man in the Moon pub." This one's a decent fella, he says he will let me know when it's time to get off. After a 10 minute ride we drive past Chelsea Football Club. It looks quite big I thought, but right now I'm more concerned with getting to the gig. The bus takes a right at the top of the road, then a left, and we swing past the World's End pub. The conductor shouts, "Next stop, mate!" I get up, press the bell and get off. I walk back down the road to the Man in the Moon pub and I'm here at last.

It's just after 8.20 when I've arrived at the pub and there are a few people milling around outside. It's not really that packed, but I notice a large group of young kids, some even look like they've just started secondary school. Now, don't get me wrong, most of us punks were young - I was only 16 myself and had just left school, but these look a lot younger than me, basically school kids; 13 maybe. Although these kids are young, they look really mad - a real ragbag crew, some in home-made, hand-painted punk gear and some wearing King's Road purchased clothes - or rather pilfered is more accurate. I watch these characters for a while as they pinch drinks and pick up anything that's not nailed down. They seem very street savvy, like street urchins. These little kids really do survive by their wits. Some football type lads walk past and make some disparaging comments, and to a man (or boy in this case), they all stand up to protect one another. I liked that. There was an air of confidence about them; a sense of self-contained solidarity, which gave the impression of a group not to be messed with.

Next thing I know my mate Sunni appeared from inside the pub. "Sorry I'm late", I said, "I got lost and then chased by a group of Teds."

I'm explaining what happened but before I could finish, Sunni blurted out, "You just missed the most amazing band - they're called the Ants. The singer, what a nutcase! He wore a rapist mask and crawled across the floor…" On and on he went, he couldn't stop talking about them. "The music was really raw, totally bonkers stuff."

"What about X-Ray Spex?" I asked. "That's who you came to see."

"Oh, they haven't been on yet. It's only their third gig, apparently, but I read a review of one of their other gigs and it said they were one of the best new punk bands." Great, I thought, at least I will see them. As Sunni and I stood about talking, I kept noticing this group of punks still up to no good. They had now somehow managed to break into the cellar of the pub and were passing bottles of beer up to the others; it looked mostly like Pils. They may have been young, but they certainly knew what to drink! Every now and again they managed to tug up a crate and they were stashing these somewhere.

Whatever these cheeky little gits were doing suddenly became irrelevant when both Sunni and I noticed these two gorgeous punk girls sitting a few feet away. I was quite shy with girls at that point but Sunni, being a lot older, was very confident. He was a black guy with a skunk haircut; he wore swimming goggles and always had the top button of his trousers open. Back home in Bradford I would often see him grab girls' hands and stick them down his trousers - he was a bit of a lad, was Sunni. Anyway, Sunni engages in conversation with these two girls and we have a right laugh. Sunni goes for the more confident, gregarious looking girl, leaving me with the quieter, more subdued of the pair. I'm quite happy with this pairing though, it suits me perfectly. I ask if she wants a drink and she asks for a pint of lager. I go into the bar but there's a bit of a queue and I get talking to a guy who introduces himself as Justin Semmens. He says he's been babysitting up the road and just bobbed in for a pint. While standing at the bar I then get talking to these two scousers called Robbo and Boxhead, who've come down to check out the streets of London. They are loud, witty and funny with their distinctive brogue. It's hard not to notice them really, but they seem okay.

Although we have not been chatting for long, I really like this girl. Her name is Penny Tration. Sunni's girl is called Anna Key. Sunni has his arm round her shoulder and (within no time at all it seemed) his hand in her bra. She doesn't seem to mind though. Sunni is up to his usual tricks, trying to put her hand down his trousers, but for reasons apparent to me and seemingly the rest of the pub - but obviously unapparent to Sunni - she doesn't seem that keen. Meanwhile, Penny and I were learning about each other, much preferring just to sit and talk. She told me about punk gigs she had been to so far, and I listened before telling her about my own experiences. As we chatted I could sense the very same passion burning inside her as was within me, about this fantastic new movement called Punk. It really did feel like we could change the world and the more we chatted, the more we felt we could achieve. Anyway, there we are, chatting away, when suddenly, we hear a band start playing, so we all go inside the pub. I see Jordan standing there in front of me.

I tap her on the shoulder and say hello and she smiles back and says "Hi, did you see the Ants?"

"No," I replied and told her what happened.

"Sounds like you were very lucky," she remarked, as I moved past her. By then X-Ray Spex have hit the stage. The singer, called Poly, is a short, slightly overweight black girl with a metallic brace on her teeth. She has a very high, almost screechy voice. The band sound great and Poly complements them perfectly. According to Penny, Poly writes all the lyrics which are great - about posing, consumerism and environmental issues - a whole bunch of stuff that seems a hundred miles away from some of the dole queue diatribe. Poly seems a very clued up young lady and her words are actually relevant. Anyhow, X-Ray Spex stormed through a fantastic, blistering set; they were very energetic and I liked them a lot. I look round for Sunni, seeing as he had come down from Bradford especially to see this band, but I can't see him. When I do eventually locate him, he's pressing himself into a back corner of the pub with Anna. It looked like he was shagging her, which, in all truth wouldn't have surprised me, but her hands were flying about all over the place, so maybe she was trying to escape. I wouldn't blame her for that either. Penny and I just stood silently and watched the band. Now being a northern lad, I had always imagined London gigs would be all sold out, and you would struggle to get in anywhere, but this gig wasn't packed out by a long way.

Shortly after, even above the band, I hear a bit of noise from outside and move over to the window to sneak a better view. There seems to be an altercation outside in the pub doorway involving the kids I'd seen earlier but I can't see who is involved so I go back to watch the band. X-Ray Spex finished what seemed like short set, I think most bands did around 45 minutes to an hour. Penny and I sat down again to resume chatting. We were getting on famously when suddenly she asked me, "Where are you staying tonight?" I suddenly realised I had forgotten all about finding a hotel.

"Nowhere," I replied, feeling quite startled.

"Oh, don't worry about that, it's OK. Me and Anna have a squat in Camden. You can stop with us if you want to." This welcoming and very much appreciated invitation then set me wondering if all London punk girls were this accommodating, or was it because we did seem to get on well with each other? I asked Penny what a squat was. Even though I liked to think I was well read, that word had never appeared in any book I ever read as something you lived in.

"We break into empty old houses and live in them rent free 'til we get kicked out. London's full of 'em."

"Wow! How can you possibly do that? Don't the police come and kick you out?" I asked, somewhat naively.

She smiled. "No, they have to catch you actually breaking in to arrest you." This concept threw me completely. I couldn't get my head round it, and it seemed crazy to me that it could happen.

"What about electricity then?" I asked.

"You just tell them you are now living there, set up an account and pay for electricity", she told me. Can it be so easy? I thought. I might have to try this in Bradford. I was still puzzling over the concept of squatting when the last orders bell went. Sunni and Anna came back over to us. They both had a gleam in their eyes, so I assumed they were getting on famously. Then almost simultaneously both girls announced, "You can both stop at our squat!" We all laughed hysterically. I picked up my clothing parcels that I had left behind the bar earlier, and we all left the pub. I said 'bye to Jordan and she nodded in acknowledgement as we walked by, "Don't forget to check out the Ants if you get chance." That word, the 'Ants' again; even Sunni was impressed. I need to see this band I thought.

Then we were out of the pub and off to catch a night bus. On our way, we bought some more food and I went straight for a kebab. Again, it was lovely. When we arrived back at their squat, we found it to be a very old, dilapidated house, with a metal gate at the side. From the street, it was boarded up and looked seemingly inaccessible which, I imagine, would put most people off trying to get in.

We entered via the metal gate at the side and round the back, and the girls used some special mechanism to make a seemingly solid door open enough for the four of us to squeeze through. We entered a very dark, cold corridor with creaky floorboards. Penny left my side to switch the light on.

Once things became illuminated it didn't look that bad. I had been expecting an empty house with maybe a bed or two in it, but even though it was quite basic, Penny and Anna's squat felt quite homely. The four of us then parted - Penny and I sat down in what had obviously once been a living room, but Sunni and Anna were practically already undressing each other, and almost straight away headed off into one of the other rooms. I heard a muffled "'night" from one of them as they groped their way noisily up the stairs.

"Do you want a drink of anything?" asked Penny.

"Oh, yes please", I replied. She disappeared into the kitchen and I started to unpack my other Seditionaries clothes to look at them, and tried them on again. Suddenly, Penny came back into the room with the tea, just as I was counting my money up. I hadn't spent a great deal; £51 for the Seditionaries stuff, plus a few beers and a couple of kebabs. I still had about £90 left.

Penny noticed the Seditionaries clothes and said, "Oh, so you're a trendy poser punk, just like in that X-Ray Spex song." She was teasing me but I didn't like to hear that comment, because I was a conscientious punk - I believed in it wholeheartedly. It was my new life. But I knew what she meant and it stung.

"Ouch!" I remarked, then continued, and whatever it was I said was as much an affirmation to me as to my own beliefs as it was to her in a somewhat feeble attempt to put her straight: "For me, punk is about a DIY aesthetic really, but there is a contradiction in my wearing all this expensive fashionable punk clothing. But then, it's also a lot more than that. It was McLaren's group, the Sex Pistols, who kind of invented punk. Maybe he did do it to sell clothes as was said, but we are what we are and we do what we will do. I do feel more comfortable in the DIY punk clothes, but charity shops are getting too expensive now, ripping off punks, and once I have had these for a few weeks and I've lived in them, then they'll look like all my other clothes. But we all have desires, we all need aspirations. These clothes exude confidence somehow, and I will always be who I am. Clothes do not maketh the man. The man maketh the clothes."

Yes! What a statement. I was smiling to myself as I was trying to justify myself. But underneath all the bravado, I was more than a little bit worried at this point - had I blown it? I wasn't altogether sure. But she smiled again. "It's OK", she said, as she went into a laundry basket and pulled out an 'Anarchy in the UK' Seditionaries muslin T-shirt. We both laughed, but I can tell you I was relieved, because I really liked Penny and I was thinking: if we fall out she might kick me out and I don't know London well enough to find a hotel or find my way about. Besides, at this time of night I'd be lucky to even find a kebab shop still open, let alone somewhere to doss. We drank our tea and chatted into the night. Above us, Anna and Sunni sounded like they were dismantling the house, not having sex.

To tell the truth, for all my time standing on the terraces; all the rucks, the rows, the holidays at Butlin's, whatever, I was pretty inexperienced at sexual encounters at that point in my life. I had only had one proper girlfriend at that point so I was looking at Penny, feeling nervous in my new threads and it all seemed a bit too good to be true. Suddenly Penny said, "You ready for bed?"

I gulped. "Yes", I replied, more than a little nervously.

"OK then, you can stay in my room, because we don't have any other blankets, and you might freeze otherwise."

As we make our way upstairs and enter her bedroom, things seem to have died down now in the other room, and the upper floor of the house appeared still intact. I enter her room as she turns on the light. Her walls are covered with punk posters; the Pistols, the Clash, the Damned - too many to recall. We tentatively undress and separately get into bed. It is freezing now so we hug each other.

Little Johnny suddenly springs to attention. Almost by accident I brush my hand against Penny's back. Her velvet skin, it was so smooth. She turns and we kiss. It feels magical. We embrace tighter than tight then slowly, I begin to kiss her body from top to toe, working my way down, lower, lower, so I don't miss one centimetre of her skin. I slow down when I get to her erogenous zone. (Erogenous zone! Ark at it. I sound like a spexpert using big words like that. They could have been near the Himalayas for all I knew about them before a punk girlfriend used it during a conversation about sex.) Stopping at Penny's clit I think for a moment. It's hard to believe this little piece of flesh is responsible for so much life and pleasure. I hear Penny breathlessly sigh. I kiss all the way to her feet then start going back up her body again, stopping at Penny's parts. I open her legs and stare for a moment.

Then I slowly stroke the inside of her thighs. She's panting now.

For some strange reason I find myself desperately trying to remember the third line of 'New Rose' by the Damned. Her body jerks, wanting contact with my tongue. I lean down in between her thighs and place my tongue on her clit and leave it there. She's writhing around the bed now then I slowly move my tongue gently around her parts as the intensity builds and her movements become more frequent. Suddenly she just shouts, "For fuck's sake fuck me!" I lunge in and we are engrossed in each other; it's pure animal lust as we roll about the bed in ecstasy until we both come simultaneously. It goes quiet as we hug. Then we look at each other, smile in the half light of dawn and carry

'79

TIME FOR ACTION
THE MOD REVIVAL
ESSAYS FROM THE FRONTLINE

BY GARRY BUSHELL

THE PURPLE HEARTS

PHOTO - VIRGINIATURBETT.COM

CRAZE
REVIVAL
THE FRONTLINE
Y BUSHELL

'79 TIME FOR ACTION
THE MOD REVIVAL
ESSAYS FROM THE FRONTLINE
BY GARRY BUSHELL

'79 DANCE CRAZE
THE SKA REVIVAL
ESSAYS FROM THE FRONTLINE
BY GARRY BUSHELL

'79 TIME
THE
ES
BY

'79 REVIVAL SERIES

RELEASES 31ST OCTOBER
NUMBERED COPIES
PRE-ORDER BELOW
CHOICE OF 5 COVERS

WWW.REDPLANETMUSICBOOKS.COM

'79 TIME FOR ACTION
THE MOD REVIVAL
ESSAYS FROM THE FRONTLINE
Y BUSHELL

'79 DANCE CRAZE
THE SKA REVIVAL
ESSAYS FROM THE FRONTLINE
BY GARRY BUSHELL

'79 TIME
THE
ESSAYS FROM THE
BY G

'79 DANCE CRAZE
THE SKA REVIVAL
ESSAYS FROM THE FRONTLINE
BY GARRY BUSHELL

2 TONE GIRLS
PHOTO - VIRGINIATURBETT.COM

on hugging. We fall asleep in each others' arms.

In the morning I'm awake first and try to get out of bed to go to the toilet. As I'm getting out I fall back onto the bed. I hear a slight groan followed by a "Morning."

I replied, "Morning! Sorry I woke you. I lost my balance."

"It's OK, I was awake anyway", said Penny. We smile then I run to the toilet and back as quickly as possible and jump back in next to her. We lie there enjoying each others' company; neither of us speaks. After awhile Penny utters the immortal words, "Cup of tea?" I have never quite understood the British fixation of not attempting the day without tea or coffee, I hardly ever drank either. It was nice in cold weather sometimes but I just fancied one today. "Oh, but we'll need milk", I heard her say.

"I'll go to the shop", I offered. "I fancy looking around."

"We'll both go," she said and we hastily dressed, and headed out onto the busy streets of Camden. Wow, I thought, it's mid-morning and the streets are bustling with people. We walk up the road to the shops; there's Camden Town tube station in the middle of the road, there's the market to the left of it. We walk around there for a while, and there are tons of people about. It's a popular destination for locals and for the Londoner from further afield. There are also quite a few skinheads about, I notice. I hadn't really come across any skinheads at that point. Although I knew about their past reputation, I didn't know what to expect of the modern day version, so I wasn't worried.

Eventually we went into a paper shop and I bought some milk and a paper before turning back from the market towards the station. As we reached the station, Penny pointed out a record shop, "It's called Rock On; it's famous", she told me. Oh, right, I thought to myself - I'll call in there later on my way home.

As we walked back down the high street toward Penny's squat, I was feeling really happy. I like Penny a lot, but I was in the punk metropolis - everything I had ever read about in the music papers was here, and here I was - Johnny fucking Johnstone - really here for the first time. It was like a dream. I didn't want it to end, but I knew it had to. Thinking positively, I still had the rest of today to enjoy myself before catching the last coach tonight. "Right", I said. "What you doing today? Because I want to go to Portobello Road to call in at Rough Trade."

Penny said, "Do you know what rough trade means?"

"No", I replied and she told me that rough trade was also homosexual slang for a rent boy.

"Oh right, well can we visit the record shop version?"

"Lot of it about down there, is there?" asked Penny.

"What?"

"Oh, nothing", replied Penny, suppressing a huge smile.

I continued unfazed, "Then maybe go back down the King's Road, check out BOY, the Beaufort Market, maybe go to Seditionaries again? Or can you suggest any other places worth seeing since you live down here?"

"Nope. Sounds good to me", she said. I think to myself that I've been reading all the wrong books. Penny seems well street savvy and I feel like a hick from the sticks.

I stand there quietly for a moment then, remembering, I turn to Penny and say, "When I was coming into London yesterday, the coach passed this big house which had 'ANARCHY IN THE UK' painted right on the front of it in big white letters. It looked amazing - and you could see all these punks were jumping around in the garden... I sat there wondering who they were. It looked like they were having fun." Penny's eyes light up but she says nothing .We walk back to the flat and put the kettle on. She makes some tea and toast; a staple punk rock breakfast. Penny finishes hers first and disappears. A few minutes later she's dressed and ready to go out.

"Come on, get ready, we're off out. I know where I'm going to take you first, on a little detour", she said. Erm... I wonder where she's taking me? I get changed really quickly and meet her downstairs. We jump on a bus; I didn't notice its destination. We seem to be heading westwards, which is where I want to be anyway.

After about 30 minutes Penny gets up. "Come on, we're here." We run down the stairs and jump off the bus as it slows down. "This way", she says. We turn a corner and start walking up this long road. I get half way up and sense there's something familiar about it but can't think what until we go round a bend and I see it - The 'ANARCHY IN THE UK' house. I smile and so does Penny. I give her a hug. She says, "When you were telling me the story about seeing the house I thought it had to be my friend's place. There can't be two houses decorated with 'ANARCHY IN THE UK'." We walk up the front path and knock on the door. After a while this attractive looking punk girl with blue hair answers. "Hi, Debbie!" says Penny.

"Hi!" says Debbie.

"This is Johnny. He's from up north," says Penny.

"Hi!" I say. Penny tells Debbie about how I spotted the house on my way into London and saw the punks dancing in the garden. Debbie is really nice. She tells me there are about four people who live there, but it's always full of other punks. They sometimes get trouble off the locals, but generally it's OK living around there. She shows me around the house. It's a bit of a wreck - spray painted walls adorned with punk posters and flyers - pretty much like most punk dwellings, I guess.

Debbie's on her own today, as all the others are out. Penny tells her it's just a flying visit as we are time restricted, as I have to get the coach back home tonight. After some tea we say our goodbyes and leave.

After that we set off to explore Portobello. To get there, we have to go back to Camden Town and jump on the tube. This is my first experience of the tube. The stairs are so steep and long, it feels like I'm descending into the depths of hell. I look at the underground map on the platform. It all seems so confusing to me, which side of the track do you need to be on to get to where you're going, because it all looks the same. I'm just glad Penny is with me. The tube journey is very quick but involves changing trains at least twice, it's also very claustrophobic. I don't like it, but I suppose it's necessary to get around in a city of this size. There should be a law against cramming so many people into such a short space. Penny says it's not bad on the outskirts, but in the centre of London it's truly awful. When we finally arrive at Notting Hill Gate, it's about a half mile walk to Rough Trade. It's in a small side street on the left hand side of the famous Portobello Road. It's great in here, I thought, looking at the fanzines and all the posters. There are not that many punk records out at the moment but momentum is picking up with more bands being signed up. We spend a bit of time wandering around Portobello, then head back up to Notting Hill Gate to take a number 31 bus to the King's Road. It's just such a great place to be right now is London. It feels like the very centre of the punk universe. We've seen punks wherever we've been today.

Eventually we get back to the squat and sit around chatting before it's time to go back to Bradford. I check to see if Sunni is still around, but Anna and

Sunni aren't replying, so I assume they are either out or Sunni has already left. After a while we go back to bed to spend a couple of hours together.

We hug, kiss, shag, and then talk about the future, if any. All too suddenly, it's time to leave for the coach. We both get ready and Penny insists on coming to the coach station with me. I gather all my stuff together and we set off. I don't really want to go back to Bradford. I would much rather stay in London with Penny watching loads of punk bands, but I have a job, and it's a big move to make. But it must be said, I'm seriously thinking about it now. We walk up to Camden Tube, it's busy and there seems to be a lot of skinheads hanging around there. "It's because of the Electric Ballroom," Penny tells me. Anyway, we get the tube to King's Cross then change for the Victoria line. King's Cross underground station is like a maze; if Penny wasn't with me, then there would be no way on earth I could ever find the right tube line. 15 minutes later and we're in Victoria Coach Station. The coach is ready for boarding. I stay with Penny for as long as I can. I'm missing her already and I haven't even left yet. We have swapped addresses and promised to keep in touch with each other. I realise that Penny is living in a squat, so she might be evicted any-time - and then where will we be? She says, "It will be fine."

We hug each other and I give her a farewell kiss but I'm reluctant to let go of her and then I have to, and walk slowly up the coach steps to board the coach. I head for the back. Luckily the coach is not very full, and so I have the entire back seat all to myself. I put my stuff on the luggage rack and settle down for the long journey home. The coach sets off. Penny waves goodbye. I start thinking about Sunni and what he'd said about that punk group, the Ants. Sunni was a well-respected character in Bradford. He was a couple of years older than everyone else, so he was more street savvy and people looked up to him, respected him. It was bugging me. I felt like I had missed the most im-portant band ever, I had to see them. The journey seemed to take forever. I try to relax, I'm laid out on the back seat of the coach and I'm thinking I really like Penny. She's beautiful, carefree, funny, and easy to talk to and we've got a lot in common, although we live 200 miles away from each other, but it's only 200 miles, not 2,000 or 2 million. But, will we see each other again? I don't know. In the meantime I would have a few more punk rock escapades. I would also have to find out more about this band, the Ants. Who are they, where are they from, who is in the band?

III
I WISH IT COULD BE
CHRISTMAS EVERYDAY

'Oh well, I wish it could be Christmas everyday
When the kids start singing and the band begins to play
Oh I wish it could be Christmas everyday
Let the bells ring out for Christmas. '

It's now coming up to Christmas 1977 and it's been nearly a year into my new life as a punk rocker. Overall, it's been a great year musically; I have seen quite a few punk bands now. The first was the Lurkers, with the Crabs supporting, then X-ray Spex and then the Clash in Leeds. Joe Strummer, reminded me of Norman Collier in his singing style. He was jumping around so much that his mouth kept missing the mic, so you only got to hear partial lyrics. The Clash seemed to be in competition with the Sex Pistols to be the number one punk band, but I think this had more to do with Bernie Rhodes and Malcolm McLaren than with the musicians. The Clash seemed to connect with the more left politically inclined. I saw them more as documenters of life, almost like voyeurs. They seemed to be writing about other people's experiences rather than their own. They weren't bringing anything of themselves to the party; it was safe. It was all slogans and telling people how they should live their lives which, to me, came across as phoney. I'd spent all my childhood reading about what other people had been getting up to, and going to school only to be told what to do. By the time I was 16 I had had enough of both. I wanted to find out about life for myself, live my own adventures and the last thing I needed was someone else telling me how I should live it.

Punk was about discovering yourself and being the person you were meant to be; to try to build a society of diversity of thought and actions, where we put people together, not in competition, but in equality and unity. I saw myself as part anarchist, part socialist, but I was still patriotic and wanted the best for my country. Anarchism was a personal issue about developing the self. Destroy the person society created and be the person you wanted to be. I never saw it as vandalism, which would be counter productive. Smashing the system would have been a better option, but everything starts with the individual. Socialism was about the well-being of everyone. We all have to live here so how else do we manage to co-exist? Communication was the key, both verbally and by listening to what people's fears and anxieties were, and why they have the beliefs they do. Musically I thought the Clash were average, nothing special. Their lyrics were great, though, in terms of highlighting social issues. But, visually, they looked bargain basement. Yes, I know punk was supposed to be against fashion - but punk was stylish and very creative in a Dystopian/Doomsday kind of way.

I was well aware of social issues and I was all for social conditions being improved for everyone. As punks we had been trying to connect to left wing politics early on, but found that the left wing seemed like hypocrites. We seemed to have more chance of getting positive change within the punk movement, which was unifying people, so a lot of punks disconnected from left wing politics early doors. Punk was inclusive, not exclusive; it was trying to tackle many taboo subjects - race, gender politics, fascism, etc. It was androgynous, so males and females were hard to tell apart sometimes. There were a lot of strong female characters in the punk music movement which until now had been a male dominated industry. Now we had these fantastic women participants like Jordan, Siouxsie Sioux, Faye Fife, Pauline Murray from Penetration, Gaye Advert, the lovely Poly Styrene from X-Ray Spex and the wonderful all-girl punk band the Slits. There were even transgender politics with Wayne County. Punk was open to anyone whether you were black, white, gay, straight - it didn't matter. It was classless, race-less, genderless.

I connected more to the Sex Pistols and Johnny Rotten. They seemed to be singing about their lives and not writing about other people. They were putting themselves on the block every day, and because of the media there were people trying to attack them on a daily basis. So they seemed much more authentic to me. 'I Wanna Be Me.' That song title resonated with me as much as their incendiary songs like 'God Save the Queen' and 'Anarchy in the UK'. Plus the energy was there; it did correspond with the energy output of the band. The clothes they wore were out of this world but of course there was a massive contradiction with the punk ethos of anti-fashion and pro-DIY, as manufactured punk clothing was bloody expensive.

I had also seen the Damned, supported by the Adverts, at St George's Hall earlier in the year. Both bands were good. It was a bit dicey getting home, though, with a lot of Teds hanging around outside the Queens pub opposite the train station, though I managed to sidestep them somehow, as there were now plenty of other targets for them. Another band I really liked during that time was Ultravox! I wouldn't really call them punk either, but there was something different about them which made them stand out and the music was interesting. A couple of their newer songs sounded as though they were maybe heading in the punk direction, such as 'Young Savage'. I even managed to get backstage to chat with them and ended up playing keepie-up football with them. I also saw Wire, another group I really liked. This was a great gig. The balcony was halfway up a wall and someone had a shepherd's crook and they tried to grab hold of members of the band with it. When I saw 999 - they gave away all their merchandise, like badges, flyers, etc. I thought they were giving everything away so I asked for their backdrop. Nick Cash, the singer, said "Fuck off. That cost us £25." There were also gigs with the Vibrators, Wayne County and the Electric Chairs, and a few others who made less of an impact.

At this point there were several punks in Bradford, but no one really knew each other. You would notice people at gigs. I always tried to talk to some of them but it's not easy at a gig, particularly when you don't know people. They would disappear into the night before you had a chance to catch them. No one stood around outside afterwards, because there were usually too many potential aggressors outside, so people went off straight after the gig. There was no focal point to meet fellow punks either. It wasn't until about August/September time that the Bradford punks started to meet socially away from gigs. Chris and I heard of a place called Mac's at the Queen's Hall, which was a student union place. It was a rock disco. A punk girl called Lynda Robertshaw from our area had been going and hanging out with these earlier punks from 1976. This lot - Ian D, Harvey M, George, Keith H - had seen the Sex Pistols at Leeds on the 'Anarchy' tour. Lynda told us about Mac's, telling us we would find like-minded people down there. So one Friday, Chris and I went down there to check it out. It was great to meet other punks; suddenly we didn't feel so alone. We met about 20 or 30 punks down there and created our own scene. The music was mostly rock all night, but they would play about five punk records together for us in the middle of the evening. It was a good place with lots of interesting people.

Although, some of the rock crowd didn't like us being there and we would have constant arguments about musical ability. "Punks can't play, man" was countered with "It's not about how well you play." But we didn't get any physical trouble off the heavy rock fans. Now bikers were another matter. Not so much the real bikers but the plastic bikers, wannabes or sometimes prospectors for the local Satan's Slaves, who were always trying to impress their elders with random acts of violence. The wannabes would get off the bus outside with their crash helmets in their hands, and would walk round trying to intimidate the punks. Then one night I had my first proper fight, when two of these wannabes started one with me. I just got angry and launched one of these lads right across the floor and he lay there, unconscious. I was as surprised as his mate. His mate looked at me. I was still in shock at what I had done, so stood there motionless, with a gaping mouth. Then, I moved, and the other wannabe just ran off. I wasn't sure what to do at that point but I wasn't about to go and ask anyone.

I suddenly realised that he might go and bring some friends back to carry on the fight, so I thought I had better use my advantage, and I ran after him. He ran into the toilets, which seemed a daft place to run; he was trapped now. I ran in after him and grabbed hold of him and he punched me. So, we had a grapple and I ended up putting him on the floor. I told him never to come back and he got up and ran out of the club… and didn't come back. Up until that point I had never shown any interest in fighting, but there were things I was very passionate about and even though I didn't want any trouble, you had to be able to look after yourself. There was a lot of trouble at the time at football matches. When I started following Leeds away I realised that if I was going to do this, then I had to be prepared to fight, because we were attacked at practically every away match. I saw people get darts in their heads, mates slashed across the face, and people hit with hammers, etc - and this was the norm, not isolated incidents. The football also coincided with me getting involved in punk and lots of people wanted to attack me for that as well. So far I had managed to stay out of any serious harm. There were some minor incidents at football; the odd slap here and there but nothing serious so far. But the frustration and anger had been building up all year. I thought I'm not taking this shit any more. This incident at Mac's gave me confidence that I could fight. I had had some altercations at football but that was gangs and you didn't necessarily have to fight one on one, it was just the odd punch here and there.

On the 15th of October 1977 I went to watch the Stranglers, the Saints and the Drones at the Queen's Hall in Leeds. I was looking forward to seeing the Drones again after seeing them a while back and hoping to meet up with some of my fellow Bradford punks at the gig. On the day of the gig Leeds were playing Liverpool at Elland Road, which was a big game with one of Leeds' biggest rivals over the last decade. I went over on the train to Leeds and bumped into Strauss, who looked like a heavy rock fan with his long hair and big army coat, but was into buying all the obscure punk singles. I always liked to see what he was buying because it was usually good stuff. It was Strauss who had told me about the Rings' single 'I Wanna Be Me.' I love that guitar hook, it is so effective. The Rings featured Twink, a 60s counter culture icon. Strauss did tapes for people, and he was sitting in the corner of the train listening to his latest one on one of those big tape players. They were a bit cumbersome, but the pockets on his army coat were massive enough to accommodate it. As I sat next to him, the Snivelling Shits' 'Terminal Stupid' came on. I wished it was louder. Following up was the B-side 'I Can't Come', followed by one of the best records from that year, Albertos Y Lost Trios Paranoias' 'Snuff Rock' EP. Then there were other gems by the Saints, the Drones, Slaughter and the Dogs, Wire and X-Ray Spex.

It was upon this day that the inevitable happened. I got arrested. I was in the Lowfields Road pen next to the Liverpool fans, and dressed in my punk clothes. Anyway, for whatever reason, this copper decides he wanted to arrest me. I wasn't doing anything to warrant this, maybe he just didn't like punks - but things didn't quite go according to plan. This copper tried to drag me over the fence onto the side of the pitch. Suddenly, all my friends see this and start to drag me back. I was being stretched right over a barrier and it was painful. This went on for a while. Eventually I caught my family jewels on the barrier; I just screamed for someone to let me go. You see, your friends are always there for you. It didn't matter how much pain I was in, they still continued to pull me over the barrier. I screamed again and eventually my friends let go. This enabled the copper to pull me onto the pitch side. There was no, "Are you alright, son?" He just dragged me onto my feet then proceeded to frog march me around the perimeter of the Elland Road pitch. As we started to walk past the Leeds Kop known as the Geldard End, to a man they started to sing, "Silly, silly, silly cunt!"

In reference to my punk attire I imagine, which was quite basic, really. Drainpipe trousers, bumper boots, stencilled T-shirt with zips, a couple of safety pins and some punk badges. I stuck two fingers up at them. How dare they? I saw a few of the Leeds firm as I went past. They just laughed at me as well. Soon I'm in the custody cell. I wasn't worried, being my first time - I was more worried about missing the Stranglers gig later that night, and I didn't fancy being locked up in a cell all night. A big burly copper banged his book on the counter and walked around me, actually staring at me with a magnifying glass, like Sherlock Holmes. "What have we got here then, the missing link?" All his colleagues laughed along. After a minute of wise cracks I'm escorted to the holding cell, then the door bangs. I look around. There are about 20 other people in there, mostly Leeds fans, but there are a couple of Mickeys sat in the corner. Everyone just sits down waiting for their time to be released.

I was in the cells for a couple of hours. Time stood still in those cells. After quite a time the coppers informed me that Leeds lost the match 2-1. That made my day even worse. Eventually they let me out at around 7pm. I was given my charge sheets for breach of the peace and I was finally free to go to the Stranglers gig, so I walked into town. It was hard to believe there had been a football match earlier with thousands of people in attendance. It was eerily quiet now, no sign of life, until I got near the city centre. The Queen's Hall was a massive building under the bridge near the train station. As I walked around looking for people I knew, I saw some familiar faces hanging around the station including Steve Marshall, one of the Leeds firm. I asked him what he was doing. He said he was looking for a fight with punks, or rockers, or anyone really. I said "Bye then" and walked on. The gig was great fun. I didn't see any trouble but I did hear of a couple of people being jumped outside, probably Steve Marshall and his crew.

The Stranglers were supported by the Saints from Australia who were quite good, and the Drones from Manchester who I thought were the best band of the three on the night. The gig looked empty, with people just around the stage, but the Queen's Hall was a big place. The Stranglers eventually came on, but to me they looked more like hippies and sounded like a Doors cover band, apart from a couple of songs like 'Straighten Out'. I loved the bass intro on that but generally I thought the Stranglers were boring. I got talking with someone who had something to do with putting the gig on. When I remarked that it seemed empty, the guy replied that over a thousand people had paid in tonight. Wow, I thought, looks can be deceiving. A thousand punk rockers! Where did they all come from? I hadn't seen more than a couple of hundred up until then, and that had been at a gig. Afterwards I bumped into some punks from Bradford and we chatted about the gig. I made my way back to the train station and met Steve Marshall, who was still hanging round looking for people to fight.

"Busy night, Steve?" I asked.

"Not bad," he replied. "A couple of minor incidents to keep me going, nothing major yet but it usually kicks off when the pubs close."

"OK, bye," I said.

Ian turns to me and says, "It was him that tried to attack us on our way to the gig!"

"He didn't seem to recognise you", I said. We headed into a noisy Leeds Station with lots of drunken people and potential for violence, but luckily not tonight for us, and we made it back to Bradford OK.

So now we are entering the Christmas holiday period. I was looking forward to a good rest, but also to getting in a few gigs, and there were some very good ones coming up, most notably the Sex Pistols, who were playing twice in a week, in Keighley on the Monday at Knickers Club and on Christmas day in Huddersfield at Ivanhoe's, which happened to be a Sunday. Although it was possible that the Pistols' gigs could get cancelled at any minute because at the moment they were banned from playing almost anywhere and we were reading in the music press that they were playing not as the Sex Pistols but as 'SPOTS', or 'Sex Pistols On Tour'. There was also the Drones, who were playing a concert at Queensbury Library. Queensbury is apparently the highest village in the UK. We call people from Queensbury mountain men; it snows in summer up there sometimes.

First up, however, are two school discos. Neither of these is at my old school, Buttershaw. We are not having a school disco because we have our discos at Westwood Park, which is the local mental health institute. At previous discos the clients or patients were allowed to come to the disco also, which seemed a strange decision. Some kids were repulsed by this, some of the girls found it scary and some of the lads were awful and started taking the piss out of vulnerable people, so the discos were stopped. Buttershaw was the biggest school in our city but only one person out of 1,200 pupils went onto university. You can read into that what you like, but I learnt very little while I was there and came away with no qualifications. Luckily I was an avid reader so I schooled myself. I even made my own school certificates, which unfortunately were not acknowledged by the job centre as validity of intelligence. My closest punk friend Chris invited me to his school disco at Grange, which is the school I should have gone to, being just up the road from my house. But no - I was sent to the enemy school and became a traitor to some in my area. How did it happen that some pupils were sent to school miles away from their home, especially when the kids had to make their own way home and there was potential for things to go wrong; meeting strangers or being attacked by other school kids, etc?

On the night of the disco Chris was still in his last year at school, so he was a bit wary of going dressed as a punk as he didn't want to get expelled, whereas I had left in April. We got dressed up in our punk attire and bobbed along to the disco. It was in a dark sports hall and there were quite a few people about, dancing to disco and pop music. After about an hour of being stared at by the rest of the pupils who reacted as though we were aliens from outer space, we were getting a bit bored. I don't think it was the reaction we were looking for. We weren't really sure what reaction we were looking for but maybe we thought in our childish, naive minds that suddenly we would become irresistible to the opposite sex, or that at least they'd find us interesting enough to talk to. Or that we'd just shock them out of their sensibilities. But none of these things were happening. We were looked upon with derision.

After a while we grew bored, so we went to ask the DJ if he had any punk records. We weren't expecting any to be honest, but we were delighted to find he had the Sex Pistols' 'God Save the Queen'. "Yes! Put that on," we shouted in an excited manner, but it was difficult to communicate in a room where you could hardly hear yourself speak. Suddenly, there it was in all its glory - the opening bar of the incendiary song that was the Sex Pistols' anthem, lambasting our head of state. "God Save the Queen, it's a fascist regime, she made you a moron, potential H bomb." As my compatriot Chris and I are leaping about the place like Spring-Heeled Jack, we suddenly find we are the focus of attention again. Everyone gathers round to check out our dance moves. The more the crowd stare disapprovingly the more we leap about in defiance.

Halfway through the song I hear a loud, authoritarian voice shout, "What do you think you're doing, laddie?" Suddenly this person grabs hold of me and Chris, he shouts to the DJ to stop the record. It comes to an abrupt halt with a screech. I am glad that wasn't my copy I thought. Then he turns his attention back to us. The house lights go on for our maximum embarrassment, or so they thought. "What do you think you are doing? This is a school disco! People come here to dance."

I shouted back, "What you do you think we are doing? This is punk, it's new - get with it, gramps. Anyway, who are you?" Looking at Chris's face I should have guessed.

"I'm the headmaster of this school", he replied. Suddenly he is frog marching us to his office.

I shake his hand off me, saying, "I'm not a pupil of yours. You can't do anything to me." So he let go of me, but not liking my response one bit, he gripped Chris harder. Punk was giving me the confidence to stand up to people and I was loving all this anti-authoritarianism. Fuck the system, I thought to myself.

Chris didn't love it, though. It was embarrassing for him, as the headmaster rang his mum and asked her to come and explain his actions. Chris's parents were quite well off compared to the rest of us. They had their own business and even had a plane, which was unheard of then. Chris's dad was a character himself - he was obsessed with the American West and dressed like a cowboy. When Chris's mum comes to pick him up, she doesn't look that concerned really but doesn't want to jeopardise his last year in school, and his exams. So they listen to what the headmaster has to say, and agree to do certain things. Then we beat a hasty retreat home. Later in the week we meet up with some of the Bradford punks in our local, the Mannville Arms, laughing about this incident, when my close punk friend Timothy Calvey says, "I am going to mine on Saturday night. Do you fancy it?"

"Yeah, OK! It sounds like fun", I said. Tim and I had this silly friendly rivalry thing going on. He supported Man United and being a Leeds fan, this was an anathema to me. Tim's brother Mick was a Leeds fan as well. We clashed on everything. We didn't like one another's favourite bands, either.

Anyway, Tim has invited me along to his school disco and his school is Catholic, so they are easier to offend. And although I liked to think I was clued up on life after all those books I had read, and being a punk trying to make a positive change in the world, I was still a kid with a sense of fun and when provoked could come across as an arrogant arse. And one of the thrills was to shock people, so I thought this could be fun. Tim has a broken leg and is struggling to get about on his crutches at the best of times and it's icy outside, but he doesn't want to miss a chance to visit his old school to show them how proud he was of being a punk. We had to get a taxi up to the school, which was situated about four miles away on the outskirts of Bradford, and the snow had been really bad the last couple of days. We got up there and went into the disco, only to find not that many people had turned up. It was a joint Catholic girls and boys' disco. They had separate schools situated next to each other; Cardinal Hinsley (boys) and Margaret Clitheroe (girls). They were never keen on boys and girls coming together usually, so this was probably a one off. As we looked around we could see nuns standing menacingly around the room surveying everyone to make sure that no one had too much fun. The music was pop/disco music as per usual. Luckily we had brought the Sex Pistols LP with us on the off-chance they might be so pleased to see us and would play one of the songs on it. Being mischievous there was only one song we wanted them to play: 'Bodies'.

Tim hated the school so he wanted to upset them. In fact, most of the Catholic kids I knew seem to hate their schools at the time. Mind you, so did everyone else. I was only on this trip for a laugh but I thought 'Bodies' was a wise choice and guaranteed to upset the Catholic authorities. So we walked up to the DJ booth and asked the DJ if he would play one of the songs from this LP. He was a friendly sort and didn't appear to realise who the Sex Pistols were.

"Which track do you want?" he asks.

"Bodies," we say, collectively. We are giggling like naughty schoolboys, knowing it's going to annoy the nuns in particular. Five minutes later the track comes on. "She was a girl from Birmingham, She's just had an abortion, She was a case of insanity, Her name was Pauline she lived in a tree." We jump on the dance floor - except in Tim's case, it's a hobble. As I am leaping around I am consciously looking at the nuns standing around the perimeter of the room like the guards of morality, expecting a reaction but not seeing one, to Tim's and my annoyance. But we knew the chorus would do the trick any minute now… BANG! "Fuck this and fuck that, Fuck it all and fuck the fucking brat, She don't want a baby that looks like that, I don't want a baby that looks like that. Body, I'm not an animal. Body, I'm not an abortion."

You can see the nuns' ears alerted en masse, eyes bulging in disbelief at what they've just heard. It's really tested their sensibilities. At first they seem a bit disorientated and are slow to respond, until their shocked faces turn to hatred. Now for the physical response. They run onto the dance floor mob-handed, and proceed to pick both me and Tim right up off the dance floor and carry us towards the fire exit doors. They open the doors and bodily throw us both out into the snow, and close the door behind them.

As this is happening I shout, "Where's me fucking Sex Pistols LP, you fascists?" A couple of minute later as I'm trying to get Tim up from the snow and back onto his feet I hear the door open again. I say to Tim, "Do you think they may have changed their minds and come back to invite us back in?"

Tim laughs and says, "You must be fucking joking. After we played that song the nuns will be damning us to hell for all eternity." Then all of a sudden and to confirm what Tim just said, my Sex Pistols LP comes flying out of the door, just missing our heads before landing in a bush. The door closes again. I finally get Tim off the floor and ask him where his crutches are. We look around and can only find one. So I bang on the fire exit door again then one of the nuns opens it.

I respond, equally angrily, "You've only thrown out one of Tim's crutches, you heartless witches! If he dies, I'm going to report you to the Geneva Convention." There is a lull in the proceedings as the nun simply turns and goes back in the venue. A minute later the door opens again and his crutch flies out and lands in the snow. We turn to each other and laugh, before heading off to find a taxi to take us back to the Mannville, where we get pissed.

Next gig up is the Drones at the Queensbury Library. It was an odd gig, this one, because they were playing in a library. It's the first gig they have ever had as far as I'm aware but it must have been a fundraiser of some kind, for them to go to all that trouble of having to move all the books out of the room in order to put the gig on. We all caught the bus up there. The only people there were us lot from Bradford; about 30 of us. I went with Sunni who as an orange streak in his hair. He was wearing his swimming goggles and, as always, had the top buttons of his trousers open and was up to his old party trick of trying to get women to put their hands down his trousers. First up was Jab Jab, a local reggae band who supported at a few punk gigs which was great, because punks loved reggae. The Drones headlined and were great, as usual. You could tell they could play a bit due to the great R&B bass lines. They had some good songs; my favourites being 'Lift of the Bands' and 'City Drones' - but there wasn't one bad song, to be honest.

There was some trouble at the gig after they let in some locals who were looking to start some. Those little villages around the country could be terrible places; very narrow minded and insular. A few punks were attacked so the promoter rang the police. As soon as the Drones had finished, we left to try and catch the last bus into town. As we set off the police still hadn't arrived. We walked outside to find there had been a really bad snowfall and it was about two foot high. There would be no buses now. We had no other way of getting home, so we had to walk. It was still snowing really badly and everyone was freezing, so we decided to have a snowball fight to try and keep warm. It was really strange because everywhere was deserted - you could hear a pin drop and it felt like we were the only people on earth. Suddenly this police car went whizzing past just as someone was throwing a snowball. Unluckily, it hit the police car, causing it to swerve and almost crash. This big sergeant got out of the car in a foul mood. He had us all against the wall and began taking our details. I think he was going to nick us, but when we all apologised and told him we couldn't get home and were throwing snowballs to try to keep warm, his attitude mellowed and he organised for a black Mariah to come up and take us back to Bradford centre, where we all stopped round mine and a few other friends' houses until the next day.

What a week so far. But the following week would be the big one - as it contained two Sex Pistols gigs. I was so excited at finally getting to see the Sex Pistols after what we'd read about them in the media; finally we would get to see what all the fuss was about. The first gig was on the Monday at Keighley Knickers Club. We, the Bradford punks, decided to only go to Keighley because Christmas Day fell on a Sunday this year, which meant there would be no transport to get to Huddersfield, no one had a car either or the money for a taxi - that's if any taxi rank would have been open. So there were no options left to get to Huddersfield. Nothing happened on Sundays in the UK. It was a day of rest or for people to go to church. There were no shops open, only pubs, but with limited opening times. So that was it, all of us were only going to go to the Keighley gig.

On the day, we all travelled over on the bus together. It was busy outside as all the local punks had been waiting there long before it opened. The Sex Pistols themselves were outside the venue at some point and people were talking to them. The promoter was handing out leaflets, telling us that the police were looking for excuses to close down the gig, so he was asking for all us punks to behave and not give them their excuse to do it. We are all talking to one another and getting drunk, until suddenly we hear Johnny Rotten speak and the whole place goes quiet. I turn round and look up and see Rotten standing there in gingham-style muslin 'Destroy' t-shirt, with goggles round his neck. Sid's wearing a black leather jacket with no shirt and Jones is also in black. Then they start to play this wonderful racket which lifts the entire roof off the place. The venue was a strange building; it was hard to even see the band as the stage was halfway up the wall and facing the balcony, which meant that the people wanting to dance to the music were underneath the stage below Rotten, who kept looking over the top to see the crowd. There was some undefinable sticky substance on the floor which made dancing quite difficult. I remember getting really drunk and not remembering how any of us got back home.

So it's Christmas Day and I dont think pubs were open and if they were it would have been a back door job.. Very few options, really, so I went round to Chris's house. We were bored stiff. Same old films, Queen's speech, etc.

We looked at each other and I said, "Fancy going to Huddersfield for the Pistols gig?"

Chris thought a minute and replied, "Yeah! Fuck it. Why not. Nothing else to do around here." "The Sex Pistols message is more important to us than the Queen's," we shouted to Chris's parents when they asked us where we were going. We realised we would have to walk, but for some strange reason it was a lovely sunny afternoon instead of the usual drab winter's day. So, we just set off walking. We both lived on the Huddersfield side of Bradford anyway, which made it a little easier. When we got to Odsal Top we bumped into another Bradford punk who came from Holmewood and was a big Bradford City fan.

He readily agreed to come with us. By the time we got near to Wyke we were really thirsty. This other lad spotted a garage, so he nipped in and nicked us a bottle of milk each.

Three hours later and 11 miles down the road, we arrived in Huddersfield. It was just growing dark by the time we got to the venue, but once we did, we were told that the gig had sold out. We were so tired from walking from Bradford that we sat down to try and get some rest because we couldn't face walking back again yet. There were about ten other punks outside, standing around next to us. We spoke to some of them; they had come from Wolverhampton, Manchester and Liverpool. The queue was just full of non-punks - old hippies, Tetley bitter men, striking firemen and people who were curious to see the band, I guess. It looked as though Keighley was going to prove to have been the better gig because that audience had been full of punks. This one might be well dodgy by the look of this crowd.

We were so exhausted that we just sat down on the floor. Shortly after, a door opened and someone passed us out a large plate of sandwiches, left over from the kiddies' party earlier that afternoon. We were starving after our walk so they were gratefully received. We passed the sandwiches around amongst the other punks. Not so long after that, the doors were opened and everyone went in the gig, except for us ten or so punks. It was a horrible feeling to have the door shut on us, especially after an 11 mile walk to see the band. We were still too tired to walk back, so we just hung around outside. A short while later, two blokes came out and had a look around. One of them was Malcolm McLaren and the other one, I assumed, was the promoter.

The Sex Pistols' manager was telling the other guy, "The Sex Pistols will not play unless you let these punks in." Then they both went back inside the venue again and closed the doors. We all kind of looked at one other and our reaction was mostly of people not expecting much at all.

But, within a few minutes, the promoter came back outside and told us, "We've decided to let you in. You can pay in on the door."

We were overjoyed and suddenly felt energised again. We formed a disorderly queue to get in and descended some stairs, paying in through a little hole in the wall on the right hand side. After I handed over my money I received a yellowish looking ticket with 'The Sex Pistols' written on it. I noticed not all the tickets were the same. Some had question marks where the band name was supposed to be. When we got to the bottom of the stairs and into the venue it appeared, as it was looking outside, that the crowd did consist of mainly non-punk types. The only other punk I could see was Simon Snake, the singer of local punk band the Jerks who were from Mirfield. He stood out from the crowd with his bleached blonde hair. He also seemed taller than everyone else down at the front. The gig was rammed. It was so full that we couldn't get near the bar - in fact we couldn't move at all. We were still so tired from walking and had no energy left, so we just sat at the bottom of the steps we had just walked down, and waited.

Very shortly after, the Sex Pistols walked on stage in good spirits and seemingly full of Christmas cheer. Once they started playing, we realised that there were far too many people in the venue, which looked as though it could hold about 400 at a push. I've no idea how many there actually were in there but it was extremely uncomfortable. The space seemed to get tighter. Sid, who was directly in front of us, displayed his scarred chest; something he seemed proud of. He was pouting and trying to look hard. Rotten spoke to the crowd and seemed like a really friendly guy. Maybe relaxing with the kids in the afternoon had put them in a good mood? Chris and I were getting shoved all over the place but we had no energy left to push back. We had to take turns at giving each other a piggy back just so we could see the band. I looked round the walls of this club and could see Pistols' posters everywhere, so I thought I would have some of them at the end of the gig. The band was on form it seemed, and enjoying the gig as much as we were. Rotten came onto the dance floor at one point to join in with the crowd. He seemed to like being close to the audience after being denied that at Keighley. It was a magical moment when Rotten shouted, "Here's your Christmas national anthem!" and went straight into 'God Save The Queen'. I thought to myself, if only the Queen could see this now.

After the gig finished everybody just left, piling past us, as we were still by the stairs where we'd come in. I was keeping an eye out for posters but with each person who passed to leave, there seemed to be one less poster on the wall. Eventually, by the time everyone who was leaving had left, from what I could see all the posters appeared to have gone. I gave a sigh of disappointment. We were still knackered by this point and could still hardly move so we just sat down again. Still thinking of the posters though, I thought I would go for a closer look on the off-chance that any had dropped onto the floor. As we were about to take a walk around the room, I spotted some posters left on the far wall, so we headed in that direction. There we bumped into some other punk mates from Bradford who were just about to leave: Sham, Nigel W, Keith P, Mark , Murph and Skin, who were equally surprised to see us. We started chatting about what we all thought of the gig.

Then all of a sudden Rotten came up to Nigel and said, "You got a spare fag, mate?" Rotten was wearing a plastic desert hat and an old suit jacket. We were a bit nervous of speaking to him really but he seemed so friendly. I asked him what he'd thought of the Keighley gig. "The crowd were good but it was a strange venue having the stage so high on a wall and the crowd dancing below us," he told me. We then asked him about the punk scene in London. He said, "You should go down and check it out for yourselves. Some places are good and some not so good but there's a lot happening down there."

I told him I had already been there and visited Seditionaries on my last trip to London, but I was hoping to go down again soon. What really struck me about him most was that he was a really down to earth guy. No airs or graces. He appeared to be genuinely interested in our opinions and seemed comfortable being around people. We must have talked to him for about half an hour.

Then I look round the back wall and shouted, "Damn! There are no posters left again."

Rotten said, "I have a 'Holidays in the Sun' poster backstage if you want it?" He came back a few minutes later with the poster and a flyer, and said, "Maybe see you in London sometime, and if you do get there I'll try and get you on the guest list." Then he walked off to talk to some other people at the bar. I went off into the toilets to see if there were any more posters there. By the time I came out only Chris was left and he had no idea where the others had gone. It had been a great gig but now we had to get home somehow and neither of us was sure we had the energy to walk back to Bradford.

We walked back up the stairs to the outside and those stairs seemed even steeper than before. Once outside, we began hearing reports from people that things were a bit hairy. The local Huddersfield Town fans were on the prowl, looking to batter some poor little punks. We weren't sure what to do but we didn't think we could walk all the way back to Bradford. So we headed across the road from the venue to the local police station. I'm not sure why, maybe to see if the police would give us a lift back to Bradford because Chris was technically still a minor so they might go for it, or ring his mum to come and get us. But luckily, just as we were crossing the road, we spotted our friends from Bradford again, who just happened to be getting picked up by their dad, so we hung around waiting with them for a lift back to Bradford. It was an extremely tight fit in the car with eight of us but it was much better than walking home. I was never sure what happened to the other lad from Bradford who'd walked over there with us, because we never saw him again once we got inside the venue. What a night though - and sober!

IV
THE MARQUEE RESIDENCY
JANUARY 1978

'Hey, you got a face like a Labrador
I don't mind, that's what I'm here for
The angel Gabriel sent me
To give you a little bit of sympathy

I'm gonna take you down to Harley Street

Such a shame you had that crash
That will teach you to drive flash
And a lorry hit you at full power
Your blood gushing like a shower

Plastic surgery – it's so plastic
Plastic surgery - fantastic.'

It's been a shit start to the New Year. I got arrested against Notts Forest, in the third round of the FA Cup. I wouldn't mind, but I didn't even do anything. As I walked past the ground someone had grabbed my leg and started shouting, "That's him!" So the police barged through the crowd and arrested me. As they marched me to a police van, they were saying, "We have your mate as well." When I arrived at the van, there was already a guy in there who I didn't know. I told the police as much, but they opened the cell door and pushed me inside. I chatted with this guy and he told me he was from Wakefield and he had attacked this Forest fan outside the ground because he was angry Leeds had lost 3-1. I was sick of being targeted by the police because of my punk attire, but there was a big inconsistency in my life. I was getting into trouble on Saturdays, but the rest of my life was about meeting people from all walks of life; and a lot of them were also football fans. This had been bugging me for a while now. I preferred to have a laugh with people; there were enough problems to deal with without creating further aggro. I was loving the punk lifestyle, so I decided to stop going to every Leeds game and only go when I had the time, with the exception of Man United games. I couldn't miss those; they were the highlight of the season.

It's been quite a while since the Man in the Moon gig in May. As soon as I'd got back to Bradford I had told everyone what a fantastic band they were supposed to be, even though I'd had the misfortune of missing the Ants entirely. I was going purely by what I'd been told by Sunni and a couple of others. Brinsley, Mel and OC said they would be interested in going to London with me to see the Ants the next time I was planning to go. So we start to plan every week, trying to work out when we would have the time and the money to make the trip. I'm still in touch with Penny; we speak on the phone whenever we can. She sends me the odd letter about the gigs she's attended. Everything sounds so exciting down in London and I'm sitting there thinking: why am I still in Bradford when I could be living in London and watching bands every night? I sit there daydreaming of walking down the King's Road, seeing loads of beautiful, creative messes. The punk girls looked so sexy even though they were trying not to be. Maybe there's a lesson to be learned there? We should not try too hard to be something we are not. I imagined all the punk groups would be hanging around outside Seditionaries; planning revolutions, travelling the world, expanding the punk family. In reality they were probably off their heads and trying to survive on their wits.

In the meantime it's back to work at the colourful world of the local Corona pop factory. I do like this job. You get a good physical workout every day, humping crates of pop up and down in customer's shops. It can be a bit frustrating at times, especially when you've delivered hundreds of crates up or down into someone's attic or cellar, then they tell you they can't pay for them right now in the hope that you will leave it there, but you can't, so you have to take them all out again. But generally it's a decent job. No two days are the same and I'm out on the road every day but I have to be careful, because my dad is the driver. He takes some stick because of me. I haven't been getting along with some of my work colleagues for a while now. Most of the blokes don't like me, because a lot of the women in the office like me; and I don't letch all over the women like the rest of the blokes do. I keep telling these blokes that women aren't stupid - they know that beneath that charm offensive you have an ulterior motive. They want more than a bunk-up in the back of your rusty old car and a pair of laddered tights. I simply treat the women how I like to be treated myself. The bosses hated me as well for that same reason. They are always all over the girls, in particular the deputy, Nigel. To make it worse, his partner works in the office as well.

The management were always trying to get me to come to work in normal clothes, but I went everywhere in the same clothes I wore to gigs - bondage trousers, sometimes a kilt; and different coloured hair every two weeks. I told the bosses to look at my hair dye as free advertisement for the pop flavours. Anyway, one day they devised a plan to either get rid of me or to get me to change my clothes. We had some new deliveries in an ultra posh Tory stronghold out in the Yorkshire Dales, so the bosses sent me and my dad, expecting a backlash. Their parting words were, "If we get any complaints, you have to change your dress code or you're out."

"OK!" I replied and waved at them. However, everyone liked my dad, who was a decent bloke. Actually there was one bloke I got on with; Arthur who was a skinhead who loved reggae and was friends with a punk mate of mine Derek Swales.

It was a long ride out to the Dales and miles away from our usual delivery routes. We arrived at the picturesque village after about four hours. As we were unloading the wagon outside this shop, the streets started getting busier. We went into the shop and the owner looked me up and down in a judgemental manner. I gathered he didn't seem too pleased to see me. So I smiled and said "Hello!" Suddenly, the shop became packed out, but everyone was looking at me, with my parachute shirt, zipped trousers and coloured hair. I don't think the existence of punk had filtered through to some parts of the Empire, yet. Someone went up to my dad and whispered, "Who'd let their son walk round like that?" Which must have hurt him, I guess; but he just carried on, not letting it show. I knew I would be judged so I was extra polite to everyone. I just love it when you change people's perceptions of you after their first physical impressions. By the end of our appearance in this guy's shop the owner was ultra-happy, because he'd made tons of cash.

My manager, John, rang the shop owner to see if their backlash plan had worked, but it turned out that the owner asked for me and my dad to be their regular delivery guys. I also learned that people may not like you but as long as they're making money out of you, they'll deal with it. The next day my dad wasn't well, so he didn't go into work. It was his first day off work, ever. I was sent out with two other drivers, Big Pete and his assistant Lee. Big Pete had just come out of the army because he had lost an eye. He was a mountain of a man. We had finished a delivery in Ilkley towards the end of our shift, and all the money from the deliveries, which had been left in the van, had been stolen. Or so Big Pete and Lee said. When we got back to the depot I found out they had tried blaming it on me, and the police were waiting to interview me. I was pulled into a room and told, "If you don't own up, you'll get 15 years."

I laughed out loud and replied, "You don't get that for murder!" The bosses were really hoping it would be the end of me but it wasn't. The following day the two drivers confessed after making the stupid mistake of leaving the stolen proceeds in their cars, only to be found out by the police. They were both sacked. It turned out they had been planning this for a while, and had just been waiting for the right moment... and when I was sent out with them, they'd decided that that moment was it, and that I would take the blame. I lived to fight another day, much to the annoyance of the bosses. The girls in the office took me out for a drink after work, which then annoyed all the men at work even more.

After a heavy week of delivering pop, it was punk gigs at the weekend; and down the Mannville and the Royal Standard on a Sunday night to finish off, before getting back on the treadmill again. I'd been trying to find out as much about the Ants as possible. 6th November 1975. The Sex Pistols support Bazooka Joe. Adam realises The Pistols are the future and hands in his notice becoming the first convert to punk. The Ants were formed in 1976; initially called the B Sides, after Adam put an ad in Melody Maker titled: 'Beat on a Bass with the B Sides', the line up consists of Adam, Andy Warren, Bid, Lester Square, Paul Flannigan and Bob Hip. They rehearse throughout '76 and record a definitive version of 'These Boots are made for Walking', then split at the end of 1976. Andy Warren joins Charlie Harper's R&B outfit, the Marauders, for a while. Then on April 23 1977, the Ants were formed at the Roxy Club after the Banshees' last gig there. The Roxy promoter Andy Czezowski was asked to manage the Ants but he declined. They then auditioned for Falcon Stuart, the manager of X-Ray Spex, but nothing happened, Lester Square departs and Mark 'The Kid' Ryan replaces Lester. The Ants' first gig is at the

ICA restaurant. They are kicked out after one song: 'Beat My Guest'. They then complete the show in the interval of John Dowie's show in the ICA theatre.

Then we have the residency at the Man in the Moon. The Ants have played a few more gigs by now. After a gig supporting the Desolation Angels at Hornsey College of Art, their drummer Dave Barbe joins the Ants. Then both Adam and Jordan find themselves in Derek Jarman's film 'Jubilee'. They record 'Plastic Surgery' with Kenny Morris of the Banshees on drums, because Dave is ill; then go to the Drury Lane Theatre to film a performance of the track, during which Adam dislocates his knee rolling about on the floor. Most of the Ants' exposure has been in and around London so far, with the odd gig in Liverpool and Birmingham. They have been playing alongside the Banshees quite lot, also with the Buzzcocks and the Vibrators, among others. I've spoken to Penny and she's told me that the Ants are now called Adam and the Ants, and they have a residency coming up at the Marquee club, starting January 5 1978, for a month. I have also discovered that the Seditionaries assistant, Jordan, who I met at the Man in the Moon gig, is now the manager of Adam and the Ants. This had happened after the third Man in the Moon gig, which they headlined. Apparently the entire audience walked out, leaving Jordan, Siouxsie Sioux and Steve Severin from the Banshees, as the only people left.

I've been dying to get down to London again to see the Ants and go down the King's Road. I did manage the second part when I went to see Leeds play at Chelsea on October 1, but it had only been a flying visit as I'd had to get back to Bradford for an engagement do. That trip down had been a bit eventful after the four of us in the car had been sussed as Leeds fans in a service station full of Sheffield Wednesday fans. They ran at our car in an aggressive manner. We'd been expecting the worst, but they just came up to the window and shouted, "You going to bribe Chelsea?" in reference to some allegations in the newspapers from old squeaky nuts, Alan Ball. We then proceeded onto London for the game, which Leeds won 2-1. We did get a chance to have a quick walk up and down the King's Road which I wasn't expecting, but I had no money for Seditionaries, so I had to do with looking and dreaming of what I might buy later. It was great to see the King's Road packed with punks even my mate Neil Roscoe and Alan Butcher thought it was fun.

I've taken it easy over the New Year. I want to save up my money for London. I'll be there for a few days to see Penny and for the first time in concent Adam and the Ants, so I will need all the money I can get. Finally the day has come and I'm off to see the Ants. I'm going down with my mates from Bradford - Mel, Brinsley and OC. They arrive really early in the morning before I've even had a chance to wake up. Mel's been telling everyone about his new car; it was really cheap, he said, but a good runner. As I look at them through the window they are all dressed in their best punk attire, a mixture of Seditionaries and a lot of DIY stuff, stencilled T-shirts with zips and X Clothes' special bondage straps. I notice Brinsley has a new hairstyle which looks like leopard skin. It looks complicated and I'm wondering how he's managed it. Brinsley probably hasn't even been to bed yet, knowing him. I'm tired, but as usual they are full of the joys of life, making noise and waking up the neighbours. They bang on the door, sledgehammer style.

"Hi, boys, looking forward to seeing the Ants tonight?" I say.

"Yes!" They exclaim in unison. I look past them to see a yellow three-wheeler car parked there.

"What's that?"

"It's my new car," says Mel.

"You serious?" I say. "Do you really think that will get us to London in one piece?"

"Sure," says Mel. As soon as Brinsley gets inside my flat he's rooting around making a mess, picking things up then putting them back in a different place until my flat starts to resemble a bomb site. OC and Mel just sit down to watch the TV. I start to make tea and some breakfast. OC comes in while I'm making tea.

"All right, OC?" I said.

"All right," he replies and suddenly he starts laughing.

"What you laughing about?"

"You making tea. You look really domesticated.

I take the tea through and ask Brinsley who had done his new hairdo. "Was it Jimmy?" We had a punk friend called Jimmy who was a trainee hairdresser alongside his girlfriend, Louise. Some of us used to go to his shop in Cleckheaton. They were always entering competitions for hairdressing - the more outrageous the better, so I would go to model for them and I would get the haircut done for free. I'd had a bleached skinhead with different coloured tramlines, and a deck of cards dyed on the back of my head once. They would take pictures and enter them into competitions.

"No! It wasn't Jimmy. I got someone to do it with felt pens," says Brinsley.

I said "What? Felt pens?" We all laughed but secretly it looked really good and showed a creative idea. Not sure whether it would stay in or come straight out, but each to their own. We're talking now about how excited we are about seeing the Ants. We've all asked Malcolm Fairplay to put them on at our new punk home the Royal Standard, but we've heard nothing as yet. I can see all the excitement they're feeling is exactly how I felt the first time I went; in fact I'm still as excited as they are. My only worry is that three wheeler car. I'm sitting there imagining us getting stuck in between two articulated Lorries on the motorway… they veer towards one another and suddenly we are paper thin and blowing off course.

Anyway, seeing the Ants far outweighs the dangers of cars and motorways, etc. On the plus side, I was only going one way. After taking some days of leave I wanted to spend them with Penny, so I would be hitchhiking home again. Finally we set off. It's a bloody squeeze getting the four of us into a three wheeled car, but we set off full of excitement and expectation. We have a battery operated cassette player and lots of badly recorded punk tapes of live concerts which sound like they've been recorded in the toilet, plus some home-made compilation tapes. We decide to play a game to make it more exciting. We call it 'Give us a clue'. This consists of playing some of our badly taped gigs and trying to guess who the hell was playing. So I pick a tape out of a carrier bag without looking and pop it into the machine and press play. As the song plays we have to guess the band. The music is playing; we are all studying hard to work it out.

This should be quite easy as we have listened to all these tapes so many times, but the quality is so bad you need to read the covers to find out, then add the sound of the engine and it's almost impossible. The tape is playing but all we can really hear are loads of London voices speaking. Then we hear 30 seconds of barely audible sounds.

OC shouts, "It's the Damned, 'New Rose'!"

"No it isn't," I reply. "That sounded like a saxophone. The Damned don't have a saxophone."

"Is it the Clash? 'Complete Control'?" asks Mel.

"The Clash don't have a saxophone either."

Mel, "It's not a saxophone. It's just a bad recording."

We keep guessing and debating and getting nowhere. In the end we have to look at the cover, only to find out it's the Stranglers. We try another tape, with similar results, so we then decide to put on one of our better recordings of songs I've recorded. After a while we are driving down the motorway, singing to our hearts' content. We stop for a cup of tea and some food at Leicester Forest motorway station. I take the chance to call Penny, who I'm really looking forward to seeing again. It seems like ages since the Man in the Moon gig. Well, it is, actually. The phone rings and I hear Penny's voice.

"Hi, how're you doing?"

"OK," she says. "But, bad news. I have to work tonight so I won't be able to come to the Ants gig."

"Shit! When will I see you then? And can we still stay at your squat?"

"Of course," she replies. "I'll come and meet you at the Marquee after I finish."

"OK, see you later," I said, and put the phone down. I was a little upset that Penny wasn't able to come to the gig, but there was nothing I could do. I was determined not to let it spoil my fun, plus I would get to spend some time with her in the next few days.

We had such a laugh going down to London, singing away, chatting about what might happen. The only concern was when we hit an open stretch of road and the wind went under us the car felt like it was about to take off, which was a little unnerving. But after four hours of part driving and part flying, we made it to Brent Cross.

We were told it was best to park up there and catch the tube into London. It's now 5.30. We park up on the street outside the station and jump on the tube. We get off at Tottenham Court Road, but I somehow get separated from the others as we hit the crowds. It's very claustrophobic on the tubes at the best of times but at rush hour it's even worse. I come out of the station but I can't see them anywhere. After a minute or two, when the crowds have dissipated but I still can't see them, I decide to walk down to the Marquee club and hopefully I'll catch up with them there. Well, I'm hoping so, as they don't know how to get hold of Penny for somewhere to stay the night.

After walking the streets for what seems like ages, I finally find the Marquee club. The Marquee is so famous I assumed that everyone would know it but apparently not. I join the queue but I can't see any faces I know. Inside, it's dark and dingy. As you walk in, there's a bar on the left hand side and it's packed to the rafters with people trying to get served. On the right is a corridor that leads to the gig room. It's not very big. The stage is to the left as you walk in and there's a DJ booth on the far wall. The place is rammed in anticipation of the Ants playing. Finally I spot Brinsley, Mel and OC at the bar, which is a relief. At the bar, I bump into one of the kids I'd met outside the Man in the Moon gig; a lad called Duncan, although some people called him Dunc, Dangerous D or Double D.

He's telling me, "We go to every Ants gig now. There's probably about 30 people from all over London following the Ants now." Dunc takes me over to a corner of the club where his mates are; I recognise some of the faces from the Man in the Moon. He introduces me to some of them: Popey, Big PD, Crazy Kev, Johnny Aggro, Red Faced and Kirby.

"Some interesting names there," I remark.

"Well," Dunc explains, "We like calling people names which describe the opposite to what their nature is. So Johnny Aggro is not aggressive and Crazy Kev is not crazy either. 'Good bloke' means he is not a good bloke. 'Slim' means 'Fat'. 'Truthy slim' means 'fat lying bar steward.' Big PD is an exception - he is big - and Joe the Collar is a golfer." There was a lot of reverse back talk. It was like our own language. As we are talking, Dunc introduces me to these two funny Scousers who have come down from Liverpool; Robbo and Boxhead. We agree that we remember already meeting at the Man in the Moon and shake hands.

"We weren't really paying much attention at the Man in the Moon but me and Robbo saw the Ants when they played Eric's in Liverpool last October," says Boxhead. "We were so impressed we've come down today to see them again." Dunc seems a really friendly sort.

As I leave the bar I say, "Catch you later."

We go back into the gig room where everyone seems to know each other. The Ants crowd are a stylish mixture of home-made Ants' clothes with 'Ants' and their song titles stencilled on, to home-made punk gear. Some people are wearing leathers like Adam and some people wore Seditionaries' clothes. The lights go off. Then a door opens and you hear a bass guitar slowly start a one note solo. Suddenly Adam's voice can be heard. "You gotttta face like a labradoorrrrr. I don't minddd that's what I'm here forrr. The aaaaangel Gaberialll sent me to givvve you a litleee bit of sympathyy. Take me down to Harrrley Streeeeet." Then the lights come on and the song kicks in and everyone is dancing in a deranged manner as Adam leaps around the stage. I notice a new guitarist. Dunc tells me he's called Johnny Bivouac so I'm assuming 'The Kid' has left. I just stand back and watch the proceedings. Adam looks like a demon, attacking his own band, jumping all over the stage like a mad man. This band is a more polished version of what I imagined after hearing about them at the Man in the Moon gig. Adam looks different to how he was described. Gone, appear to be the 'rapist style' mask and the badly designed bondage straps. Adam stands there staring menacingly at his crowd of deranged Antlings. He's wearing all leather, Seditionaries' 'Anarchy' shirt, white-soled Kung Fu slippers and Kabuki style Japanese make up. I could now see how much more had gone into his image; he was quite stylised. I thought Adam looked really good and his behaviour was both angelic and demonic in equal measure. It wasn't camp; there was something more menacing, an underlying sense of excitement and danger maybe? I thought, they sound great. The audience look like they're having a mental breakdown; there's people pulling on their jaws in anguish, there's people rolling about on the floor, people ramming into each other like they're fighting. This is so different to any other punk gig I've been to. Nothing compares - not even seeing the Pistols.

The other thing I notice is the same as at the Man in the Moon gig - that this closely knit gang of kids are tight as a group - they are all looking after each other's backs. To the causal onlooker it just looks like an unruly group of people who can't dance, but it's well organised in its chaos. The ones more capable of looking after themselves are on the outside of the group, protecting the smaller ones on the inside. But everyone looks like they are off their heads, or something. It's very aggressive in nature. Some people jump onto the stage with the band and roll about. Some of them are stage-diving back into the audience. It's audience participation at its best. Adam's facial expressions change in an instant as he switches from angel to devil. God knows what's going on inside his head, maybe internal malfunction or something. Then he attempts to kick a guy called Justin, who is rolling around on the stage, in the head. Everyone seems to be in some kind of demonic trance. The energy is unbelievable. It feels like a train about to crash. How can so many people put so much energy into a gig? Adam then launches himself into the audience; arms outstretched as the Ant kids jump all over him and overwhelm him until he hits the ground. Then in the same instance they drag him back on his feet and throw him back on stage.

Next up we have Jordan, who enters for one Ant track 'Lou', a New York coke joke song about Lou Reed. Jordan bellows out inaudible words, much to the crowd's delight. She is dressed in a black wig and twin-set and pearls, belching out the lyrics. I'm down at the front, rolling about on the floor. I'm totally immersed in the Ants now and saying to myself, as the gig's going on, this is the best band ever. Watching the Ants is the best experience of my life to date. I need more of this. I feel like an addict. I can't get enough. Fantastic songs like 'Red Scab', 'Send a Letter to Jordan', 'Dirk Wears White Sox' - based on Adam's favourite character Dirk Bogarde - in his favourite film, 'The Night Porter'. I look down and see Dunc, kneeling on the stage in his home made Ants T-shirt, at the feet of Johnny Bivouac. He's also totally immersed in the Ants. Jordan looks down towards him to see if he's OK.

Accidentally, I bump into some of the Ant kids who I hadn't been introduced to earlier. They all turn round to have a go at me, their faces grimacing like they mean to do me serious damage. It's a split second, but time stands still for that second and stretches it out, giving the illusion of a much longer period. Sound shuts down. You're in the present; everything outside your peripheral vision stands still. I'm waiting for the onslaught. From nowhere, Dunc appears and says, "He's OK." Then everything resumes as normal. Everything is back in sync, the music is now audible again, people are moving, and everyone carries on dancing. People are jumping on stage with the band then leaping off back into the audience. That whole sequence felt like ages but in reality, was only a second or two. Adam is now bare chested and still leaping around.

Suddenly, a gang of skinheads appear from nowhere and try to crash through to the front of the gig. As these skinheads charge through, initially causing a rift in the crowd, there's a split second before people respond in what looks like a well-practiced manoeuvre. Immediately the skinheads become engulfed by the Soldier like Ant kids, who are heavily under the influence of Ant music, in a frenzied attack. In the background you can hear: "10, 9, 8, 7, 6, 5, 4, 3, 2, 1, at the Screen on the Green, fall out." These Ant kids neither show nor feel any fear, it seems. It's carnage. From somewhere, weapons appear. A guy who Dunc had introduced me to earlier, Popey, who looks like one of the older ones, suddenly hits this skinhead over the head with a plank of wood. Where the wood comes from, I don't know. But the skinhead falls to the floor, his eyes now dazed with 'Out of Order' signs across them. The Ant kids use whatever is at hand, and relentlessly steam into the skinheads. How can these skinny school kids chase a group of older skinheads out of the gig room and into the safety of the bar area?

One skinhead gets up off the floor and picks up a chair. He is behind the Ant kids now; he sees a chance to get revenge for his mates by attacking from behind, but it's not a very clever tactic because he still has to go through the Ant kids to get out of the building. Maybe a clever person would have stayed quietly at the back of the room until it was over then leave. He is about to hit Popey on the back of the head. Quickly I respond by punching him full on the side of the head, which sends him sprawling back across the floor. Popey turns round to see the skinhead flying across the room. He stares, says "Thanks," and moves on. I look round and the Ants are no longer on the stage. I can't help wondering if they'd played the last song, or the band was upset at the fighting? Right now it's an experience I will never forget and I can't wait for the next Ants gig. I see Dunc on my way out and thank him for stepping in. I get introduced and chatting properly to some of the Ants crew who I'd seen earlier; Johnny Aggro, Stevie Parker, Chukka, Vince, Joe the Collar, Big PD, Crazy Kev, Spud, Kev A, Dave P, Pete Vague and Justin Semmens. I shake hands with them. They ask where I'm from.

"Bradford," I say. Dunc gives me his telephone number which I put in my wallet.

He says, "Give us a bell when you're next coming down to see the Ants, or I'll give you a bell if the Ants are playing up north, then we can all meet up."

It's time to leave the Ant kids. I try to find OC, Mel and Brinsley. None of them are fighters, although Brinsley has a knack of starting them. As I look around the venue I suddenly see them standing at the back of the room, as excited as I am. Almost in one voice, we all say, "That was fucking mental." We were all talking over each other to get the best bits out. As we are leaving the Marquee, I hear Penny calling to us from the opposite side of the road. I rush over straight away and give her a hug. It's reciprocated in kind. I can tell she is pleased to see me, but something doesn't seem right. I introduce her to my friends.

"This is Mel, OC, and of course, Brinsley." Brinsley is under strict instructions to behave. We walk up to Tottenham Court Road to try and catch a night bus to Camden and grab some food on the way. I'm wanting a kebab. I couldn't believe you could only buy these in London. Anyway, we find a takeaway and give the guy behind the counter our order. I can't wait for my greasy kebab to arrive. When it does, I tuck in like I haven't eaten for a week. I have grease running through my fingers and all down my front like an infant child. Gosh, this is lovely. Brinsley follows suit with a kebab. The other two opt for chips and gravy. Penny says she ate in the pub.

Suddenly a bus appears outside. "Quick!" shouts Penny, "We need to get that bus." As we run, chips and bits of kebab fly through the air as we struggle to catch the bus. I don't want to lose any of my kebab so I try catching hold of it again, which is not easy in full flight. We just manage to catch this bus. I love the fact you can just jump on and off London buses without them stopping. We run up the stairs and sit on the back seat. After a ten minute journey we are in Camden. We ring the bell and run down the stairs just as the bus is slowing, and jump off like paratroopers, taking the plunge one after another. Luckily we all land safely down the 2 foot drop. When we get to Penny's we all just fall where we stand, some on the chairs and some on the floor. Penny asks if we want a drink. "Tea please," we all shout. I wasn't a big fan of hot drinks because you have to wait for them to cool down, but occasionally I will have a drink in winter to get something warm inside. It's the same with food; I don't see the point of boiling hot food you can hardly eat, but I fancied the hot tea tonight. We put the TV on and just lay about, too tired to talk as Penny finds some blankets for us.

"Where's Anna?" I asked her.

"She moved out a while back."

"Who you living with now, then?"

"This skinhead guy." Then almost in the same sentence, "He's just a friend." I suddenly feel quite anxious about this situation. My mind is racing.

"Where is he, then?"

"Oh, he's away right now with some mates somewhere." I could tell from Penny's behaviour that something was not right. As the others crashed out,

Penny and I went to bed. We couldn't keep our hands off each other. It's been so long that pure lust takes over; instead of foreplay we just shag the living day lights out of each other. Then we fall into each other's arms. I gently stroke her arm then move over her body and proceed to kiss every inch of her skin, stopping between her legs and teasing her by gently touching her clit then removing my tongue, until in frustration she grabs me and pushes my head and tongue deep inside her. As the climax builds, her back arches, her eyes are closed. Suddenly she's trying to stop herself from crying out as her body goes stiff then gives way to relax on the bed. We cuddle up, exchange a kiss, and just lie there.

After a minute or two, though, I feel I have to ask about this skinhead lodger. Penny just says he's a friend but I can tell from her voice that she doesn't want to discuss it, so I don't pursue the matter. After a while we both fall asleep. The next day we wake in each other's arms. We lie there quietly as the sun shines through the window. Suddenly I can hear Brinsley on the prowl, banging about. I get up and go downstairs to see what's happening. The reasonably tidy room now has books strewn all over the floor. The other two are somehow still asleep, but Brinsley has moved to the kitchen and is now making a mess in there.

"What you doing?" I say.

"Just making tea and toast," says Brinsley.

"What about the mess in the living room?"

"Oh, don't worry. I'll tidy it up later. I couldn't sleep." The other two wake up and while I'm waiting for the kettle, I nip upstairs to see Penny.

"You OK?"

"Yeah," she replies, "I'm just gonna lie here for a while."

"Do you want to do something later, after they've gone?"

"Sounds good."

I know it's not a good thing to do but I just want to be alone with Penny right now, so as soon as I have made the tea and toast I ask the others what time they are setting off back to Bradford. No one looks like they want to go any time soon. I ask Mel, the driver, "I thought you had to be home early?" Hint, hint.

"No," said Mel, not getting it.

"Me neither," smiles Brinsley, realising that I want to be alone with Penny.

Everyone sits around feeling tired, trying to gather momentum to make a move. We sit there watching TV.

After an hour I say, "Come on, you lot. Making a move yet? I want to spend some time with Penny."

Mel sparks up, "We don't know how to get back to Brent Cross tube."

"Just walk up the road to the Camden tube and get the Northern Line to Brent Cross." They don't look confident. "OK! I'll come with you," I say. I run upstairs to tell Penny I'm taking them to the tube.

As we walk up the road, I let slip about Rock On Records next to the tube being a great record shop. As soon as I've said it I think to myself, why did I mention that? Damn. So we find ourselves in Rock On. Mel is diving into the records for stuff he hasn't got. The other two have no money but still look. After what seems like another hour I'm shouting, "Come on, lads!" Eventually Mel's bought half a dozen singles and two LPs, after listening to what seems like the shop's entire stock. As we make our way to the tube station next door, Brinsley pulls out about 12 singles from inside his jacket.

"Oh, look what I found," he giggles.

"I don't really want to get banged up for nicking singles, not today of all days," I sigh. We look hurriedly behind to see if anyone is following. "Right. Get your tickets, go down the escalators, then look to see which side goes north, OK?" I begin, before I suddenly realise I've left some stuff in Mel's car, so I need to go with them. "Bugger."

I buy my ticket and make the long, steep descent into the bowels of the tube. We get to the bottom and check which side goes north. Luckily a tube pulls in straightaway and in seconds we are flying north through the underground tunnels, swerving as we go. After what seems like about five minutes we're at Brent Cross. Luckily the car is still there and I pick up the small bag I'd left. The three of them get in the car, still looking a little tired and hungover and I say goodbye.

"See you all back in Bradford when I get back." Then out of the blue a copper comes up and asks Mel if this is his car.

"Yes!" Mel replies. The copper asks him his name. "Brendan Mellon," Mel replies. The copper turns to OC beside him.

"So what's your name? Charlie Banana?" Me and Brinsley burst out laughing. A policeman with a sense of humour. Whatever next? There should be more of them. Even OC starts laughing along. Mel was furious though. The copper asks him for his licence, which he inspects carefully. Satisfied, he gives Mel his licence back and moves on, saying "Bye, Mr Mellon."

Within 15 minutes I'm back in Camden. I come out of the tube to beautiful sunshine. There are lots of people milling about. I look up and down the street. Down to my right there's a skinhead sniffing glue, half off his head, just about to pass out. I walk past him, noticing a few shops and a bit of a market but I'm looking forward to spending some time with Penny so I just head on back to her squat. When I get there she is still in bed. I get in next to her and we hug. "Fancy doing something?" I ask her.

"OK, if you like! What do you want to do?" says Penny.

"I don't know, we could go for a walk to Regent's Park, or go for a drink maybe, then go to a gig later?"

"If you like," she says. I just can't get rid of the sense that something is not right. Penny seems preoccupied and deep in thought about something. We get up out of bed; Penny goes to the loo while I get changed. She comes back and starts to get dressed. I go downstairs, stick the kettle on and put some bread in the toaster then sit down to watch TV.

After a couple of minutes Penny comes down. I get up and pass her some tea and buttered toast, then I ask her for a bit more info about this skinhead who's living with her but she seems a bit defensive.

"Oh, he's just someone from back home wanting somewhere to crash 'til he finds somewhere to live," she says, but the tone of her voice is that of someone hoping I'm not going to pursue the matter any further. "Anyway, I haven't seen him for a couple of days. He said he was going to visit friends and didn't know when he would be back." I still sense there is something not quite right about this but I don't want to cause any problems.

"OK, then. Right, let's go out. It's lovely out there." Penny puts her cup and plate in the sink and we head out of the door, making sure the squat is secure first. Regent's Park is not far away from Penny's, back up the high street, turn left past the Dublin Castle and it's at the top of the road. The park is full of young couples lying next to each other and kids playing. I see a group of people playing football. We sit nearby and I ask her what gigs are on tonight. "The Banshees are playing the Nashville tonight and tomorrow night, not sure what else there is."

So that night we go over to the Nashville to see Siouxsie and the Banshees, which is a bit of a trek, but they are quite good. The Ants used to support the Banshees a lot back in '77. They are another band trying to find a record deal that have a big following among the London punks. I'm really enjoying my time with Penny. We seem to get on quite well; everything just seems so natural. We manage to spend nearly a whole week together. She has to do her shifts at the pub where she works, but we have a lot of time together. There's still no sign of Jamie the lodger yet though, which is good. We manage to get around London, checking out all the key punk places. I manage to pick up some good records - the new Raw Records compilation and a couple of bootleg LPs down Portobello Road, one by the Banshees and one by the Pistols - so I was well pleased. There were always tons of live cassettes which were much cheaper, but the quality was often quite poor unless they were taped through the PA system, which was rare. Most of the other tapes were recorded by people on cassette players which you had to sneak into gigs with, and these things were not small. People would hide them in girls' bags, or wear long coats. There could be half a dozen people recording any particular gig, and when you listened back there were always lots of people talking most of the time, overpowering the music. As this is still the early days, and few bands have record contracts to put out their music, these tapes were often the only way to listen to what bands sounded like.

Penny and me spend a whole day down the King's Road going in all the shops: BOY/Acme Attractions and Beaufort Market. We stop off for a drink in the Roebuck before we go to Seditionaries. The Roebuck is still lively during the day with a mixture of punks and people working close by. After an hour, we head on down to Seditionaries to say "Hi" to Jordan. I ask her about the Ants, telling her I thought the last gig was great and I'm looking forward to the upcoming gig at the Marquee. After a general chitchat I go to look at the clothes. I'm still after an 'Anarchy' shirt but there is no chance now of getting one. I end up buying another t-shirt. Penny and I wave goodbye to Jordan then head off home. After spending an enjoyable week together getting to know each other, the time is just flying by.

Then it's the second instalment of Adam and the Ants at the Marquee club. Penny has managed to get the night off so we can go see the Ants together, but there's more bad news. Two of the staff are off sick for the next week so

Penny is going to have to cover for them, which means I will hardly see her over the next couple of days of my visit. This puts a dampener on things but we try not to let it get to us. We get down to the Marquee at about 8 o'clock; I immediately clock Dunc with some of the Ants kids. There are some people I didn't get a chance to talk to at the last gig. Dunc introduces them: Steve Shaw and Godfrey and Metin are from the East End. A nice, friendly lass comes over called Fiona Cartledge. I introduce Penny.

Fiona says, "I've seen you around at gigs somewhere?"

"Probably," says Penny. They try to work out which ones. Some of the Ant kids ask where I'm from.

"Bradford," I tell them.

"Long way to come for a gig, mate!"

"Yes, but it's the Ants," I say. After a while the other Ant kids turn up. There's about 30 of them, now. Johnny Aggro and Popey say "Hello." We drink, chat, play pool. I like this lot. I get the impression that they don't mix that much with others, but I enjoy their company. After a while we all go inside the Marquee to hang around and chat some more. I get talking to some other punks at the bar, but the Ant kids just stay in their own corner.

The Ants are about to come on so we make our way down to the front. It's pitch black. Then, again, the single bass note starts 'Plastic Surgery'. Dunc turns to me and tells me to listen to the full, sinister sound from right next to the PA. It's the greatest intro of all time and it sends us mental. As the song picks up momentum the Ant kids start jumping around more vigorously and I join in. This is only the first song and I'm knackered already. The band go straight into 'Puerto Rican'. It's just like the last gig - everyone is rolling around in trance-like states minus the skinheads. The Ants are so good I don't want to leave here, I just want to stay listening to them all night. But the gig doesn't seem to have been on for two minutes before it comes to an end. As we're all leaving, Dunc asks if we'll be down again next week.

"Sorry, I have to go back to Bradford in a couple of days' time, but I'll get back down as soon as I can," I say and there's some north/south banter as the Ant kids wave goodbye.

"Off back home to see your whippet?"

We're back at Penny's from the Ants gig, really tired, and we go to bed. I'm just about to fall asleep when suddenly the door opens and this figure jumps on to the bed, waking me with a fright. My instincts react immediately. I grab hold of this person and turn them over. They react back and next thing we are both rolling about on the bed. I shout for Penny to get the lights on so I can see what's happening. Seconds later the lights are on. Suddenly Penny shouts, "Jamie!"

"Who's the northerner?" he shouts back at her.

"It's Johnny. I told you about him," says Penny. I let go of him.

"So you know this bloke then?" I ask.

"Yes! He's Jamie, the lodger I mentioned."

"More than just a lodger though, innit, Penny?" Jamie shouts. Then he walked away. I tried to get up to go after him to see what he meant by that remark.

"Leave it," shouted Penny, as she grabbed hold of me. I stopped but I wasn't happy.

"What did he mean?" I said.

"Oh, nothing. He's a windup merchant," she said, and then we went back to bed and fell asleep.

The next day we both got up together and went downstairs. Jamie was already awake. When I went to make a cup of tea, he followed me in, chatting to me in an inquisitive way, trying to suss me out and test me. He started going on about these big fights he's been in with his skinhead mates, trying to impress me. I let him know that I didn't like him. Jamie stood back, surprised I wasn't impressed by his tales of heroism in the name of the skinhead cause. Anyway it was clear to me that Jamie and I were not going to get on. A few minutes later Penny walked in the kitchen and Jamie grabbed hold of her. She tried to break free.

"Stop it, Jamie!" she cried. I grabbed his hand and pulled him off her.

"OK mate! I'm only playing. We are friends, you know. I've known her for ages. We grew up together, didn't we Penny?" Penny looked really uneasy around this guy; she wouldn't look at him.

"Yes, Jamie," she said. He walked out of the kitchen laughing and I heard the door slam shut.

I can't put my finger on it. Penny seems scared of him, maybe. It's certainly not the friendly relationship she's tried to paint. I don't want to fall out with Penny, so I said nothing for now. Jamie keeps shouting things which sound like veiled threats. He stares at me like he hates me but hasn't quite worked out in his head yet if he's confident enough to have a go at me, so he keeps making cheap comments to see how I will respond. I don't respond, because he wins if I do. I just smile at him like I'm not bothered, but I am really. I'm going to snap soon if this carries on. This goes on all the next day and I can see it's affecting Penny and I don't like it. I keep saying to her, "Are you OK?" or "I can have a word with him if you want?"

"No! Please. Just leave it," she says.

"What's he got over you?" I ask.

"Nothing, please just drop it," is her reply. I walk off, totally frustrated. I feel that Penny and I really get on but this Jamie situation could drive us apart. I don't know what else to do so I decide to go for a walk.

"I'm off out," I shout and leave the squat. I remember I still have Dunc's telephone number so I give him a bell; luckily he's in. Dunc himself answers the phone.

"Hi! What you up to?"

"I'm at a bit of a loose end so I thought I'd give you a ring," I told him.

Dunc says, "You can come up to mine in Wood Green if you like?"

"OK, that would be good."

I get directions and head on up there. I'm still not that familiar with getting around London on my own. The buses are confusing and the tubes are a nightmare. Anyway I jump on the tube at Camden and change at King's Cross for the Piccadilly Line which takes me to Wood Green. I get lost a couple of times, heading south instead of north, but I eventually get there. I get to the house and bang on the door. A girl with a lovely, warm, friendly smile opens the door.

"Hello," she says.

"Hi, I've come to see Dunc."

"Dunc! Your friend's here."

"Show him up," shouts Dunc. So this lass who I presume is his sister takes me to his room. I walk in to see Dunc lying on his bed. I smile at his sister as she walks away.

"Who's that?" I ask him. "It's my sister, Linz," says Dunc.

"She's nice," I said. I look around his room and it's covered in the new Marquee poster and other Ants flyers. There's a poster which says 'Adam and the Aunts' with the 'u' crossed out. The design looked like some scantily clad

Nazis, looking like aunts, all in a line. "What's that poster?" I asked.

"It's from a gig at Colchester last year. I think there was a mistake with the printing or something."

"I noticed the Ants posters on the wall at the Marquee but I didn't manage to get one," I said to Dunc. He said Adam gave him a load after the gig then he asked if I wanted one. He gave me one signed by Jordan with the inscription 'Love and Rubber, Jordan.' "Nice one, Dunc," I thanked him. We talked for ages. He showed me some pictures that someone had taken of people dancing to the Ants. One photo of Justin looked really mad. The people in it looked like they were having a mental breakdown. Dunc told me his dad was a jazz musician called Stan, who'd played with Acker Bilk in the old days. He then said that he himself was a bit of a drummer, who was looking to get into a band at some point. It's a really relaxing afternoon at Dunc's, chatting away about punk rock and the Ants, but soon it's time to go back to Penny's, so I say my goodbyes to Dunc. As I'm leaving his sister Lindsey says goodbye. I say goodbye and smile at her as I leave.

I ask Lindsey if she likes the Ants but she replies, "They're OK, but I'm more of a soul girl."

I get back to Camden quite quickly and walk to Penny's. Suddenly I see Jamie coming out of the squat. I start to walk faster, sensing something's not right. I walk in to find Penny on the floor, crying. I go over and give her a hug. "What's wrong?" then in the same breath, "Is it Jamie?" She says nothing, but I'm assuming it is Jamie. Penny asks if she can borrow a fiver. "Yes, of course, but you only got paid yesterday," I said.

"I lent it to Jamie," she said. I tell Penny I'm off to the shop. As I get there, Jamie is stood outside with a mate.

"All right, northern boy," he shouts with a snigger. I go into the shop buy a pint of milk and some cans. Jamie sees the cans in my hand.

"I'll have one."

"You've got the money Penny gave you, go buy your own," I say, walking off.

"I spent that. Maybe Penny will give me some more," he sniggers.

"No, she won't." I go back to the squat and sit with Penny, but the atmosphere has changed for the worse. I can't get through to her; she's shut down. I try talking to her but it's no good. I don't want to keep going on, as that could make things worse.

Eventually Penny says, "I don't think we should see each other."

"Why not?" I say. She says it's because we live too far apart, but really I think its Jamie. "But we get on fine." Then she makes more negative remarks about why this and why that, but you can just tell they're excuses. I try in vain to highlight the positives, but to no avail.

After an hour she goes to bed, saying she wants to be on her own. So I sit up with all these things going round in my brain until I can't think any longer. After a while, though, Jamie comes in.

"All right, northern boy."

"That's not my name."

"Well, I don't know what it is and I ain't interested anyway." I jump up and grab hold of him.

"What is your problem?" I shout.

"Nothing, me ole' China," comes his reply.

"What you got on Penny? She looks scared to death of you."

"Oh, hasn't she told you?" he sniggers. "You see, northern boy, me and Penny are related. She's my half-sister." I looked shocked. "No, she didn't tell you then. Ha ha. You see we have the same whore of a mum. She left my dad and moved in with Penny's dad and then they had Penny. In the meantime my dad committed suicide so Penny feels guilty I guess. Or she's going to, after I've finished with her."

A menacing grin comes on his face and the tone of his voice becomes more sinister. Then he says, "I will never let her forget what our mum did to my dad. Penny owes me, and I aim to make her pay. Big time." I grab hold of him by the throat.

"If anything happens to her, I will hunt you down." He smiles with hatred in his eyes.

"Go on then, northern boy. You'll be gone soon and then she'll be mine."

"You sick, warped bastard. No! She doesn't owe you anything. She's innocent in all this." He takes my hand off his throat. We square up to one another, but then Penny walks in.

"What's going on?" I tell her Jamie has told me everything. She runs off upstairs.

I follow her, but she just says, "Keep away." Jamie goes out into the night.

Suddenly I'm sitting there on my own, wondering what the fuck has just happened. Yesterday, life was great. Now that's gone. I stay there thinking and rethinking, going over and over things, trying to make sense of it all. I try to go into Penny's room later to sleep, but she asks if I'll sleep on the settee. "Fine," I tell her. "But I'm going home tomorrow and I won't see you for a while."

"We're not going out together now, so it doesn't matter," comes the reply. I'd been hoping she wasn't going to say that, but she did. I get all my stuff packed to take downstairs, ready to go first thing in the morning. There's no point in hanging around here now. As I'm leaving the room, I ask her if we are still friends. "I don't know," she says. "I'll let you know later, when I've thought about it."

"Right, I'll say goodbye now then, as I'm going back to Bradford first thing. If you ever need me, ring me. I'll be there. Take care." I go back downstairs and bunk down on the settee, thinking how can this happen? My head's all over the place now, I can't stop thinking, over and over again. What could I do to make it better? What if I tell Jamie to leave? She can come and live in Bradford with me. I could move down here? All these things are going round and around in my head. Next thing it's morning. I wake up on the settee and what happened the day before hits me again. I feel depressed, but there's nothing I can do but go home and let her have her space. Hopefully things will change. I have a wash and get myself ready to leave. I pause as I'm heading for the door. Should I say goodbye again? No. Leave it. I can call her later.

I'm deep in thought as I leave Penny's. I would miss her, but we can't have a proper relationship when we live so far apart. My main concern is Jamie, but hopefully Penny and I will remain good friends and maybe even get back together later, who knows? But for now, it's done. I catch the tube up to Brent Cross and walk on round the ring road to the M1. I was stood at the bottom of the M1 Northbound for what seemed like ages, feeling a bit rough and just wanting to get home.

There were quite a few other people hitching. One was this pretty looking lass who was standing next to me. Almost immediately, this van pulled up. I think his intention was to pick the lass up instead, but by the time the van stopped he had pulled up right in front of me. As I opened the door, the driver was looking back in the direction of the female hiker, but she had already assumed that he had stopped for me, so she was looking the other way. I said, "Where you going, mate?"

"Leeds," he said, not really concentrating on me. I jumped into the van and shut the door before he could change his mind. We set off and I could detect straight away that this guy was feeling quite uneasy. I suppose I did look quite intimidating, in my punk gear and with red, blue and white hair. And my nose stud.

We got to the first service station, which was only about 3 miles on, and the driver said, "I need to stop a minute." He got out of the van and went to the phone box, looking over at the van constantly. I'm not sure whether he thought I was going to try and hot wire his van or something. I got the feeling that he was describing me to whoever was on the other end of the phone, in case something happened to him. Anyway, he came back and we set off again. I thought I would strike up a conversation to try and put him at ease, and to show him he hadn't picked up a potential homicidal maniac.

After about half an hour we were getting along famously. In fact we got on so well that when we got to Sheffield, he asked me if I fancied a pint. I told him I was skint; that's why I was hitching home. "Come on," he said. "I'll buy you a pint. So we stopped off at this pub just off the motorway where we enjoyed a pint or four. It was then he told me that he had originally stopped for the female hitcher, and hadn't even noticed me until I was in his van. He also said he had felt intimidated. He had never met any punks before, but could remember reading a particularly negative article in the Daily Bullshit (The Sun) or the Mail - one of those rags - about punks spitting and attacking people with weapons, or something similar.

"You're nothing like the punks they mentioned in that article," he told me.

"Don't believe what you read in the media. It's all rubbish," I said. "The establishment always try to turn people off anything that might benefit them. They rule by division, not unity." We left the pub at last orders, after having a great time. This pub was somewhere he usually stopped, and he knew a lot of the locals. He had introduced me to all these regulars, telling everyone, "Here's my punk mate."

By the time we got back to West Yorkshire we realised that if he dropped me off in Morley, I would have missed the last bus, so he said he would drop me off in Bradford. Not only did he take me to Bradford, he dropped me off right where I lived. He waved goodbye and drove off back to Leeds. I arrived back at my bedsit and lay on the bed, thinking of the next Ants gig. Although I was still missing Penny, perhaps it was all for the best right now.

V
RUBBER PEOPLE

'Gagged in discipline, bound in bondage
Feast until this treatment ends
Spanked in satin, whipped in Wigan
For they are our fettered friends

Rubber boots, rubber cap, rubber bars, rubber head
Rubber cat, rubber sheet, rubber doll, rubber bed
Rubber people, rubber people
OK, rubber people'

What's been happening in the insect world? The Ants have been busy playing lots of gigs. On the 23rd of January they did their first John Peel show, playing 'Lou', 'It Doesn't Matter', 'Deutscher Girls' and 'Puerto Rican'. The next day they recorded 'Deutscher Girls' for the 'Jubilee' soundtrack LP. The Ants are starting to play more gigs further afield from London these days, but my work commitments mean it's not that easy getting time off, except at weekends. But Mel, OC, Brinsley and I have managed to get to some Ants gigs up north, so it was great for us to be able to see them at the Nottingham Sandpiper, Sheffield Limit club and Doncaster Outlook club. I met another northern Ants fan at Doncaster; Dean Parko from Cleethorpes. The Outlook was the nearest venue outside of his home town and they got more bands to play there, so he came over when he got chance. The Ants were one of the bands that Dean wanted to see again.

Another gig was at Eric's in Liverpool. Dunc, Fiona C, Popey, Johnny Aggro and a couple of the others managed to make it to some of these gigs. I asked Dunc how they got up here. He said, "We take it in turns to ring Jordan up to ask if they will give us lifts to gigs in the van." They were all nervous of asking, which was why they would take it in turns. One of them would ring and say, "Hi, it's the Ant kids. Can we have a lift?" Jordan would reply, "Oh, it's the minions." Sometimes they were lucky, sometimes not. In the van, they would chat with the band while Adam sat on his leather cushions reading a book. I asked Dunc, "Whose turn was it to ring and ask this time?" "Johnny Aggro's", he said. I ask how they get there when they don't get a lift in the van. Dunc replies, "When we can't get a lift we go by coach, and sometimes Scottish Lloyd takes us in his van." I was talking to Popey and he was telling me about when they'd all gone to Bristol the other week, and it had been quite scary. The Ants had played in a place called Barton Hill Youth Club, and the crowd didn't like them. The crowd just took the piss so Jordan got angry and threw a pint pot on the floor, but it bounced into the audience which angered the crowd. It was touch and go all night with the band, and the Ant kids had to tread carefully after that incident. Dunc then chips in, mentioning a gig in Brighton. The Ant kids went all the way down there and the gig never happened, so they had to blag a lift back in the VW Ant wagon and were dropped off at Victoria Station. Popey was also telling me that he and Dunc had had this idea for the Ants crew to start wearing blue prefect's badges, but by then too many people were going to Ants gigs so the idea never got started.

The gigs are always great, but there are no particular stand out moments. The Ants were pretty consistent. It was a bit weird because not a lot of the locals had heard of them. They were pretty much dismissed in the media, so the gigs are not as crazy as the London ones because so few people turned up. We had a bit of trouble once in Liverpool after the Damned played. We ended up in a club called the Swinging Apple after losing Boxhead and Robbo back at Eric's. Someone told us this was a punk club but there seemed to be all sorts in there; Teds, punks and lots of skinheads. We had our old Keighley punk mates with us, Stan and Eggo. Eggo was 6 foot 7, or at least he looked it compared to the rest of us, but he wasn't aggressive. You would have thought his size alone would have put people off but then again it can sometimes attract trouble, especially if there's a gang of them. Anyway, tonight, it did. We only wanted a beer. We got to the bar, ordered our drinks and some skinheads must have heard our accents. As we walked towards a table to sit down we were attacked from behind. It was over in no time and it wasn't prolonged. They were just sending out a message that we were not welcome. We quickly finished our beers and left.

The Bradford punks have a big London trip coming up - the Rock against

Racism gig on Sunday 30th April 1978. With the Bradford punk scene being from many different ethnic backgrounds; Muslim, eastern European, black, Indian, etc, everybody wanted to go to this gig as a show of solidarity. There was the added bonus of watching some good bands as well; the Clash and X-Ray Spex, among others. Someone in the Anti-Nazi League, who drank in the Mannville, helped to organise this trip to Victoria Park - possibly Geoff Robinson, my old history teacher, who was big in the movement. There were nine coaches going from Bradford. They were due to set off from outside the college on Great Horton Road. We had our own special coach, which would be full of just punks and local eccentrics; and not forgetting the 'Blockheads'. The 'Blockheads' were a little group of Ian Dury and the Blockheads fans and pissheads, who resided at 'Blockhead Towers' on Merton Road, Alan, Keith Haste and Kendal, who all drank in the Mannville. The plan was, we would all go on our usual night out, but about 20 of us decided we would stay out so we wouldn't miss the coach which left at 6 am. We were not sure how we were going to achieve this because last orders were at 10.30, and you had to leave by 11 o'clock. Then, it was onto Mac's 'til 2 am. Then, we were spoilt for choice - as in - nowhere to go. As we were leaving Mac's, someone told us there was a late night drinking club next to the army recruitment office up the top of town. We would be leaving our comfort zone and usually, when we left our comfort zone, it meant trouble. But, with nothing to do for four hours until the coach arrived, we thought we would chance it. So we went along to this club and surprisingly, they let us in. Usually our dress code alone would guarantee a negative response and no entrance.

When we got into this club we went upstairs and my first impression was that it was tiny. The music they were playing was reggae and soul. To make it more interesting, some of Bradford's dodgiest clientele were in attendance. We all sat at one side of the room, having a chat and a couple of beers. We were a bit wary of the people around us because we were so used to getting some sort of reaction when we went off our turf, but everyone seemed sound with us. Anyway at some stage of the evening someone complained that someone had spat at them. So we all looked around, but no one was even paying any attention to us. This kept going on for a while and after a few more drinks we started getting a bit pissed, annoyed, and brave with it. We were sure someone was spitting at us. At one point Tim Calvey jumped up and shouts, "Who's spitting at me?" Everyone stared at us wondering what we were on about. The management came over to see what was up. We told them we thought someone was spitting at us. The argument went on for a while. Eventually the music stopped and other people started getting annoyed with us and it seemed we were on the verge of getting involved in a fight. Then Tim said again, "I have been spat on." But everyone was looking at us and no one seemed to be making any spitting gesture. All of a sudden someone looked up and realised there was a bloody big hole in the roof and it was rain that had been landing on people. Everything calmed down then and we were all laughing along with the others. The music started again and everyone was happy.

After the club finished at around 4 am, we waited outside to think about what we were going to do next. We had nowhere to go. Suddenly Mick Calvey remembered that one of the local eccentrics, Benny, had said earlier that we could stop at his bedsit in Mannville Terrace, which was by the college. So we all went up there and spent about 20 minutes throwing bricks at his window - well, missing, mostly, and hitting other people's windows instead. After a while we managed to wake the whole street except for Benny. Eventually one of the bricks hit his window and smashed it. We all cheered as Big Rick celebrated a direct hit. Suddenly Benny's angry face appeared, looking to see who'd broken his window. He was shocked to see about 20 drunk and smiley punks in his garden. He shouted down, "What do you lot want?" "You said we could stop at your flat!" Benny said, "I thought you meant a couple of you, not this many. It's only a bedsit!" "We can't get home and the coach sets off to London at 6 am!" Eventually Benny lets us in. It's a tiny bedsit with just a bed, cupboard and a wardrobe. We can all just about fit in the room. "You'd all better try to find somewhere to get your head down till 6." About ten people got onto the bed. Some tried to sleep standing up in the wardrobe. The floor was full. Someone tried getting inside the chest of drawers. Luckily there was only just over an hour until we had to meet the coach so people did the best they could to sleep. Obviously, no one did. At 5.30 we all got up and went on to the end of the street to get the coach instead. As soon as it came, we loaded on all the beer that we had left in the Mannville, and we set off. The coach was lively with excitement except for those of us who had been out all night. We all fell asleep. When I awoke we were on the outskirts of London.

As we got off the coach at Trafalgar Square we were told everyone was marching to Victoria Park. We started to walk down towards the Lyceum along the Strand. Every few yards a loud shout went up, which I thought was to signify the National Front had turned up for a fight. This went on for two or three miles and we were told it was to signify we had completed a mile. Suddenly we realised we would miss X-Ray Spex if we marched all the way there, and they were the only band I was really interested in seeing, so a few of us decided that we would go the rest of the way by tube. It took us a while to get there as none of us had been to east London before and the tube system wasn't easy to navigate, even though I did have some experience of using it on my other trips to London. The tube is not easy to figure out if you're not used to it; one wrong move and the system can devour you and it could be ages before you find yourself back on track. So anyway, we got on the wrong tube and went the wrong way a couple of times. The tube stations were like massive subterranean dwellings with lots of long, maze-like dark passages. They probably haven't had a lick of paint since they were built. Some of those around the centre had been modified a bit, but when you go out to the suburbs, they still look very Victorian. Finally, we made it to Victoria Park in Bethnal Green just as X-Ray Spex were coming on.

They were great and so were their songs. Poly Styrene was not one for copying others; she had her own unique style of dress. Today she was wearing what looked like a light coloured old granny suit and a turban on her head. Her lyrics were fantastic; lots of humour but very observational as well, about consumerism and how we're manipulated into buying crap. No one else was writing about stuff like that. After they finished we went and looked around for the others. It took us a while but we found some of them near the perimeter of the park near the toilets. We decided to go to the pub for a pint or two then made our way back towards the park to see the Clash. As we approached we noticed a few gangs of skinheads. They were just walking round the perimeter of the park shouting "Skinheads!" while trying to look menacing by very aggressive posturing. There was the occasional 'Sieg Heil!' but to the annoyance of the skinheads no one was challenging them, so some of them started a little skirmish with a mixed group of student-looking types who wouldn't say boo to a goose. Being the multi-cultural bunch that we were, we jumped into help them out, eventually backing the skinheads off.

The crowd inside the park was massive. Some were saying there were about

80,000 people there. We watched the Clash come onto a huge roar from the crowd. I didn't really like the Clash for reasons already stated; plus signing to CBS had a negative affect on punk as a whole - yes, I know the Pistols were doing it as well, but they just seemed to be ripping off record companies. We were watching the Clash, when we realised that if we watched their entire set we may miss the coach back to Bradford, as we had been told by the coach driver that he would not wait for us if we were late. I was more interested in getting back to Trafalgar Square for the coach, but quite a few of our lot liked the Clash so we opted to watch their whole set, then leg it to the tube as soon as they finished and hope that we caught the coach. The Clash didn't appear to be as good as they had been when I saw them at Leeds Poly in '77. Even Jimmy Pursey of Sham 69 couldn't save them when he came bouncing on stage to sing "White Riot" with them. When they finished we all met back at the toilets and made a hasty retreat back to Trafalgar Square for the coach. We managed to get there just in time. A few people did get lost though and the driver wouldn't wait. The rest of us sat back in our seats and fell asleep again. After about an hour I woke up and remembered the beer we had stashed, so we cracked them open. By the time we got back home we were all pissed. We pulled up outside the Mannville for a nightcap. After a couple of pints I went home to my beautiful bed and the end of another exciting adventure.

I was still really tired the next day at work, which was nearly fatal. I was half asleep and was reversing my dad back up the road in his lorry, not really paying attention. I was just waving my hand back because that's what you did, but I wasn't actually aware of my surroundings. Next minute, Bang! I can't move any further. I shouted out in pain. "Stopppppp!" Everyone comes running out of the depot to find that I'm stuck in between two lorries. Most of the blokes didn't like me, because of the office girls - and I could be a bit cocky and dismissive of them at times, so these blokes loved this situation. They were all standing about laughing, making no attempt to try and help me. John the manager and Gilbert the warehouse manager gave a wry smile. They would savour this moment. I'm thinking how the hell did this happen? Suddenly I was very awake. I couldn't move an inch; my chest was trapped and I was scared for my life. I thought I was going to be crushed. Sweat was pouring down my brow. My dad got out of the cab and started having a go at me, to prove his point about concentrating. "Dad! I get your point, I really do. Now can you get me out of here?" He wouldn't let it lie though, and didn't seem as concerned as I was about this situation. He couldn't start the engine again to drive forward, because the lorry would start with a sharp reverse before going forward. In the end I think he just let the brake off and Arthur, one of the few blokes I got on with at work, came to help push the lorry and then other people pushed it into a forward motion. I was so relieved. My chest was killing me. I thanked everyone then went and sat down in the cab. My dad said, "Are you OK to carry on?" "Yes! Let's just get out of here." My humiliation was complete.

So we were driving along. I was just trying to compose myself after that scare and I started thinking to myself that I really wanted to go down to London for the X-Ray Spex gig at the Roundhouse with the Ants supporting. It was the Ants' first gig at a big venue in London but I couldn't get time off. To be honest, I didn't have the money either after going to the Rock Against Racism gig. I really wanted to see X-Ray Spex again, as well as the Ants obviously. I was just glad I'd got to see them at the Victoria Park gig. Anyway, the gig passed, and I became even more gutted that I hadn't gone because I'd found out that Jordan, the beautiful, buxom Seditionaries assistant and Ants manager had announced she was leaving the Ants to concentrate on other projects. Not only that, but Johnny Bivouac had announced he was leaving the group too; a double blow for the Ants. They hadn't wasted time in getting another guitarist in, though. Mathew Ashman stepped up to the plate at the Hard Rock Café on the 6th of June for a D-day gig. The Ants had also recorded a demo of 'Young Parisians'/'Lady'/'Catch a Falling Star' in May.

In the meantime, between Ants gigs, there were one or two other gigs worth noting. One Sunday night we went down to the Royal Standard to see a band called Bitch. I thought Bitch were quite good. At this gig my friend Delia came up to me with this lad and introduced him as Paul. She said, "Paul's a big Ants fan also." We got on like a house on fire. Paul told me he was seeing the singer, Charlie Green, who was a famous punk face from the early days down the King's Road and featured in lots of pictures at the Roxy Club. Paul ended up stopping at my bedsit for a few days because Bitch were heading back to London. Paul then went back to Middlesboro. I think Paul was 15. Most of the punks I met were school kids or had just left school, like myself. We were hitching all over the country watching punk bands; some had left home and were squatting or living in bedsit land. Paul and I arranged to keep in touch and meet up at future Ants gigs.

At the end of May the Buzzcocks played at Bradford George's Hall, supported by Penetration. This was a lively gig. We had already had a few run-ins with the local NF in Leeds, but we were quite a solid bunch and would all stick up for each other. More alarmingly, some of the Bradford punks had a run-in with some Nazi punks from Leeds called the Dentists and the Vents. To put this in some kind of context; it's impossible to be both a punk and a Nazi. The two ideologies are incompatible. Also, as far as I'm aware, there are no other NF punk groups anywhere in the UK but these two. After watching the excellent Penetration, I got talking to a punk from London called Phil, or Trigger, as he was known. He was from the East End of London but was a big Chelsea fan, not good in a West Ham area. I was talking to him at the back of the gig when a mass brawl started to the right hand side of the concert hall. Suddenly the house lights went up. After a while the announcer told everyone that the gig was being abandoned. This was because one of the Leeds Nazi punks had been stabbed, in the mass brawl during the Buzzcocks' set. Then the Nazi punks were chased back to the train station. Trigger ended up staying at my bedsit for the night. I always put people up who visited Bradford, as people put me up on my own travels. Bradford was like that generally though, lots of us put people up who visited our city. That was one of the things I loved about punk; when you visited places, punks were just pleased to see other punks and would look after you. My only other experience at that time of meeting people from other areas was at football matches, and that usually ended up in a brawl. The morning after, Trigger set off on the next part of the Penetration tour. We said our good byes and hoped to bump into each other at a gig somewhere.

South Bank Poly, Elephant and Castle Rock Against Racism gig 17 June 1978

I've been waiting for this day to see the Ants again. After speaking to Dunc on the phone it seems the Ants have signed up to play some Rock Against Racism gigs, because they have been coming in for some stick for quite a while regarding their lyrics and song titles. Some journalists such as Nick Kent, Garry Bushell - in fact, loads of them - are calling the Ants a 'Nazi' band; so the Ants decided to get involved with the RAR gigs. The Ants can't be racist; they have a black half-Jewish drummer and Adam himself has Romany blood. They are signed up to play Ealing College on the 10th of June and this one at the South Bank Poly on the 17th. Brinsley and I get the coach down. OC and Mel can't make this trip. Brinsley spends the whole journey winding people up, or testing them, as he calls it, which basically means he sees how long it takes before someone wants to beat him up, then he gets me involved in saving his arse. I've spent the whole journey trying to relax. Just as things are nearing kick off time with Brinsley and our fellow passengers, we hit London. Suddenly, everyone switches off to sit back and watch the sights of London. We arrive at Victoria and get to the front of the coach so we are first off. Then, we leg it down the road and jump on the tube. We meet up with the Ants crew in central London for a drink before descending upon the gig. Someone is handing out pills so we all down a few. We've got so blasé about drugs that nobody even asks what they are; uppers, downers, or what. They could be Paracetamol for all we know.

I look around the bar and see Brinsley. He has the triangle from the pool table which he has attached to a piece of string, and he's dangling it through the serving hatch. We hear a female voice scream "Arrrgggggghhh!" We turn to look at Brinsley laughing his head off at the bar staff's plight, and decide to leave before the police arrive and we run the risk of missing the Ants. We jump on the Northern Line, south bound tube to the Elephant and Castle. The tube is packed with punks and skinheads heading south. Can they all be going to the Ants gig? It is a Rock Against Racism gig so it will attract non-Ant people. We pull into Elephant and Castle tube and everyone gets off. It's going to take ages waiting for the lift upwards so we decide to take the emergency stairs, which is a long way up and won't be easy, but it will be quicker. We emerge at the Elephant. The South Bank Poly is across the road from the roundabout. This whole roundabout is a shopping precinct with subways. The tube is on the opposite corner to the Poly.

There are lots of people about; student types, punks, skins. I even see some Teds and soul boys/footy fans, but they are mingled in with the crowd in twos and threes, so they are not as noticeable to security. There is potential for trouble here, I think to myself. We hang around outside talking, and notice that there appear to be more dodgy looking geezers turning up than punks and students, so we decide to go into the building. As we get near the front of the queue, security are knocking back some of the skinheads and some of the other potential NF-type people, but they are also letting a few skins in as well, probably on the word of some punk bird saying, "He's OK." Eventually it's our turn. We are told the gig is on the second floor in a bar/concert room, so we scurry up the stairs. The venue looks full. We look at each other. Who are all these people? Where did they come from? Dunc turns round and says, "I think the Ants are starting to get big. Just look at all these people, where did they come from? They ain't been to any other shows. Look at all the birds, there's loads of them. Lots of other outsiders here as well." Popey shouts out, "Fuck the skinheads! I hope they're not gonna try and get on board or they'll get some beat on a bass from the B sides." We all agree, laughing to ourselves. It's not a little cult band any more, now the Ants are taking off. Popey makes sure everyone sticks together. He's the silent but deadly type; he has that aura of 'don't mess with me' about him. It's the look he gives people. He was a lot bigger physically than the others, except for Big PD, of course. He doesn't say much or mix freely with everyone but he's best friends with DD and Johnny Aggro as they grew up together.

We retire to the bar to get some drinks and hang around chatting. I notice Brinsley; he seems to be having a heated debate with one of our skinhead friends. Oh no! I thought; here it comes. Suddenly this skinhead turns round to look at me, as Brinsley has just pointed me out. The little bar steward, he's set me up again! Why does he do it? The skinhead walks over to me and says, "Your cocky little shit of a mate says if I hit him, you'll smash this glass over my head." "Why do you want to pick on him? He can't fight", I said. "Because he's trying to get off with my girlfriend and he's saying skinheads can't fight", says the skinhead. "Just ignore him. He's a wind up merchant", I tell him and turn away. This skinhead is not going to leave it though. Really, I should be angry with Brinsley, not the skinhead. He's always doing shit like this, causing fights then leaving someone else to deal with it. Maybe I should just let the skinhead beat him up? Turning my back on the skinhead had maybe given him the confidence to have a pop. He's now shouting at me but I'm trying not to take any notice of him. I'm watching the Ant kids who have moved over to the other side of the hall for some reason.

Abruptly I'm back in the present. Brinsley may have started this but this skinhead wants to pursue the matter, and if it's not with me he will be causing trouble somewhere else this afternoon, so I might as well get it over and done with and save someone else from the aggro. This guy is full of ego and he thinks everyone is scared of him because he's a skinhead. He's still shouting at me. I'm sick of this shit, so I just shout back at him. "Oi! Arthur Brain! Give me the fucking glass then, if you want it smashing over your head. Or fuck off. I can't be arsed arguing the toss with people like you." The skinhead looks shocked at my response; he senses that I mean business, and I do now. I just want to have a laugh and get on with people, so when anyone wants to cause trouble with me that makes me aggressive, because it's uncalled for.

The skinhead is unsure what to do now. He wasn't excepting this reaction. Popey, who is stood behind me, turns as he hears all this and asks if I'm OK. He looks at the skinhead as if to say if you're looking for trouble you will get it. Within seconds this skinhead is surrounded by Ant kids. Pete Vague suddenly appears. Now he is a big lad. A lot more physically developed than most of us. He doesn't say anything but his physique alone is menacing. Even though he's not a fighter, he looks the part. Stevie P stands behind the skinhead, ready to attack. Stevie's family are north London villains so he's used to a rumble or two. The skinhead looks uncertain about what to do now he's on his own, but he makes a wise move and beats a retreat. Brinsley is laughing at him, so I grab Brinsley and take him away so as not to make the situation worse. "I should hit you; you're always getting me into trouble", I said. I can't help smiling though. I do like Brinsley, for all the trouble he causes. Hopefully it will end here, but if the skinhead has friends with him we can expect a repeat performance - only next time, there will be no warning. No one likes to be taken for a mug.

A girl comes over and introduces herself as Rosie. She asks where the loos are and I point to some stairs. Rosie dashes off to find the loos; she needed them badly - after all the alcohol, everyone was rushing around like headless chickens. Suddenly I needed the loos too, so I followed Rosie up the flights of stairs - but there are no actual signs for the toilets. I couldn't go any further. I looked around and saw another door with no sign on it but it was ajar. I pushed through to see Rosie standing on a roof. She was looking over the edge. She saw me and gestured to me to hurry towards her, so I went. We both looked over the edge. The whole building seemed surrounded by quiffs and bald heads - rows upon rows of Teddy boys and skinheads, trying to gain access into the gig, probably to fight the punks and the students. "Wow, look at all that lot.

You'd think Elvis was playing or something." It seems we've stumbled into an old Teddy boy stronghold. Teds were quite racist, as well as the skinheads, and I'm assuming the soul boys/footy fans are with the skinheads, so we could be fighting racism on its own ground. I wonder whose bright idea it was to have the gig here? So far, security is doing a good job of keeping most of them out of the gig, but for how long? Surely they need the help of the police?

It's getting close to the Ants coming on, so I go back to the gig and we all go down to the front of the stage; all the smaller ones in the middle, bigger lads on the outside - because of the larger than normal crowd at this Ants gig we are expecting trouble, so we are prepared. We look around for potential candidates. There are a few skinheads dotted about - who you always have to watch anyway because they just love spoiling people's fun if the opportunity arises. I'm also on the lookout for the skinhead from the earlier incident because he's a potential trouble maker. Security's being kept busy; there have already been a few people, mainly Teds and skinheads, who have been ejected from the gig. There is a really nasty atmosphere in here. I'm looking at the balcony on one side of the room, and there are lots of skinheads hanging around with the soul boys and Teds. This is going to kick off, I'm thinking. There has already been a rumour going around that the less frightening of these people, i.e. the straight looking ones, are the main Millwall and West Ham firms - which should prove interesting, because they loathe one another. So the big question is: are they fighting each other, or are we the intended target?

For now, though, the Ants come on stage and start their set with 'Plastic Surgery', followed by 'Puerto Rican', 'You're So Physical', 'Fall In', 'Deutscher Girls', 'It Doesn't Matter', 'B Side Baby' and 'Lady'. On 28 minutes and 28 seconds Adam suddenly shouts "Stop!" as flames shoot out of the left PA. Longfellow and Robbo are scurrying around the stage trying to deal with it. It's chaos trying to put the fire out. The band try to carry on for a bit longer. People are saying someone flicked a fag in the bass bin. I look around. A small group of Teds have managed to get back in the venue and they are fighting with a small pocket of students and punks in the entrance. It's mayhem. People are either panicking or fighting. Suddenly there's a big fight on the balcony where the skinheads and soul boys are. I haven't a clue who's fighting who, unless it's kicked off between the Millwall and West Ham firms. Next minute it's going off everywhere. Robbo is on the stage taking hits to his head and back as he tries to keep people off the stage while there are still flames all around. The band disperse quite suddenly as it's now becoming too dangerous.

I look around the room. It's chaos. The temporary bar has been flattened to the ground and the bar staff have done a runner. After a minute or so, I see some police come into the building to try to escort the Teds and the skinheads out, and to stop the violence. It's not that easy, though. The fire is still alight and everyone is running around in panic. I go back up onto the roof, because in a worst case scenario where the building is burning down and we can't get out of the gig, then maybe there could be an escape route onto another building. When I get up there Rosie is still watching what's going on. I join her and look over the side at the big crowd below. We can see the three main gangs in their own groups; the Teds, the skinheads and the soul boys/footy fans. There is plenty of tension in the air between these three groups. If these NF types put their differences aside and join together that would be bad news for us lot - and for the row of shiny helmeted coppers who have now turned up and are protecting the building, standing in front of them like a beacon of hope.

This was mental, I thought. If all those Teds/skins were to get into the gig, it would be mayhem. I take a peek back inside. Security are trying to still clear the concert room and get everyone outside but it's not that simple. The PA was still on fire, people are still trying to get out of the building and the fire brigade are struggling to get in; it's chaos. Not only that, but someone has set fire to all the chairs in the room downstairs, so there are now two fires. Suddenly, some of the people who were evicted from the gig earlier have taken up positions on the top of the flats opposite, and are throwing bricks and bottles down onto the crowd below. People are diving for cover. There are people getting hit on the head with bricks and bottles; some with blood gushing down their heads. There's a lone police van parked further along the road from their other vans. The police have nicked two punks and put them in the back of the van and handcuffed them to the spare wheel. Suddenly the bricks and bottles are raining down on the police van. The front window goes through, followed by more bricks and bottles. They make a right noise, bouncing off the roof of the van and nearly hitting the Old Bill, so the police hide under the van. All you can see are the coppers' boots sticking out from under the van.

The two punks see their chance to get away. They kick the police van doors open, pick the spare wheel up between them and run off down the road, dodging bricks and bottles as they go.

Next thing, we hear what sounds like a shot. Everyone ducks or hits the deck, including me and Rosie, even though we are certain we are not the targets. After a couple of minutes we sneak a look to see what was happening. Everyone is still laid on the floor below. No one knows who the intended target is. Does it have racist connotations? No one knows. So we are all playing it safe, it seems. The police have to do something; it is their duty. We see a copper trying to attract a motor cycle rider, but he rides off into the distance. After a minute we hear police sirens in quadraphonic sound as loud as you like, all over the London skyline. I say to Rosie, "This will be the armed response unit. This is where it could get naughty." A van pulls up and a load of heavy duty coppers leap out, wearing body armour and carrying guns. They start spreading themselves about the area as the shots continue. After a while the armed response unit run across the road. They seem to be heading for the old tenement flats next to the Poly, which is next to the tube. Suddenly we're on lock down. No one can get into the building, or out; we've got a potential lone gunman doing a Lee Harvey Oswald number but we don't know who the intended victim or victims are.

Rosie and I are standing there looking at the scenes below in disbelief as the events unfold. After a few minutes the Old Bill bring down the people who'd been throwing bricks from the roof of the flats. Upon which, the skins, Teds and footy fans try to storm them, because they'd been the ones getting hit with the bricks and bottles - but the Old Bill back them off. Then from a different block of flats, a lone copper brings out a young kid with what looks like a rifle. I'm thinking it's more likely to be an air rifle but those pellets can still cause a lot of damage. I tell Rosie I'm off back into the gig to see what everyone is doing and to see if they are OK. At the top of the stairs I look around to see if I can see anyone. I spot Dunc and Popey in the crowd so I head back down into the gig. I lose sight of them for a second until Dunc comes up to me, off his head on the pills from earlier. He's looking out at what's in front of him; chaos, basically. There are still one or two people fighting. Some are running around panicking, not knowing which way to run to get out, but no one can get out anyway. We've already had snipers and people throwing bricks and bottles; what else can go wrong? It's the full menu for chaotic situations; only thing left is for the building to fall down around us. The security are still trying to clear the concert but people don't want to go outside - but they don't want to stay in here, either. So we carry on looking around to see what we can do.

Suddenly, my eyes catch this striking platinum blonde figure in the corner, with stiletto heels, green army trench coat, and smoking a cigarette. She oozes style and sex appeal. She knows what works and she's working it. She looks great and appears to have the self confidence to pull it off. She's surrounded by other attractive punk girls who have been following the Ants for a while now .They are called the Ant ladies. They are trying to talk to her but her eyes are firmly on the playing field in front of her. She has that determined look of searching for something. I nudge Dunc and Popey who in turn alert some of the other Ant kids around us. "Look at her", shouts Joe the Collar, "she's OK for practising on!" It was followed by a collective "Wow." "What I could do to her given the chance", Stevie P exclaimed. Then the fire brigade come rushing into the building. We try rounding everyone up so we can all go out together. Alberto is charming some dishy punk lass off her feet; Johnny Aggro, Joe the Collar, Huw, Justin, Big Paul D, Red Faced and Godfrey are looking around the bar for anything alcoholic which hasn't been broken. Jerry Lamont was standing next to Clanger and Frenchy; both seemed to find everything funny. Remarkably the search of the bar comes up trumps when Red Faced finds a crate of beer and passes them around.

The Ant ladies, Fiona, Annie Dayglo, Caroline and Sandy are trying to find the women's toilets. I tell them to try making their way over to the corner where Dunc and everyone are. Popey starts taking control; we were going to try to get out together. I pull Sandy to one side and say, "Who's the platinum haired punk girl over there?" Sandy looks round. "Oh, her! Her name is Si-mone. She's been around a while, but this is her first Ants gig. She doesn't mix very well with the other punk girls sometimes. She seems to be quite secretive, or arrogant, or aloof - take your pick. Well, that's what people say about her, but not a lot of people know a lot about her either. She keeps herself to her-self." "Oh, thanks for that." Sandy follows the other girls out the door. I don't know what to do now. As I look around I notice Grant Dell and go over to tell him the plan. "What you doing, Grant?" He whispers in my ear, "This guy over there has got an amazing Seditionaries collection and he might trade or sell it cheap. He says he's bored of punk now." I reply, "How can you be bored of punk? It hasn't been going long enough to get bored of it."

We are finally moving outside the gig. There's a gang of Teds, boxed in so they couldn't get to the punks being escorted from the gig. A few moments after the Teds had gone, a copper announces that everyone would be leaving under escort via the tube - and there would be no exceptions. If you had come in a car, you would have to collect it later. All the Ant kids leave en masse. I notice the lovely Simone is just in front of us with her friend. I keep looking at her. She looks stunning, with lovely long legs. As we march through two lines of police we can see and hear the abuse from the NF types. We are all watchful of our surroundings. There must be hundreds of police there now; it's a major incident. The NF gangs are getting more daring now, out of frustration at not being able to get to the punks and students. Out of the corner of my eye to the left, I see a group of Teds make a lunge forward and catch a couple of coppers off guard, so they lose their balance. As they're both trying to stay upright, even more police lose their balance. Suddenly there is a gap for the Teds to break through. A large Ted bird is the first to break through. She leaps straight for Simone and catches her unawares, trying to drag her down on the floor. Here is my chance to get to know Simone. I leap to her aid; noting that this Ted bird is built like Giant Haystacks, I take no chances and trip her up. As she falls she bangs her head on the concrete floor and seems spark out. I drag Simone away.

Before we know it, more Teds force their way through the gap. Popey has a chain round his waist. He takes it off and whacks a Ted right across the face with it. The Ted falls to the ground, clutching his face. Red Faced is having one of his moments, jumping straight into the Teds, along with Big PD. They are doing well, for two guys being vastly outnumbered. I stick Simone to one side then go back to help the Ant kids fighting the Teds. After what seems a while but was probably only about a minute, one of the Teds catches Brinsley over the head with a bottle; blood spurts out of a wound on his left temple and he's staggering about shouting, "Oh, I'm gonna die, I'm gonna fucking die; help me." He seems to be exaggerating a little and I can see Brinsley looking to see what an impact his performance is having on any women in the vicinity. I know his game. Then suddenly he does keel over. The coppers have regained their composure and start to break up the fighting by hitting the Teds and forcing them out of the gap and back with all the other Teds. What looked like a pantomime now looks serious. We gather round Brinsley to see what we can do. Someone shouts, "Put him in the recovery position!" "What's that then?" Another voice returned. "I don't know. Put him on his side or his back or something. Or with his legs crossed and his mouth open. Oh, I don't fucking know. I'm not a doctor." "Or we could just leave him 'til someone turns up who knows what they're doing", shouts Big PD.

We feel like we should do something so we turn him onto his side. Then we all start frantically shouting for an ambulance. I go to find out if Simone is OK. She seems to be fine, but now the coppers are taking the last of the punks down into the tube. Simone's friend appears and hugs her, looking relieved to find her in all the chaos. I say to Simone, "You'd better go. It still may get ugly round here. We have to stay with Brinsley 'til the ambulance gets here." "OK", she says, then walks off, saying, "I hope we get to meet again sometime." "Me too", I say. Then as she walks off she turns to smile at me. Bugger! Why now? I thought. She's disappeared into the tube now; it's just us, the coppers, and the NF types. There are bottles raining over the top of everyone and smashing all around us. This one copper who looks like he's in command walks over and says, "It might be better if you leave first, then we can disperse them." The reply is a collective "No! We can't. Our friend is badly hurt. We're waiting for an ambulance." We move out of the way so the copper can see for himself. "OK then. Wait here."

The copper then directs his troops to start advancing at the NF, away from where we are. Within seconds we hear an ambulance on the horizon. A few more seconds and it's coming up the road. Some skinheads are throwing bricks at it because they know it's coming for us. The coppers eventually get the ambulance through and within seconds it's parked in front of us. The paramedics put Brinsley on a stretcher, into the ambulance, and shut the door. We sit around waiting for the verdict. After about ten minutes the paramedic comes out. "It could be serious. He may have a haemorrhage, so we're taking him in." We all look at each other in shock. He is one of my closest friends and he's got me into lots of trouble in our lives, but I would miss him dearly if he died. Suddenly the grief turns to anger. I asked the paramedic which hospital they were taking him to. The paramedic gives me a card with the details on and I put it in my jacket pocket. Popey shouts, "We need revenge!" We all shout "Yeeesssss!" "Right, what's the plan?" says Dunc. Popey says, "Right, we get on the tube to Kennington; it's only round the corner. Then we get off and come in round the back of the Teds. We find a similar sized group as ourselves then batter them." "OK!" Then we're off. We run down the road and try to bunk the tube by jumping over the barriers, but in a lot of stations you could just walk onto the platform. No one paid for tubes in London, well, we didn't, anyway. When you got to your destination you just told them you got on at the last stop, or jumped the barrier if there was a chance. But my luck's out today. A big ticket collector catches me as we try to run through the barrier. I struggle but he manages to hold on to me. "Right, you, where's your ticket?"

In my slowest northern drawl I try to act thick and more northern than normal, and hope he falls for the northern stereotype routine. The idea being, it makes him feel superior and he lets me go. "I don't have one... I was... just... following... that... lot", I said. "So they are your friends?" "No! I never met them before in my life. I just thought I would follow them and see where they're going," I said. There's a pause. I follow up with, "I has never been to London before and I don't know what to do down here. It's big, in't it?" I'm now doing my best Benny from 'Crossroads' impersonation. The ticket collector's bitten. He's smiling to himself now, possibly thinking 'You thick, Northern bar steward.' All followed by a patronising tone and finger wagging ceremony. "OK then, I'll let you off this time but next time you come to London you have to buy a ticket to travel on the tube before you can get on. OK?" "OK! Thank you, mister", I say, smiling to myself. I walk off. Result! He's even forgotten to ask me to go and buy a ticket to travel. Double result. I run down the emergency stairs to try and find the others. As soon as I get to the bottom I see the Ants crew waiting. "Good to have you back", shouts Big PD. A south bound tube pulls in and we all jump on. There are about 30 of us altogether. There were more of us earlier but we seem to have lost a few in the chaos. Alberto's lost, along with T Smith, Krazy Kev, Godfrey and some of the East End lot. But we have plenty of fire power. Kirby's a big lad; Stevie P, Big PD, Paul Rochford, Popey, Dunc, Paul W, Boxhead, Spud, Chuckka, Red Faced, Dave H, Joe the Collar and Huw Griffiths .

Kennington is a two minute stop. In no time, we're on the streets again looking for the Teds or the skins or whoever we come across first. We can hear the commotion but can't see anyone. Then, when we walk to the end of the street, it's all in front of us. The Teds and the police are still fighting and it seems the skinheads have returned to back the Teds up. The footy/soul boys are not committing themselves yet, they just sit and watch the Teds and skinheads put themselves on the line. We watch the fighting in front of us but no one notices us. Some of the buildings around Elephant and Castle are old Victorian dwellings with flats facing inwards. We notice a gang of about 20, maybe 30 Teds and skins leave the fray with the police and enter one of these dwellings. There's a derelict house just near to where we're standing. Popey gives a signal to go towards the dwelling. We all pick up ammo on the way; bricks, planks of wood whatever we can find. We follow the Teds into the courtyard but stay out of sight for a minute to weigh up the situation and the surroundings; looking for potential escape routes if it goes wrong. We realise we can escape through the other side if it goes wrong. Then we spread out along the balconies of the flats quietly; we're trying to surround them before they know we are here. Eventually we're all in position. The Teds are looking for ammo to fight the police. As they make their way through the tunnel, we pounce. It's such a short space so they can do very little. We just steam into them, hitting them with whatever we have in our hands. I'm sure everyone is thinking of Brinsley as we steam into this gang of skins and Teds. We catch them off guard; they become disorientated and are vanquished. They lay on the floor moaning and groaning. Someone looks outside the tenement to make sure the other NF types haven't heard anything and are coming to their aid.

Nothing happening. Great! Popey whispers, "Right. Let's get out of here." In no time we're making our way back down the road to Kennington tube. As we're running away anxiously, we keep looking back to see if anyone is in pursuit; mainly, the police - because a couple of those Teds and skins looked in a bad way. Anyway, it was too late now. It's done. In minutes we're gone from the area, revenge exacted. We get back on the tube and into central London and settle down in a pub to chill out. "It's been a mad day, but great fun", shouts Red Faced. "I love it when my blood gets boiling." I look at the card the paramedic gave me. Brinsley is in Lambeth Hospital, Brook Drive, SE11. I notice the telephone number below, go to the bar and ring the number on the card. After a while a women answers the phone. I hear a faint voice. "Yes. Can I help you?" "Yes. I'm trying to find my friend, Peter Armistice." "Oh, yes, he came in earlier with a head injury", says the nurse. A pause. The nurse carries on. "It seems everything is OK. It was feared it could be a haemorrhage but after a scan and some tests it appears to be just concussion", she said. "Can I visit him now?" I asked. "You're best leaving it until tomorrow. He's still unconscious." "OK. I'll ring back tomorrow then. Thanks."

I returned to the table with the others, feeling totally wiped out. I couldn't stop thinking about Simone and that smile she gave me. I was in there, I thought. After a couple of beers everyone looked dead on their feet, so we all decided on an early night. I asked if anyone could put me up for the night and Spud said I could stop at his in Edgware. We were both that tired when we got there we just crashed out. Next day I thanked Spud and left early to find a phone box to ring the hospital. They told me that Brinsley was OK and could go home, so I went to pick him up. When I arrived he was up, but not feeling too great. He told me they were going to keep him in but they'd decided to let him go as long as he went to casualty when he got back to Bradford. On that note, we had to hurry and zoom across London, just in time to catch our coach home from Victoria. The last thing we needed was to miss that. We boarded the coach and snuggled up to the back seat. It's a quite journey back home. I'm totally knackered and Brinsley just doesn't look well. I tell him I'll take him straight to the hospital when we get home. "Oh, I'll be all right", he says. When we get back to Bradford I offer again to pay for a taxi to the hospital, but he declines again so I pay for a taxi back to his mum's. On the 10th of July the Ants play their second John Peel session, doing 'You're So Physical', 'Zerox', 'Friends' and 'Cleopatra'. On the 29th of July the Ants sign to Decca Records for two singles.

The Rock Garden, Covent Garden 10 August 1978

I got a phone call from Dunc saying the Ants had finally signed to Decca. "That's good news", I said. The Ants have so much material now, we wonder which songs they will record. I tell him I'm coming down to London for the Rock Garden gig in August and we try to sort out where's the best place to meet before the gig. Then I contact another northern Ant fan, Dean Parko. He says he's going down so I tell him where we are meeting. Paul W, Boxhead and the other northern Ants already know about the gig. I'm travelling down with Brinsley and Mel on the coach . We also have Baz, who likes the Ants, with us. We have already arranged to meet some of the Ants crew after the gig, at a fetish club at the Maitresse Club at Falconberg Court off Tottenham Court Road. This was situated through the arch next to the Astoria, downstairs on the right. Some of the Ants crew had visited this place in the past. The guy on the door, Lal Hardy, is a tattooist who does a lot of the Ants crew's tattoos. He lets them in for free whenever he's on the door. The Rock Garden is quite a small venue, situated at Covent Garden near the old Roxy Club. The Ants crew meet nearby, outside the tube. All the Hatfield boys were there already; the North London crew were marching up the road - Bradley with Terry S behind him, Grant Dell from Croydon was coming up right behind them, followed by Alvain and Roy, Dave from Bromley, Mark and Paul Harding. Getting off the bus from the East End is Godfrey, Metin, Metin's brother Cetin, Big PD, Pete Vague and Tom Vague, who were unrelated. Mannie Zerafi ,Steve Lawrence ,Ian Rouault ,and Debden. My mate Dean Parko is from Cleethorpes, but everyone has started calling him Grimsby. Paul's got here from Middlesboro with Denis O Neil , and Boxhead from Liverpool. It looks like being a busy night.

The last to turn up are the Lady Ants - that group of beautiful, seductive ladies who follow the Ants everywhere. They could steal your heart - or your wallet - depending on their mood. Simone stood out in front with her platinum blonde hair, perusing the area for threats. She's been to every Ants gig since the South Bank one. I stood there staring at her. How beautiful was she? She looked like bliss and gorgeousity. I've been doing some digging on her and there are some really disturbing stories doing the rounds about her getting men who like her beaten up by heavies; attacking a man with a baseball bat; attacking another woman who took a bloke she liked. How much of this stuff is true, though, is another matter. We all know how rumour mills can get out of hand, but no smoke without fire, they always say. I stare across at her and think to myself, how could so much beauty be so cold inside; what happened to her for her to be that way? We may never find out because from what I hear, she never says much about her past. It was a closed door never to be entered.

Besides Simone is Sandy C and Caroline, who's with Paul Rochford, Lesley, Anna and Fiona C, along with Annie Dayglo, Wendy G. So it looks like everyone's going to be there tonight and we weren't expecting any trouble. We all hang around catching up with what's been happening since the last Ants gig then we make our way to the Rock Garden round the corner. We're all stood there waiting to go in, but the queue just isn't moving. What's going on? It seems to be taking ages. We start to get impatient and people start making grumbling noises. The security shout, "Don't worry, it won't be long now." At this juncture I'm starting to feel really unwell. I've been off my head for the last two days on speed and I just want to get into the Rock Garden and get a drink. My throat is like the Sahara desert. I feel like I'm going to pass out and my impatience at the situation is palpable; sweat is pouring down my face. Some of the other Ants crew come over to ask what's wrong. "Been off my head for two days on speed. I haven't slept or eaten and I'm dehydrating. Has anyone got any water?" "No!" comes the reply. There is still no movement in the queue. Then out of nowhere the police turn up and steam into the club. Some people make a discreet disappearing act.

After about ten minutes the police come out with about four people hand-cuffed. We're all wondering what's happened; apparently they are drug dealers. Someone asks, "How did they get in before us then? It's not even open yet." A police inspector is seen in deep conversation with the owner and the door-men. Then the inspector comes over and asks if any of us know these people? We're asked to give our names and addresses to one of his officers and they'll be in touch. It feels like this gig is never going to happen. I would give anything in the world just for a drink right now, any drink, I don't care. Meanwhile the Old Bill come up to us individually and ask if we saw anything. The general mistrust of the police means they get very little response, and those who do offer to help give false names and addresses, usually punk rock stars: Adam Ant, Joe Strummer, Savage Pencil, etc, much to the amusement of the others. We've now been outside the Rock Garden for what seems a lifetime, but it's probably only about 40 minutes. Everyone is getting impatient but it's another ten minutes before we start moving forward. We all pay in. It's difficult to get on the guest list for London gigs because the bands only get about half a dozen places to give out and there are too many of us tonight.

Now we're descending into the depths of the Rock Garden. I notice a pile of tins of what looks like paint, but think nothing of it. It's not very big down there. I head straight for the bar to the left side of the club, but there are so many people waiting to be served due to everyone having to wait outside, and then coming in all at the same time. It feels like I'm never going to get a drink.

I feel so unwell right now; I'm anxious and I can't stop fidgeting. There are so many people at the bar now. As soon as someone gets served it creates a space. I try filling that gap, only to lose out to someone nearer. This is going on for what seems like forever, darting from one gap only to lose out again and again. Dunc and Popey come over and tell me they are going back outside for a bit, as it's boiling down here. "OK, I'm stopping here." I need a drink badly but the queue is just not going down. Just as I'm about to give up and go with them, a gap appears and I get in there.

Relief. It can't be long now. A couple of minutes later a barman asks me what I want to drink. I'm just about to reply when this flame comes out of the bar somewhere. It's nothing major but the fire alarm goes off and we all have to leave the building. Fuck! I cannot believe what's going on. I turn to leave the building. I'm looking for any discarded drinks as I go. There's none. Shit. We all leave in a fairly orderly queue. No one seems very perturbed that the bar is on fire. Now we're all back outside. I'm still gasping for a drink. I'm really badly dehydrated. I lean against the wall. Suddenly Simone comes over. "You alright?" "No! I need a drink badly", I said. "Oh! I see. Alcoholic, are we?" Simone giggles. "No, I've been off my head for two days and I haven't had a drink all day. I'm dehydrating badly. My throat's like the Sahara desert." "Why didn't you say?" She pulls out a bottle of water. Simone didn't drink a great deal. She liked to be in full control of her faculties at all times; she preferred to take uppers like speed or coke than drink. Not as though coke was readily available; more for the posh clients around London. We had to do with paste, which was great when you're up there but can be a very horrible experience coming down. I liked to come down with alcohol. It made it easier to cope with - and you could sleep.

Simone knew all the Ants crew secretly admired her, and she didn't want to end up compromised by getting drunk, then maybe pregnant - then it's all over for her. She liked that power she had over men - and the other Ant ladies were jealous of that fact. This could sometimes strain some relationships within the group. Anyway, she's a lifesaver tonight. "Thanks for the water. You don't know how much I needed that." I gave her a peck on the cheek then she started to walk off. Suddenly, she turned round and said, "I heard you and some of the Ants crowd are going down to the sex club later?" "Yes!" I replied. "I might see you there then?" I wondered what she meant. The Ant ladies didn't usually go there. You couldn't really call the lads regulars to be honest; we went down there because our tattooist did security there, so we got a freebie. The nature of the place was not really our thing but we were hardly likely to be bothered in a fetish club, and it didn't bother us. We could have a quiet drink and a chat there. Anyway, I thought no more about it as Simone turned and walked off, knowing full well my eyes were burning into the back of her head with lust.

We're all standing around in disbelief at how this night is panning out and wondering if this gig will even happen. No one in the club is telling us anything other than that we have to wait for the fire brigade to come. After a short while we hear heavy boots coming along the road as they turn up. To cheers, they steam straight into the club and down the stairs. After about 10 or 15 minutes they come out again. Another couple of minutes and we're all going back inside and cheering some more. We're all excited now after the night we've had and just want to see the Ants. Strangely, the bar is quite clear on re-entering, so I take my chance to get a drink. "Two pints of lager, please." I'm still nervously looking around in case I get coshed on the head or another fire breaks out, or whatever fate might decide should happen next. Bosh! They arrive and I gulp both straight down, just to be on the safe side in case anything unexpected happens and I miss out again. There is some tension in the audience now, probably due to tonight's events, rather than any prospect of trouble. It would just top the night off now if a load of skinheads came in to disrupt the gig. But we're lucky; none here tonight, so we're free to revel in the Ants.

I'm talking to this girl who is a friend of Penny's. She tells me Penny's gone to a Sham 69 gig. I tell her that's probably where all the skinheads have gone tonight. I ask her how Penny is, because I haven't spoken to her in a while. "You two not seeing each other anymore then?" says the friend. I can't remember this girl's name as I never ask people their names. "No", I replied. "We lived too far apart from each other to have a proper relationship but we're still friends though… I hope." I didn't want to tell her the proper reason for our fall out, because Penny might not want people knowing about that. Next moment I hear the Ants on stage. I turn round to see Adam with a gold-painted face, not his traditional Kabuki make up. He's also wearing a long green army-type trench coat and what looks like a pair of tights being used as a top, with the crutch ripped for access. Maybe he fancied a change, I don't know. The Ants crash through their set to the delight of the Ants crew, who do their best to give 100% on the audience participation front. People throw each other all other club. Some people roll about on the floor. Visually, it really does look like a mass mental breakdown. 'That crazy beat drives you insane' was a popular Ants catchphrase. It's turning out to be a classic Ants set with a mixture of old favourites like 'Plastic Surgery' - one of my own favourites, 'Send a Letter to Jordan', and some newer songs like 'Animals and Men' and 'Never Trust a Man With Egg on His Face'.

Between the break in the songs we hear a bit of a commotion behind us. I hear Dunc say, "Shit, it's Smithy. He's one of the main faces at the Arsenal. What's he doing down here?" Dunc looks round again. "He's arguing with the bouncers." There are plenty of words being exchanged. Then, Smithy turns, goes behind the door and starts throwing the tins of paint that were stacked there at the bouncers. There's white paint flying everywhere. "Oh, shit", I shout as paint splashes onto my clothes; others are in the same predicament. Alberto, who always looks immaculate for a punk, is now covered in white paint from head to toe. Not one of us has been spared, it seems. The Ant ladies appear to get the worst of it. This is going to be a messy gig. Some people discard paint-splattered clothing; luckily a lot of the Ants crew wear leather or plastic clothes so it's a bit easier to wipe off. In the meantime, Smithy starts trying to box with the bouncers. They laugh at first; these bouncers are big bodybuilder types. Other bouncers try grabbing hold of him but he knocks one of them out. There's a stand-off. Smithy's mates stand there as backup, but he seems to be doing OK on his own. Then someone shouts, "The Old Bill's on the way!" Within seconds they're gone, out of the door in a flash like nothing ever happened.

After the gig we make our way outside. First, I bob over to say hi to Andy and Math, who were in great spirits. It was these two who sorted out the guest list for the Ants crew. Math loves Dandelion & Burdock; he says he can't buy any in London, so whenever I go to Ants gigs I try to fill a bag full for him, although I haven't brought any today. And if I did I would have drunk them earlier, when I was gagging. We chat briefly. I tell them everyone is going down to a sex club on Tottenham Court Road. Dave was elsewhere, and apparently Adam was just sitting in a corner of the dressing room in a world of his own. He put so much into gigs that he was physically wiped out afterwards. But there were two Adams - the crazy guy on stage and the quite shy, reserved

Adam in real life. As we left the gig, there was another big commotion. I was thinking it may be skinheads come down from the Sham gig, but the word coming back was it was Arsenal. Must be Smithy's mates. But why come back here? All of a sudden, these Arsenal fans are charging at us. We get all the main faces to the front: Big PD, Dunc, Metin, Paul W, Steve Shaw, me. There's a good few of us and we manage to hold our own. Dunc even ends up talking to one of them he knows from watching Arsenal, just as the police sirens are heard on the horizon. The Arsenal fans scarper again and we make a sharp exit as well. There's been too much going on for one night, tonight. I follow Dunc down an alley and I ask what that was about. He said, "They came back to do the bouncers again, because the police stopped them earlier and nicked Smithy."

We had already pre-arranged to meet everyone after the Ants gig, at the sex club off Tottenham Court Road, so we walk up through central London and turn off up Shaftesbury Avenue towards Oxford Street. Dunc and I turn off Tottenham Court Road and approach a dark, dingy alley, where some of the Ants crew are already waiting. There's Johnny Aggro, Joe the Collar, Big PD, Krazy Kev, Spud and Kev, Steve Shaw and Popey, Justin Semmens, Stevie P, Dave Holloway and Huw. Some of the others have already gone inside. I'm with a friend, Baz, waiting for Brinsley and Mel to arrive. 'Oh bondage, up yours...' We see Lal on the door outside. He's a stocky rockabilly guy and a big Spurs fan. Lal says, "Alright, geezers, how you doing?" "Could have done with you at the Rock Garden tonight, mate", Dunc replies. "It was mayhem down there. Smithy came down with some Arsenal geezers and steamed the bouncers, throwing paint everywhere." Lal laughs and replies, "I love an old ruck with those Arsenal boys."

We walk into the club and go to the bar. I buy a drink from the beautiful, bare-chested barmaid, and just stand there, transfixed. The club is spacious, with cubicles running off the main hall. These are where people can go off to do what they like in private. The club itself was fitted out like a dungeon. It was dark, with gas lanterns in each corner. The walls looked like they were decorated with rubber. There were chains attached to the walls, all spaced out. There was also an area where sandpaper was attached to the walls. I think the idea was that someone would drag or push your body over the rough surface, to draw blood. In one corner there was a stocks; also bowls you would put water in for your dog or slave. The flooring was a rough exterior like granite, perfect for dragging people around. There was some quite interesting design that had gone into this place. We headed towards the rest of the Ants crew over at the bar that had come in earlier; passing a tangle of rubber clad bodies in one corner, who looked to be fiddling about with one another's nether regions. There was a woman wearing a gimp mask, dragging this naked, chain-bound guy around the floor like a dog. Every now and again she would stop, whip his back until it drew blood, then sprinkle it with what looked like salt, and rub it in. Then she would clap her hands and another slave would come and give the 'dog' a drink out of a gold plated bowl. I looked over into one corner and there was a naked woman tied and bound to a rack on the wall; her boobs were all bound together like red balls on her chest and they looked like they were about to burst. Some people were dripping hot wax onto her breasts. Not everyone, though, was engaged in sexual activities. Some rubber clad people were stood adjacent to us, just chatting away.

After about half an hour, Mel went to the toilet. After about 30 seconds he came running back through the door with his old man hanging out. We started laughing and asked what was wrong. He said, "I just went to the toilets. I was stood there having a piss, when suddenly from the side this head manoeuvred itself in front of the latrine, waist high in front of me. All I could see was this open mouth and wide open beady eyes. I went into shock and legged it, calling him a dirty pervert." Mel sat down, seemingly still in shock, but after a couple of minutes he regained his composure and wanted to go and do this bloke. "You can't go around doing that! It's perverted!" he said. I said, "Look, Mel. We are on their turf; it's their club, not ours. They don't mind us being here. It's their rules. If you don't like it, don't come in." For all Mel's punk rock credibility, he came across sometimes as a sensitive, shy lad, unless he was drunk. He seemed awkward around sex, even though it was the Ants' main subject matter. I guess that doesn't make it easier to deal with, direct. More importantly, Mel was a good, loyal friend, and that meant everything.

Brinsley, on the other hand, was the polar opposite. Everything was fair game; wives, girlfriends - anyone who would have him. I really liked Brinsley. He was a survivor; he would do whatever he needed to do to survive. He was quick, bright, intelligent, with no boundaries. I look around and Brinsley is hovering near some people dancing. He's wearing this Adam mac. It seems odd looking at these rubber clad people, dancing around their handbags in a fetish club. Suddenly these people are distracted and it's now that Brinsley makes his move. When the rubber people turn their heads, he flicks his foot through the handles of some handbags on the floor then flicks them up in the air in one movement. The mac opens as the bags are in the air then it quickly shuts around them. Then he carries on dancing like nothing has happened. It's such a quick movement that you hardly see it. He then scurries off to the toilet to see what's in the bags before anyone has even noticed. If he comes out with a wry smile on his face, it was a success.

I found this place fascinating but it didn't do anything for me sexually, or at least I thought it didn't. The mind, like the body, is there to be explored and in this environment you're bound to find some intrepid explorers on a similar journey, I guess. It wasn't intimidating or anything, just people doing their thing; this place was a fetish club and you had to wear leather or rubber to gain entrance. Most of the Ants crew wore leather; some wore all leather. Apparently, from what the bar person was telling us, the main attraction was a pretty Aussie sex slave called 'Subby'. The name had a dual purpose. One was she was Australian, so 'Subby' was an abbreviation for subterranean. The other reason was she would crawl around on all fours, and would spend most of the evening under the long tables with their long-sided tablecloths, to prevent people from seeing what was happening and to conceal her identity. These tables went around the whole circumference of the room. There she roamed, only coming up for air. She was rarely ever to be seen by human eyes. She would spend her time giving pleasure to both men and women. You would never know she was there until she targeted you. Some of the other Ants crew who had been here in the past had mentioned this mysterious woman; it all sounded intriguing, I thought, but I didn't focus too much attention on it.

Anyway, we were sitting at the table. I was talking to Duncan and Popey about a possible, forthcoming Ants tour for the release of the first Ants single, which might be 'Young Parisians'/'Lady', rumoured to be coming out in November, when suddenly I felt a cold, smooth hand, which had run up the inside of my trouser leg and was now stroking the inside of my thigh. I wondered who this was - a practical joker, maybe? At the same time I think: where is Brinsley? Then I thought: even he wouldn't try that. I looked under the tablecloth. It was really dark down there. I could see what looked like a head. The only features I could make out were some blue, piercing eyes and a pleasant smile. As soon as they noticed me, though, they turned away. I was thinking: is this the girl who was the main attraction? I suddenly jumped up, startled by the thought that it could be a bloke. Oh, please, don't ruin my evening by being a bloke. I may be open minded to what others get up to, but I only like women. As I calmed down, I tried to look again under the long, black tablecloth to see for myself again. What looked like a woman's thin, tapered hand pulled the cloth back down and a voice whispered, "Don't worry." It was a soft, dulcet tone which sounded like a woman's. I started to relax a little now. Then the stroking started again and it felt as if the whole club was looking at me, as this hand began to slowly unzip my fly while stroking my inner thigh. I was wearing a pair of Seditionaries bondage trousers, so the zip went right up the back above my arse. These trousers were designed for sex.

I was dying to know who was under the table. Suddenly I felt a cold liquid on my cock as these hands slowly rubbed in what felt like oil, as my cock started to get hard. I then felt a blowing and cool air on my cock. A tongue started to slowly but gently lick the base of the shaft, slowly, up to the head. The feeling was unbelievable. Popey and Duncan were unaware what was happening to me as I tried to maintain our conversation. "Yeah! So we're going to… oh eerrrr… Sorry guys, lost my concentration there for a minute." "You OK?" asks Popey. "Yeah, I'm OK, think I'm just tired", I replied. I thought, well, I can't tell them I'm getting the life sucked out of me. It was so hard to focus on what they were saying while this was going on. I was a bit self conscious thinking could they tell? Suddenly it happened; that ten second climax. That uncontrollable surge left me drained. I felt a soft caress on my leg as I felt her move away. I tried to stroke her hair as she went past. After a couple of seconds, I was back in the room. "What were we talking about?" "The gigs", said Dunc. "Oh, right", I said. I'm feeling tired. "What gigs?" There's news of some gigs abroad in Belgium and Germany, and Italy later in the year. I thought I would love to go to those but it won't be easy to get the money or the time off. I wasn't sure at that point, to be honest. It was something to think about.

I go back to the bar for a drink. Brinsley's being really generous with the money he's nicked from the ladies' handbags earlier. He was like that. Money was just a means to survive, but it seemed to be a bit of a piss take now. Here was Brinsley, buying all these ladies a drink with the money he had nicked off them earlier. As I'm standing there waiting to be served, Brinsley starts talking about the size of his cock, and then asks the ladies if they want to see it. "No thanks!" comes a unanimous reply - which seemed strange, considering the environment we were in; but he took it out anyway and started waving his proud manhood around. Then he tries to put it into the hand of the lady next to him. He used to do this round my house, scaring all the ladies. They would be sitting there watching TV or listening to music, then would look to the side and Brinsley would be there stroking his cock like a pet. I'm not sure he mentally gets what's going on here. Do I? On the surface this whole scene just seems, to the outsider, to be people with weird sexual tastes. But I figure this whole S&M thing is a lot deeper than it looks. It's about stimulating the mind as well as the body and also being in some kind of control. Also, trust must play a vital role here - but it doesn't look like any of the Ants crew are getting much attention.

I noticed Mel earlier, sitting in the corner looking nervously about him. But after a few drinks, he's happily dancing on his own for all his worth on the dancefloor, which isn't a traditional dancefloor really; it's more for parading. But, this is not a traditional nightclub. Is it a night club at all? Baz is sitting with Johnny Aggro, Big PD, Joe the Collar and Huw. Some of the others are just enjoying a quiet drink at the bar. I'm knackered. It's been a very eventful evening, more so than a normal Ants gig. I'm too tired to move so I just sit watching the others. As I sit there, I feel the warm hand on the inside of my leg again, slowly caressing me, teasing me; as the hand stops just before it gets to the groin area, I laid back and let them get on with it. After a while the hand gently made its way to the zip on my bondage trousers and started to unzip me, ever so slowly. I was getting hard. I wanted more than just a blow job this time, though. But by then, I thought, I'm too tired to make a decision. Oh, I'm just going to lay back and enjoy it. But I was getting frustrated now as my interest increased. I decided to look under the tablecloth to see if I could get a better look at whoever was under there. I thought this must be that 'Subby' character. As I look under the tablecloth I see someone in a mask; I can see an open mouth and beautiful, soft blue eyes. It has to be the same person as before? I say "Hello!" I'm not really sure what to say in this situation. I was thinking of maybe saying "Imagine meeting you here", but that seemed a bit clichéd.

Then this person reaches out, holds my hand, and whispers in a seductive tone, "Hello, my name is 'Subby. I live under the tables. Have you heard of me?" "Yes!" I reply. "Was that you earlier, as well?" "Yes" came the reply. Her voice sounded familiar, but I couldn't quite place it. Then she proceeded to drag me under the table. No one can see us under here and most of the other people were at the far side of the club, so they wouldn't hear us, either. I look into her eyes in pure lust that seems to be reciprocated, in kind. All she is wearing is a peep-hole leather bra and matching panties, stiletto boots and a leather mac. We embrace in deep lust, hands and fingers probing, tongues investigating each and every part of our bodies like explorers; seeking out erogenous zones. Trying not to miss a single part of flesh, in the hope we hit the jackpot. The noise we make seems deafening under the table. For a split second I think that people must hear us, but the pleasure is so intense I just think, "Fuck 'em!" I know for a fact that all the Ants crew would love to be under here.

Suddenly she puts some handcuffs on my wrists and I can't move; then she puts a hood over my head. She parts my legs as far as they would go and gets down in between them. We're back to the leg-stroking routine again, her hands moving ever so slowly; millimetre by millimetre slowly approaching the groin area. She stops and plays with my pubic hair and my cock again. I feel her blow on my cock again, then a pause… then a lick… a pause, and then a lick again. As I lay back, I thought how lucky I was but by now I wanted to know what this person looked like more than anything. Her nails dug into my skin; it was painful but not enough to want her to stop. After a few minutes I was feeling ready to explode. Then, she just stopped and moved away. It felt like the tablecloth had moved, as if someone was leaving. I moved my legs around frantically, trying to connect to see if she was there but I came into contact with nothing. I was handcuffed and hooded.

What do I do now? I didn't really want to start wriggling about to free myself because people would become aware of what was happening if I tried to wriggle out from under the table. Maybe the table would collapse and it would be really embarrassing. So I just laid there and waited to see what would happen. As I became all deflated, I started to hope that maybe Subby would come back and finish me off. Well, I bloody hoped so, otherwise I was in a mess. I waited there for what seemed like ages, but was probably only about five minutes. I wasn't pleased that she'd just buggered off as I was about to come. There is no worse feeling than being aroused with no end product. What made it worse was being bound and hooded, so I couldn't bring myself off either. As I lay there feeling dejected, I jumped at a cold hand on the inside of my thigh once more. I recognised the voice again; the woman I understood to be Subby. Again, she started to slowly rub inside my leg and my cock started to get hard again. I was now thinking only for my cock. "Please don't start this again and bugger off. That's cruel." I can feel some kind of oil being rubbed on it which feels nice. While she's gently rubbing my cock I hear her whisper in my ear. "I noticed you at the Ants gig tonight." This news startles me. Suddenly I'm on alert. What, who, where? I was completely caught off guard. I don't know what to say. Do I play it cool and nonchalantly play it down, or panic and wonder who the fuck it is? I decide on the first option. "Oh! So you like Adam and the Ants then, perfect job for an Ants fan, ha, ha!" I said.

"Well, there are a few reasons why I like the Ants", she says. "I suppose it gives me greater insight into what the fuck Adam is singing about, I guess. And their gigs are much more exciting than most so-called punk bands; they have a style I like. Also, Adam looks sexy. But the fans also have a style I like - dark, edgy, and unpredictable. Not like most of the other punks." "I agree, there is something special about the Ants", I say. Just as I'm about to be drained yet again, she asks, "Did you see anyone you liked at the gig?" as her lips surround my cock. You what? Not now. What sort of complicated shit is that at a time like this? I can only focus on one thing - the drain game. It kills the whole fantasy trying to think of other people. Seconds later I slumped onto the floor. Drained... of life. I pause. What was it she had asked me, again? Oh, that was it. "There was a nice looking lass called Simone who I've seen about. Why?" She raises her head, and says, "So you liked a girl called Simone, then?" "Yes", I reply. Suddenly she removes the mask. "It's you! Simone!" I screeched. "That's such a coincidence it being you, as I was only having a fantasy about you seconds ago", I said. I then thought to myself, you lying bar steward. Well, it would have been her if she had asked me the question before my balls were about to be drained.

I can't believe my luck. "I've wanted to get closer to you since the South Bank Poly gig", I admitted. "Me too!" she says. I try to hold onto her but she pulls away. I ask if I can return the favour of making her come. She says, "No one has touched my body for ages; I don't allow it anymore." I'm quite shocked really, and not sure what to say to that. I fancy her, but I'm not so sure what's happening now. I don't want to push her on this so I just lie back and we lay there chatting. I ask her about her 'Subby' tag. She says she was born in Australia but moved to England at the age of six. "Also, it's because I work under a table." "Oh, right", I said. Simone carries on, "No one knows any of this, so I used it to remain anonymous, knowing people wouldn't put two and two together; but certainly no one knew about this part of my life anyway, until now." "Why do you do this job?" I asked. "I love sex without the commitment. Plus, I like lots of men, so I can't be faithful to one man alone anymore", she said. There's a pause.

"Look. I don't really talk about this, but I was in an abusive relationship where I had to have sex whenever they wanted to, and I hated it. I swore then, when I finally got courage to leave, that that would never happen again. Now I enjoy giving pleasure which pleasures me also, but I don't have full sex with men anymore as it reminds me of that time, so… I just pleasure men. And women. Depends how I feel at the time." I'm looking at her, thinking she must have had a tough time, but I think I'm making her nervous, because she adds, "Look. It's about me having control over my body. The power my sexuality gives me is a turn on for me. I love to be wanted. Which is better than not being wanted, but I don't like doing it behind people's backs." "I suppose you're right, but it seems a waste", I say. "So we're not going to see each other again, then?" "Who knows? You've gotten further than anyone since I started my new life", she says. "I quite like you being a northerner. I don't get to see you that much so I'm kind of intrigued, I guess? I see all the others regularly, now I go to all the Ants gigs." On that note I'm confused and not sure what to say anymore. Simone says, "I'm working now, so see you around." She puts her mask back on and moves back under the table. I sit there and try to take in what just happened and what was said.

After a couple of minutes I still can't think straight. I take a quick look around and it seems a lot of people have gone now, so I look for my friends. A few of them are crashed out around the club. It's winding down time. I go into the toilets. I open the door to find quite a few people in there. "This is where the party's ended up, is it?" I shout, and walk in to join them. There are a few people doing lines of coke and sniffing poppers. There's this guy shagging the hell out of this other guy in a cubicle… oh, hang on, there's a queue, it seems. This middle-aged woman gets in front of the guy being shagged and takes his cock in her mouth. The guys waiting their turn for the rear entrance are becoming slightly frustrated; maybe it's the drugs which are kicking their adrenaline. I'm not that keen on watching a guy get butt-fucked against a cubicle door. The whole toilet smells of poppers. I hate the stuff. You're supposed to take it when you're about to orgasm, apparently, because it relaxes the soft muscles like the anus or vagina so its use is both sexual and for the high. All it did to me was make me violently nauseous and feel disorientated, so it wouldn't work either way for me. If I took poppers while having sex I would forget what the hell I was doing. I'm ready for home. I go to look for Brinsley. I go round near the bar area and he's sitting there chatting this woman up. Alberto is still there at the side of him but everyone else has gone. "Right, we're off, Brinsley." "OK. Where we staying?" he asks. Alberto says, "You can stop round at mine. I'm only up the road and it's easy for the tube back to Victoria tomorrow for your bus." "Nice one!" We say goodbye to Lal on the door as we leave. "Bye, boys. Keep out of trouble." We get to Alberto's and crash as soon as we get in. The next day we're up early for tea and toast and a bit of a wash. We say our goodbyes to Alberto and head off back to Victoria. Five hours later we're back in Bradford.

VI
DEUTSCHER GIRL MEETS IL DUCE

'Five foot two, he's proud as a stallion
A Popeye chin and very Italian
He's... Il Duce
Benito Mussolini
Il Duce

We'll do the tango
We'll try the foxtrot
I'll eat a mango
You'll drink a straight Scotch
You know I told you
You could be classy
So why did you have to be so Nazi?'

Part 1 'Jubilee'

There's been an advert in the local paper for the Bradford Playhouse which shows obscure niche films: foreign, leftfield, art house, etc - basically, not your mainstream films. And this month they are showing 'Jubilee' - the Derek Jarman film starring Adam Ant and Jordan. The Bradford punks have been hoping to see this film since its release in February '78, but that never happened on its original release. It would never have been shown at the local Odeon cinema as it had no commercial value; it was too niche - so I had to go to Leeds to watch it. We're all excited. It's on a Friday night, as well. I'm wondering if this is going to be the punk version of the Bill Haley incident of the 50s, with lots of punks smashing up the cinema.

I mention it to some of my peers, Timothy Calvey and Big Rick Jankowicz. You can see the ideas formulating in their heads. I don't think it will happen though as we're not vandals, but it might get messy as I imagine people will be trying to sneak drinks in and some people may be off their heads on various substances.

On the night we arrange to meet in the gay pub the Junction at the bottom of Leeds Road, just across the road from Little Germany where the Playhouse is situated. I catch the bus into town. The Junction is heaving. I've only been a couple of times before when I was meeting some of the gay punks: Andrew, Nora, Tallulah et al, to go to a gig, and the place always seems to be heaving. It's even more so tonight, with the 60 or so punk rockers filling what little space was available. The film doesn't start until 8.30 so we have time for a couple of drinks to get us in the mood before we head over to the Playhouse. I head to the bar to try and get a drink. The gay punks are holding court at the back of the pub. We're on their turf now. Andrew walks over to me and looks me up and down. Andrew is such a handsome lad but with lots of make up on he looks like a beautiful woman. He gets followed by both men and women. He's loud, gregarious and camp, but friendly. The gay punks are always trying to snare a straight punk; it seems to be the ultimate conquest, to turn someone. It's all done in a friendly, bantering sort of way, maybe so they can say it's a joke if it goes wrong, but hoping really that it'll be successful.

Andrew sidles up next to me in this tight space. "Oeer girl, you looking for me, handsome? I hope you're standing to attention if you are." He pecks me on the cheek. Nora and Tallulah are waving frantically as more of the Bradford punks enter the pub. We all feel comfortable in this environment. We're all out-siders of society in here. There are so many little groups of people in here, I don't know how we all got inside. The young lesbians congregate in one area of the pub laughing and joking. Some of the punk girls are moving around both groups. The older lesbian and gay male groups congregate by the bar on the chairs, so they don't have to walk anywhere. I finally get a drink and head over to where Andrew is holding court. Debbie Nicholson, 'The Night Nurse', walks in with Mick Calvey, her boyfriend; followed by big Alex and Harvey Caswell. It looks like Mick and Debbie have been arguing again.

I want to go to the toilets but I can't move. I try to navigate my way, eventually getting there only to find about ten people in a queue. This pub is packed out to the point of being uncomfortable. I wait for what seems ages to have a piss. As I'm standing there, I notice that one toilet door is never opened. After about five minutes, though, it does open and two young gay guys come out. Everyone shouts, "Fucking hell, Cinders. We haven't got time to look for the ball! We need to piss. Come on, make way, or you're gonna stink when I piss down your leg." The gay crowd are all bitching now. It seems just as bad in the Ladies. When I get back in the bar I drink up and tell everyone I'm off to the Playhouse. It's far too full in here. A few follow me over. I've never been to the Playhouse before. We pay for our tickets and are directed downstairs to the cinema area, via the spiral staircase where there's a foyer, toilets and a bar. It seems different to mainstream cinemas; it's quite quaint, as though we've travelled in time back to the 1920s or 30s.

We all buy a drink and sit in the small bar area. I notice a film poster on the wall with Adam and Toyah on it which is different to the original film poster, so I ask the guy behind the bar if I can have it. He lets me take it so I fold it up and put it in my pocket. It seems 'Jubilee' is one of two films by Derek Jarman being shown tonight; the other being 'Sebastiane', which appears to be a gay version of 'Spartacus', which is based on fact. The Spartans used to have sex with younger soldiers as part of a male bonding session. We had a couple of pints and went in to watch 'Sebastiane', but it wasn't for me. The gay punks stayed for the rest of the film but I went back to the bar. After an hour or so everyone was getting a little tiddly but eventually it's time for 'Jubilee'. Brinsley and OC walk through, followed by Mel, but Mel seems to feel the need to tell me he doesn't feel comfortable around Andrew and co. "Don't get me wrong, I've nothing against gays, but they always try to fiddle about with you!" "It's only banter, Mel", I laughed.

The crowd are getting a little boisterous now, as 'Jubilee' starts. The film begins with a guy called Ariel, who's dressed in black tights and holding a crystal ball. He's setting the scene of the story through the eyes of Queen Elizabeth I viewing England in the 1970s. A few people start shouting "Adam!" It's not Adam, but he looks like him with his black curly hair. Jordan looks very attractive in her twin set and pearls; she's a looker. There are plenty of other punks in the film. People start dancing in the aisles, but when the Ants do come on, they've missed out the intro to 'Plastic Surgery'. However, this is the best part of the film and people start rolling around in the aisles as though they're at a gig. The manager of the cinema strides in and tells us if we don't get back to our seats the film will be stopped, so reluctantly everyone sits back down. Unlike the Teds, we don't throw a wobbler and smash the place up. We moan and groan a bit, but carry on watching the film in our seats.

Quite a few other punk bands also appeared; Chelsea, Wayne County and the Electric Chairs, Toyah, and Siouxsie and the Banshees. When the film finished we clapped and shouted "More, more", then the house lights went up and we saw a young lady in between her boyfriend's legs with her head going up and down. Everyone started shouting. Men: "Lucky bar steward!" and from the women a mixed bag of comments, from "Put it away" to "Show us your cock then!" The girl's head lifted, red faced and embarrassed and they both hurried out of the cinema. What the owner noticed was the amount of mess we had made. Around the floor between the seats were strewn empty bottles of cider, crisp packets, fag packets and empty cans. The manager shouts, "Are you lot going to take your rubbish with you?" Some of the less drunken of us pick up our rubbish and take it out. Then we're gone. We all head back to the Junction for another drink and a discussion about the film. I wasn't sure what to make of Adam's acting. He didn't actually say much, and seemed to find it hard to keep a straight face most of the time. To the Ants fans among us, the 'Plastic Surgery' scene was the best, but others had their own preferences.

The first part of the Ants' European gigs has been announced but I can't get any time off to go; most of the Ants crew are in the same position. It turns out in the end that only six people are going to the Belgium gigs. Pete Vague can go because his boss at the vegetable store across from his mum's in Kilburn is very accommodating. Pete would work long hours and save his money to go to all the Ants gigs. There was also early Ants stalwart Frenchy, who Adam called French Marc, even though Marc was Romany and didn't like the French. Frenchy was born in San Marino but grew up in France. His family are Italian Romani; Vlax Piedmontesi to be exact. Adam also has Romany ancestry. The others lucky enough to go were Denis Hogan and his girlfriend Siobhan, along with two geezers from Banbury who were friends of Siobhan's. That was the Ants crew for the Belgium tour. It was such a pity a few more of us couldn't get over there. It would have been great to go abroad because I had never been, and after reading so many books about history I often wondered what life was like outside the UK. While these gigs are going on I can't help but wonder what was happening over there, but we would have to wait until Pete and Frenchy returned to give us a rundown. I imagined it was exciting and wondered what the locals thought of the Ants.

A couple of days after the Belgium gigs, I ring Frenchy and ask him, "So what was it like?" He tells me, "Well, we missed the first gig because we were given the wrong date. But we were there for the rest and I tell you the second night was the best I've ever seen the Ants play, to date; Matthew was on fire and Adam just seemed to feed off him. Dave is always good and Andy, well, Andy is Mr Cool but that night, he had a little smile on his lips. There weren't many people listening to the band so Adam just asked us what songs we wanted to hear and they would play them. We had them play 'Plastic Surgery' three or four times one night. But the rehearsals were best. You could really see how good they were, especially now Matthew has joined." "I was hoping you were going to say it was a non-event because I couldn't go", I said. "Did you meet Pete Vague out there? He said he was going." "Yeah", he replied, "Big Pete Vague, who I didn't really know that well until this tour; he was good fun. He wore a pink drape coat, a kilt, pink trousers and blue brothel creepers the whole time." I said, "I saw Pete once in a drape jacket with his hair in a big quiff and long side burns. It suited him; he looked like a proper Ted until you looked down and saw he was wearing Seditionaries bondage trousers and Anti-Christ boots." Frenchy went on, "On the ferry back, we were out of money and we were starving. Matthew, Dave and Andy were sitting a few metres away from us, eating. When they finished, Andy picked up everything they had left and brought it to us. We were so grateful. I kept telling Andy I would repay them when we got home." "That was good of the band. Andy and Maff always look after the fans." "When we got back, the police didn't want to let me back into the UK because I was wearing the RAF colours (Red Army Faction), Chelsea chapter, and they didn't like that one bit. So they sent me back to Calais and I jumped on a plane and made it to the Roebuck that evening!

"Wow", I said, "it sounds like a bit of an adventure. Bit shitty about the police sending you back to Calais because of your T-shirt, though." Then Frenchy recalled past Ants gigs. "The gig at the Roxy was shite really", he exclaimed. "In fact all the bands that played at the Roxy seemed to sound bad as the compilation album shows. Even X-Ray Spex sound horrible on that and they were always good live. Ditto the Subs. The one Ants gig that really sticks in my mind was the Hope and Anchor one with Jordan, and the Man in the Moon because we knew he was going to be good, but like I said, on the second gig of this Belgium tour, they just clicked." "Right", I said. "I'll see you at the next Ants gig. I can't get down to Margate on the 16th so my next one will be Salisbury Tech College on September 21st." He told me he couldn't make Salisbury but may go to Margate.

Frenchy was actually living in the same house as Adam at this time last year, along with Julien Temple. I once asked him what it was like living with Adam. He related lots of little stories; one in particular about smuggling Mandy (the actress Amanda Donohoe), who was Adam's girlfriend at the time, into the house, and Clanger, another old Ants stalwart, somehow getting into the bathroom while Mandy was having a shower and saying, "Frenchy, I love coming here!" "We lived at Redcliffe Gardens, five minutes away from Stamford Bridge, and even though I'm a Chelsea fan we didn't really go out much on match days. There was too much trouble, and we might become targets if the Chelsea fans couldn't find any opposition fans to fight. The Sex Pistols lived two minutes away at that time as well, in Edith Grove. We used to bump into them at the newsagents. But Adam, he never really mixed much. Mandy did though. Julien Temple lived in the basement flat and he had wild parties - but not Adam; not much, anyway. I can remember maybe three times when he really sat down and listened to music and had a chat with us. Most of the time, he sat in his bedroom. Even back then, he was so sure that one day he was going to be a star. It was slightly disturbing to hear so much self-belief; so much certainty in his conviction. I mean how could anyone be that certain? The thing is, that offstage, he neither looked nor acted anything like he did when onstage. He wears glasses, and is really shy and friendly, but very reserved. He would always stop when we met on the staircase and have a quick chat, and he'd tell me what was happening with the band."

Part 2 Salisbury Tech College 21st September 1978
'Well, tie me up and hit me with a stick
Beat me, beat me
Yeah, use a truncheon or a household brick
Beat me, beat me
There's so much happiness behind these tears
Beat me, beat me
I pray you'll beat me
For ten thousand years
Beat me, beat me.'
We were all looking forward to this gig. It was near Bournemouth. I loved the seaside so I thought we might go a day earlier so we could get a bit of sun, sea

and vagrancy in. While we were there we could also catch up with Tom Vague, another Ants stalwart who lived locally and could maybe show us round and put us up for the night. I give Tom a bell before we set off; he told me he was at his mum's somewhere in the west country, but he would meet up with us in Bournemouth. Mel, Brinsley, OC and I decided to drive down. We didn't think Mel's cheese-wedge car would make it so we hired one from a local notorious car firm, 'Rent a Wreck', whose cars were famous for breaking down. I could hear what people might be thinking, "Erm... that doesn't sound like a good idea..." And just to prove that making one bad decision was not necessarily an isolated case, we followed it up with the possibility of another and potentially more life-threatening one. Brinsley had been taking driving lessons so we decided to let him drive for a while, to build his confidence. We had to be careful in case we got pulled by the police, because of course you're not allowed on motorways on a provisional licence.

As we are driving down the motorway, it's lovely and peaceful. We are all sitting there listening to music, and I'm thinking to myself that Brinsley has not said a word. This is quite odd; Brinsley is never quiet. Suddenly, as if he knew I was discussing him in my mind, he starts talking about a film where the driver pulls on the handbrake of his car. Before anyone even has a chance to think, he pulls the handbrake. Now everything becomes psychedelic, like we're inside a kaleidoscope tube, going round and round. Then we stop dead. I slowly open my eyes to see if I am still alive, or whether I've passed over into another world. I look around and we are all just sitting there, silently, eyes popping out of our heads in shock. Then I look out of the window. Miraculously, we and the car are still intact and residing in the middle of the central reservation of the motorway, facing in the wrong direction. I look at Brinsley. He's got a grin on his face as wide as a Cheshire cat. "That was fun. Shall we try it again?" Brinsley got a rapid indication that we might not be best pleased with his latest stunt when my outstretched hands tried to strangle him. He broke free and escaped out of the car. I got out to go after him and tried walking round to the other side of the car, but I felt wobbly on my feet. The others got out and did the same.

By now Brinsley was starting to realise he might have gone too far this time. As we proceeded to chase him down the middle of the central reservation, he shouted out behind him, "Come on, it was only a laugh!" After a couple of minutes we're tired of chasing him and sit down on the floor. "What if the police come now? It's my fucking licence on the line. We can't say Brinsley was driving", says Mel. So we went back to check whether the car was still working and carry out a few routine tests. When I say tests; we just copied what we had seen other people do in films, whenever their car broke down. We walked around the car to see if there was any damage to the exterior. Then we lifted the bonnet and looked inside, even though none us had any idea what we were looking for. It seems we were lucky. To the untrained eye, there appeared to be no damage. We climbed back into the car and Mel drove towards the motorway service station, which was luckily about 500 yards away, leaving Brinsley in the middle of the central reservation. We waved as we drove past him. For once, he looked shocked. We pulled into the services because we needed to get our heads right and have a quick rest and a drink.

After about five minutes Brinsley walks in through the door. We all give him a disapproving look so he skulks away to the tuck shop. Suddenly we see him rush across the café and into a toilet with what looks like a briefcase. I follow him in to see what on earth he's up to now. I walk in and he's opening the briefcase. "Where did you get that from?" I ask. "Some bloke over by the till", he says, "It's really heavy. It must be full of cash or something valuable. The case alone must be worth a few bob." "What the fuck? We're trying to get to a gig, to see the Ants. You've just nearly killed us and now you're nicking briefcases off people? Why?" I exclaim. Brinsley replies, "I haven't got any dosh to pay for petrol or anything." "Why didn't you say?" "'Cause I didn't think you would let me come", he replied. Just then he opens the case and in it are four house bricks. We look at each other and simultaneously say, "What the fuck?" Brinsley is in a rage now. He picks up the case and walks out of the toilet. "Where are you going?" "To give him his case back", he says. I stand and watch as he approaches a man in the far corner of the service station.

He taps him on the shoulder and the guy turns round. Brinsley says, "Excuse me. Is this your case?" The man says "Yes! Where did you get it from?" "I nicked it", says Brinsley. The man looks at Brinsley in disbelief. "You what?" Brinsley then tears into the guy. "Excuse me. I have a reputation to uphold of nicking top quality items. Can you explain to me why you are walking round with an expensive suitcase full of bricks? You've just wasted my whole morning. I don't mind getting nicked for pinching quality but fucking bricks? Explain yourself!" The poor guy sits there in disbelief at what's happening. Brinsley does have a lot of cheek but this is unbelievable, even by his standards; but quite funny in a serious way. To say he's just nearly killed us, written off the car and driven without a proper licence, you would think any sane person would like to think about their actions, but not Brinsley. He's on a roll. He's even excelled himself today. We all look round for the police - surely they have to arrive soon. We shrug our shoulders. The Ants gig in Salisbury is looking more and more doubtful. Suddenly I snap into action and go over to Brinsley.

"So what's so special about these bricks, then?" Brinsley throws the suitcase back towards the guy. The guy is still in shock with mouth wide open. He still can't speak as we drag Brinsley away. The man's eyes are still following us in disbelief. Brinsley's still ranting, but our need to physically kill him for his earlier actions has subdued. We want to see the Ants and not spend a night in a cell, so we just throw Brinsley in the back of the car. OC gets in next to him, I get in the front and Mel drives off quickly before anything else can stop us getting to Salisbury. We drive for a few miles then we pull off the motorway for a short while. We see a dirt road, out of the way, so we drive up there just in case we're being followed. We sit in the back of the car taking a collective deep breath, then we all look at Brinsley and, as one, we attack him with a collective, "Why do you do it?" The thing is, it's too hard to really dislike Brinsley for long periods, because he is funny. After things calm down a bit we set off again, hoping the coast is clear. We decide not to stop again, just so Brinsley can't continue his anarchic roll. Things are a bit more relaxed now. We only stop once more for a quick toilet break but chaperone Brinsley so he has no human contact outside of us. Sometimes, though, OC can be a bad influence when he gets together with Brinsley. They are like kindred spirits of chaos. OC is more sporadic though; Brinsley is full time.

As we set off again, we notice a punk guy, walking with his back towards us. On the back of his jacket he has 'Adam and the Ants' so we pull up and ask him if he wants a lift. "Yeah", comes the reply. "Where are you going?" OC asks him. "Bournemouth", he replies, "OK. Jump in", says OC. The bloke takes off his jacket first and jumps in the car. "Thanks for the lift", he says. "No problem. What's your name?" Mel asks. "Richard but everyone calls me Rick." Brinsley's straight on it. "Hi, Dick." Rick doesn't respond, maybe he doesn't hear him but knowing Brinsley there will be plenty of other occasions.

I say to Rick, "I see you like Adam and the Ants?" "Who are they?" Rick replies. We're all shocked at his response. "Eh? You've got it written on the back of your jacket, mate", says Mel. "It's not my jacket. I nicked it off some punk the other day", Rick replies. This is going to be fun, I thought to myself. He's nicked a jacket off an Ants fan. First thing I notice about this guy is that he has 'I Hate Chips' tattooed on his forehead, spelt backwards; which reads perfectly when you look in the rear view mirror of a car. We all notice it and snigger to ourselves but none us want to ask him about it - except of course Brinsley, who shouts, "I love chips, actually."

Rick looks at Brinsley with a menacing glare and says, "I hate chips." "Really?" says Brinsley, followed by "Enough to get it tattooed on your forehead?" Rick says nothing and just scowls. Brinsley is in mischievous mood now. I ask Rick, "So why is your tattoo back to front?" Rick looks at me disapprovingly and pauses like he's weighing up his options. "I did it in the mirror in the bathroom at home when I was off my head on glue." I can see Rick starting to get frustrated. It must seem to him to be like an interrogation now. Not to let an opportunity go to waste though, Brinsley inquires as to why Rick hates chips. Rick stares at Brinsley. There is silence for a second. Then he starts. "I was going to marry this girl from Plymouth. It was the longest relationship I ever had. Most of my others lasted a couple of days, sometimes a week or two, but this one lasted for ages - at least a month, maybe even two. I really loved her, but the strange thing was, all she ever ate was chips. Crinkle cut, chunky, French fries… that's all she ate. Bloody chips." There was a collective, "So what happened next?" Rick carried on. "She ran off with a guy who owned a fish and chip shop." We all said at once, "A fish and chip man?" Brinsley, quick off the mark again, "Did you go round and batter him?" Rick didn't find this amusing; although we did, we tried to show some reserve. After another pause Rick continued.

"Yes! We lived together in a flat. One day I came home and she had left me a note saying she was leaving me, and not to try to find her, and that she had found someone else. I spent ages wracking my brain trying to think who it could be? But I couldn't think of anyone. I mean, I never let her go anywhere on her own so how did she manage to meet someone else without me knowing? I spent a whole week looking all over the place trying to find her. Then one day I was walking down this street near where I lived, but I had never been down before. I saw a chip shop and thought I fancied some fish and chips. So I went across the road to this chip shop. I looked in the window to see if there was a queue and I noticed her serving. So I steamed in to find out what she was doing. As I walked through the door she looked up and saw me. She looked a mixture of scared and surprised. She froze and didn't know what to do. She was stood there with this piece of newspaper half filled with chips. The little old granny who she was serving said to her, "Come on, dearie. I want to eat my fish and chips before I get called in for my hip operation next month." She carried on serving the old granny. Her new bloke saw what was happening and said, "Can we sort this out later? It's not an ideal time now." Then she just said to me, "I'm sorry I just left, but you couldn't give me what I really needed so I found someone who could. It wasn't planned, it just happened." I was going mental in my head but I didn't want to do something in a shop full of people so I stormed out."

We were all transfixed by the story. Another collective, "So what happened next?" "Well, I can't say too much else because the police are looking for me in connection with the fish and chip shop that got burnt down not long after." We all look at one another. Mel's trying to concentrate on driving, but in the back we're all trying to stop laughing, holding our hands over our mouths as he's talking. Suddenly Rick takes a knife out of his pocket and starts picking his nails with it. We're all alarmed, and look at each other. "Yow! What the fuck is the big knife for?" "Oh, it's OK. It was in the pocket of the jacket I nicked", replies Rick, and continues to pick his nails. I look at his arms and notice he appears to have about 20 different football teams and girls' names tattooed on each arm and, now he doesn't have the leather jacket on, he looks more like a skinhead. For fuck's sake. This could be interesting. Cue the fun. We start looking at the tattoos on his arms. "What team do you support, mate?" "Chelsea", comes the reply. "But you have a West Ham tattoo there. Oh hang on - and Millwall." "Yeah, I used to support those teams at one point", Rick replies. "You supported a lot of teams then", says Brinsley, giggling. He's in his element here, testing people. "Yeah!" Rick replies. I say, "What other teams you got tattooed, then?" "Millwall, West Ham, Arsenal, Spurs, Man United, Liverpool, Southampton, Portsmouth, Aston Villa, Birmingham City, Newcastle, Sunderland, Sheffield United, Sheffield Wednesday, Norwich, Ipswich, Bristol City, Bristol Rovers, Exeter and Plymouth." "That's a lot of teams", I say. "How comes you support so many rival teams?" asks Mel. "And how come there is a woman's name under each team?" says Brinsley. I'm wondering whether Rick has the capacity to cope with all three questions at once.

Suddenly he speaks. "I travel around a lot, so when I get a girlfriend I support the team where she's from, and when they fall out with me or they get a police injunction out on me for my behaviour, I support the rival team to piss her off." "OK", we all say. Then Mel asks, "If you have an injunction on you then you can't see the ex?" "Yeah, that's right", says Rick. Mel replies, "Well, how would they know you have their rival team tattooed on your arm then?" Rick sits there scratching his head, deep in thought. After a minute or so he replies, "That's a good point. I never thought of that. I did once send an ex a picture of my new tattoo of the rival team but she didn't respond, so I thought it had pissed her off." He follows up with, "I also have a really bad memory so the tattoos also act as a reminder not to revisit any of these places I've already been, or go out with a woman with the same name; because I'm still wanted in a couple of those places by the police." We all look at each other in disbelief and think 'Oh fuck!' OC says, "You'll be running out of options soon, mate." I say, "We should call you 92 after all the football league clubs tattoos; you're not far off the lot there." Rick doesn't reply as he continues to pick his nails with his knife.

Everything goes quiet for the rest of the journey; luckily it's only about five miles to Bournemouth now. We finally get there in the late afternoon. It's still sunny, so we park up and go and sit on a beach. We get out of the car, lock it then walk the rest of the way. Our skinhead friend Rick follows us. "You got nowhere to go, mate?" "No, I'll hang about with you lot for a bit." We all look at each other. This guy is weird, but we're too tired to say no, so we say, "OK, you can for a bit then we're off to meet someone." Brinsley was still in testing mode though, so we had to be careful - and Rick did still have his knife. We were all quite tired now, so we just lay back on the beach and listened to the waves crashing. It really was beautiful as the sun started to go down. After a while we were all feeling hungry, so after a brief discussion we decided to go and get some food. Rick says, "I like fish…" We all looked at each other. Brinsley saw his chance to keep testing Rick. "What! No chips with that fish, Dick?" Rick just glared at Brinsley but didn't respond. But Brinsley wasn't going to let it lie. "So, Dick! How can you seriously hate chips? They are delicious." "My name is Rick, not Dick." Brinsley replied, "Yes, but Dick, or Dickie, even, is a derivative of Richard." "Well, I prefer Rick", came the reply. Brinsley said, "OK, so what about your career choice as a chip-hater? It's such a niche market. I don't think I've ever met a chip-hater." "I don't want to talk about it anymore. I explained earlier", said Rick. Then he stormed off.

So we took this as our cue to avoid looking for food and to go instead to book into a B&B we'd spotted earlier near the car park, hopefully ditching our new skinhead friend along the way. In a way I did feel kind of sorry for him. He didn't seem like your normal aggressive skinhead. He seemed quite lonely in the world, like a lost soul, to be honest. Yet he had a knife, and had nicked a leather jacket off an Ants fan; so he was probably unpredictable with violent tendencies, but didn't use violence as his first course of action - otherwise we would have been fighting with him after all the piss-take remarks he'd taken off Brinsley in particular. There was definitely something not quite right with him. Maybe he had learning difficulties? So we went to the car for our stuff and booked into this B&B. We were lucky there were two rooms left, but we would have to share a double bed. We paid the lady, dropped our bags and I rang Tom Vague from the B&B and arranged to meet him in the pub down the road in an hour or so. Then we headed back towards the beach.

As we walked to the pub we were hoping that Rick had seen we had gone and moved on. We saw the beach in the forefront but we couldn't see Rick. "Great. Let's go to the pub, have a few beers, meet up with Tom then have an early night before the Ants gig." We all say, "It's a plan." So we get to the pub door, open it, and see that Rick is standing at the bar looking in our direction, which was quite freaky. Mel says, "Oh, no. Richard Head's here. Or Dick to his friends." "What you doing here?" I ask Rick. "I guessed you'd want a few beers, and I saw you clock this pub earlier, so I chanced it that you would be here." I thought to myself, maybe he's not as dumb as we think. We all sit down for a pint. After a couple of beers Rick seems to have come round a bit. He doesn't seem so bad and we're having a laugh. Brinsley's on the prowl for local talent. But there is none. Out of boredom he comes and sits back down with us. And I see he has that glint in his eye which in my experience spells trouble. "I'm bored," says Brinsley. "Let's play 'guess what women's names are on Rick's arm and for a bonus point the reason they kicked him into touch'."

There's a silent pause; we're all expecting the worst. Rick puts his head up like he's thinking. He pauses then bursts out laughing, but after that just goes back to his pint. I don't think he understands Brinsley's humour. "Shut it, Brinz", says Mel and Brinsley walks off in search of a plaything.

Suddenly the door opens and Tom Vague comes in. "Hi Tom", we shout, except for Rick who looks at Tom with suspicion. I say, "Tom's OK, he's one of the Ants crew." After a few beers Rick is drunk but cheerful. There's a lot of noise at the back of the pub by the pool table, so we go and investigate. There's a group of lads playing pool for money. We watch the game until it gets to the last ball. As the guy is about to hit the final ball and claim his money, Rick sticks his head in between the guy's legs and lifts him up into the air, so the cue misses the ball. These guys are livid but Rick seems to be unaware he's done anything wrong. As these guys are about to go for him, Rick's finally worked out that there could be some trouble. He stands there with his hand in the pocket where he keeps his knife, looking a bit bewildered. We try and calm things down but we're struggling, because there's money at stake. Eventually the guys agreed to let this guy take his shot again. As everyone is watching the game we take that as our cue to escape, leaving Rick there.

We haven't got the patience anymore and Rick is a liability we don't need in our lives. Tom says, "Where the fuck did you meet that idiot?" So we told him the whole story. "We picked him up off the motorway. He was wearing a leather jacket with the Ants on so we thought he was an Ants fan, but it turned out he had nicked it", said Mel. We carried on with the tale of the fish and chip girl and all the footy teams tattooed on Rick's arms." Tom's eyes are wide with disbelief at what he's hearing. "Fucking hell. What a bell end." Then Brinsley starts moaning. "I was well in there, then. That barmaid fancied me!" As we walk down the road with Tom, suddenly, as per usual, Brinsley, the man with no money, shouts out, "Are there any decent nightclubs around here with birds in?" "There's women in all nightclubs, Brinz", says Tom. "Yes, but birds who let you shag them without having to introduce yourself or buy them lots of drinks?" says Brinsley. "Why are you so derogatory towards women, Brinsley?" I ask. "Maybe I'll tell you one day, but there's a good reason, believe me", replies Brinsley. Tom says, "There's lots of clubs but they won't let punks in. Oh, hang on, there's a new punkish place just opened down near the beach."

So we head off down there. As we approach the place we can see a light in the doorway. Then Tom says, "I'll have to leave you to it now, I've got to be off. I'll catch you tomorrow then." We pay in and head to the bar. It's not too full, but I'm quite tired so I get a drink and sit down with OC and Mel. Brinsley has other ideas. He's on the prowl. His overactive groin muscle is on the look-out for someone cheap and available. We find a corner and listen to the mixture of punk and reggae sounds. This DJ is good; he's playing US 60s garage punk, We the People, the Music Machine and the Chocolate Watchband. I watch in the background as Brinsley tries to ingratiate himself into some ladies' - well, any ladies' - knickers. All he seems to be doing is winding the local punk blokes up and we can see the glares he's getting. I know what happens then. He gets in trouble, then I have to go and defend him, and that gets tiresome. I don't want to be falling out with people because of him. Anyway, we sit there quietly, just listening to the music, daydreaming really about the Ants gig to-morrow night; who's coming down, what will happen, what songs will the Ants play, etc. I'm getting a round in at the bar and have a friendly chat with the owner, who's called Frank. He seems a pretty relaxed guy. We talk about his club, and he asks what it's like in Bradford. He then introduces me to his daughters, who are the barmaids. "Hello", they shout. "Are you from London? We would love to go up to London." They looked at each other and smiled. I've seen that smile before on many an excited face, craving the excitement of old London Town. Suddenly Brinsley appears. "Hi! I'll take you to London", he says. Both girls have that mischievous glint in their eye which could spell trouble. Frank shouts to his daughters, "Get serving! There are people needing serving." I notice that look in Brinsley's eyes that usually means fireworks in my experience. I say to him, "Leave it!" "OK", he says, and walks off. I sit down again. Everything is peaceful, for now.

At the end of the evening we start to make a move. Suddenly Frank's run-ning towards us with an axe in his hands, looking serious. I'm looking around for what could be the problem. OC and Mel sense trouble also and quickly make themselves scarce outside. Frank runs up to me and shouts, "Where's your fucking mate Brinsley or whatever he's called?" "Oh fuck! What's he done now?" "My 15 year old daughter is missing." Oh, shit. I shrug my shoulders to indicate that I don't know where he is which doesn't help matters; Frank's incandescent with rage. "I'm gonna kill the little shit!" He turns to look elsewhere like a man possessed, as people are hurrying out of his way. I'm looking around and thinking where the fuck is Brinsley? I try to get out of the door of the club but suddenly I feel quite pissed. Well, not so much pissed as tired, and my legs are going all over the place. I finally make it outside and OC and Mel are feeling a bit the worse for wear also. It's getting a bit heated around here; we can hear Frank shouting his daughter's name out as he runs round the club looking for them. Suddenly I hear Brinsley saying, "Shhhhhhhush, over here!"

We run across to him. "What the fuck are you doing?" "Just shagging that guy's daughter. She's dirty, man." "She's only 15!" "What's his problem? I'm only 14. She knows some right tricks that lass. It should be my mum running around going ballistic. Anyway, I was shagged at 13. You didn't hear me calling for my mum", says Brinsley. "Where is she now?" "She's gone back inside. I told her I'll take her and her sister to London, so go pack some clothes." "Are you fucking mental?" we all shout. "Oi! Hang on a minute. You're 14, then how comes you're having driving lessons? You need to be 17, don't you?" Brinsley replies, "Well, technically I can apply when I'm 15 years and six months but, I just told you I was older so you would let me drive, but it wasn't technically a lie either. I've been getting driving lessons off Dodgy Dave. He teaches getaway drivers. He's the best in the business. Well, you need to be when you're a bank robber." "So how old are you then?" I asked. "It depends on the situation", replied Brinsley. "Right, let's get out of here. It's getting dangerous. I'm not going to be able to save you if Frank catches you with that axe." Brinsley goes, "What axe?" "He's running around the club with an axe looking for you, saying he's going to kill you." Brinsley suddenly looks scared. "Fuck that. Let's get out of here." OC says, "You're not waiting for your new girlfriend then, Brinz?" "Fuck off, OC." "What you like?" OC says, mimicking the gay punks back home.

Then, unbelievably, there's another shout from inside the club. "Someone's nicked my records!" We all look at Brinsley. "What about the records?" "I haven't got any records", protests Brinsley. I look at his face and I believe him. If he's done anything wrong he kind of gives you a wry smile, but here there is none. "You know how much I love music. I would never nick someone's records." We decide it's best to leg it down the street. We haven't a clue where we're going, but after about half an hour we stop and we're stood in front of the beach. We sit down against this café, under some kind of roof, to catch our breath. As we sit there recovering, we can hear the sea washing up on the beach. It sounds really relaxing - so much so that next thing, we're being woken up by these people doing exercises right in front of us. "Come on! Let's have some squat thrusts!" shouts the instructor. "Fuck off! We're trying to sleep!" The exercise enthusiasts quickly get the message and rapidly move on.

After about five minutes the café opens. As the shutter goes up, suddenly a hand appears on the counter from below like Thing from the Adams Family. "Four cups of tea, love. And some toast." The woman shrieks. "Aaaaarghhh!" Four heads appear. "Morning, missus!" "You silly bleeders. You scared me to death", says the café lady. There's a collective, sheepish "Sorry!" "We would like breakfast in bed, please, madam; the crumbs from the toast will blend in nicely with our new sand bedspread", says Mel. We lie on the sand feeling like shit. It's red hot and we're in the sun but we don't have the energy to get up, so we lay there for a while longer. I fancy getting in the sea. It might wake me up, so I trudge off down to the water's edge, which is a bit of a way off now. When I get there I look out over the ocean. I love the sea; it represents freedom. I take off most of my clothes and jump in. It's fucking freezing! The others come down to join me and do the same then we splash each other and mess about. After a while we go and sit on the sand to dry out. We're feeling a bit better until we try to get dressed; then our clothes get full of sand so we go back down to the water's edge to clean the sand off, only to go back and get covered in sand again. Mel shouts, "This is doing my head in." "Me too. I bloody hate sand now." In the end we go down to the sea wash our feet and arses and legs, and get dressed there. We figure the sun will dry our clothes out. Half an hour later we decide to try and find our B&B. Luckily we weren't too far away. We apologise to the lady at the B&B and ask if we can get our money back but she argues that someone else may have come looking for a room, so we just collect our stuff and leave.

As we approached the car we noticed that the back window has been smashed. We all look shocked. We walk towards the car and notice our lovely skinhead friend Rick is asleep in the front. We bang on the car door and he opens it. "What the fuck happened here?" shouts Mel. "Morning, lads", says Rick. "Well?" "I lost you in the pub somewhere and I had nowhere to sleep and I was cold, so it seemed like a good idea to smash the window so I put a brick through the back window to get inside." Brinsley says, "So was it warm then?" Rick says, "No! It was bloody freezing, because there was a draft coming in through the back window." I say, "Why did you have to put the back window in? Couldn't you have just got in through a small side window?" "Well, I was pissed and things were blurred and it was dark, so I just went for the biggest window", says Rick. "For fuck's sake!" We're all getting mad now. Rick senses this. Just as the mood was about to start to get darker he suddenly shouts out, "I can pay for a new window. I have tons of cash." I say, "Why didn't you get a hotel room then?" Just as he starts getting on side with us, he makes another comment that makes us just want to kill the bar steward. "Oh, it was too late. It was too dark and I couldn't be bothered looking." But then he pulls out a massive wad of cash. There must be about £500. He asks, "How much will it cost?" Mel answers, "I don't know?" I ask, "Where did you get all that money from?" "Oh, the last place I was at in Ipswich they left the safe open when I was leaving, so I took a bundle", says Rick. "Right", says Mel. "Let's find a garage and get this window sorted."

OC and Brinsley are in their own world as usual, not caring either way what happens. OC is a really nice lad; lovable and stupid in equal measures, but a joy to be around. But he can be frustrating. He was great at restoring furniture. He's one of those people who has so many ideas, you wonder where he gets them from. The downside is, he's too busy thinking of ideas so he never finishes any of them, or even starts any of them in most cases. Mel turns round. "Right, let's go find a garage." As we set off, Rick suddenly says without thinking, "Can we stop at a shop? I'm starving." Our patience is wearing thin but then Brinsley says, "Good idea. They might know where there's a garage." So we head for the nearest shop/garage, whichever came first. We drive down the main road and there is a garage. We go in and ask about having the window repaired. "Sorry, lads", says the owner. "No one is going to repair your window straight away. They would need to send off for the window and then fit it."

Rick's gone inside to get some food and we're all looking despondent. He comes back and starts eating his food. After about five minutes there is a gulp and Rick is sick all down the interior of the car. "Sorry, lads." Rick looks at us apologetically. "Right, Rick. Give us some money for the window, then it's time to say goodbye before we end up killing you." Rick goes in his pocket and pulls out his wad. "How much?" Mel says. "I don't know, give us £70 for the window and for the inconvenience." Brinsley, not to miss a chance, adds, "I want £20 as well or I'm going to tell the Old Bill where you are." Rick glares at Brinsley but what can he do? So he hands over the cash sheepishly. "Thanks Rick. This is the end of the journey", says Mel. We all nod in agreement. Rick turns and walks off with his head bowed. We were kind of expecting him to have a go at us and use his knife or something. He looks a forlorn figure walking away with his head down; I felt quite sorry for him but we haven't time to dwell on it. The greatest band in the world is hitting this part of the world tonight.

"Right! What we going to do about this window?" says Mel. We found some plastic sheets with holes in so we could run the rope through the holes and fasten to the car. It's a bit of a struggle but we manage to fix it, of sorts. We all jump in the car and fuck off before we get pulled. After a while we pull up at a telephone box and ring Tom. We have a brief conversation, telling him what has happened. He laughs nervously. We arrange to meet by the beach in a couple of hours and head down to the centre of Bournemouth, looking around the shops as we go. It's a really nice place, is Bournemouth. I wouldn't mind living there myself. After a while we go into a pub for a drink, and there are some punks over in the corner. Suddenly I see Chris Beanland. Chris was my best punk mate in Bradford. He and Russell Hitchcock disappeared in early '78 and no one knew where they went. I shout at him, "So this is where you went then? There were loads of rumours about you being all over the place. I thought it might have been something to do with that lass you got pregnant?" Chris just said, "I came down here to get away for a while with Russell, and just stayed."

It was really good to see Chris. We had already had a lot of adventures together. We went to the Sex Pistols' gigs together, as well as plenty of others. Unfortunately Chris was a big Man U fan, but punks never fell out over football. We stood in the Stretford End together watching Leeds win 1-0 with a goal from Allan Clarke. He came with me to watch Leeds at Birmingham City once because he missed the coach to Ipswich to see Man U, but I got arrested after being in the ground for five minutes for fighting, after we were attacked by a load of City fans in the Leeds end, and he had to go home alone on the Leeds coach. I had to walk it. I was the only Leeds fan arrested and I was beaten up by all these black Brummies in the cell. The police let me out of the cell and said, "Catch this bus; it will take you to the ground." Police being the lovable jokers that they are, the bus took me to Aston Villa's ground. Then I got a lift off some Liverpool fans who dropped me off on the M62, and I got arrested again for walking on the motorway. The police dropped me off just outside Manchester where I got talking to this girl, who asked who I was and where I had been. She went away and came back with loads of young Mancs with baseball bats and I was chased down the motorway to Birch Services. I had had enough by that point so I asked some coppers where I could get a taxi and told them what kind of a day I had had. They took pity on me and took me back to the police station, gave me some food, contacted my parents and got me a taxi from Rochdale, which is where I was. The taxi cost me £14. Then I had to go back to Birmingham on the Monday to court and was fined £100. That was a bad weekend.

"Where's Russell then?" I ask Chris. "I don't know. He was here for a while, and then he just disappeared again." I tell him I couldn't keep in touch because he had just disappeared and left no number. He asks why I'm here. I tell him, "I'm following Adam and the Ants and they are playing in Salisbury tonight." Chris introduces us to all his punk friends from Bournemouth. One of the girls is wearing an original Ants 'Plastic Surgery' t-shirt. These are really rare, so I ask where she got it from. She said it was from a friend who knew the Ants. I ended up buying it off her for a couple of pints. I ask if she is going to the Ants gig in Salisbury tonight but she isn't sure. I tell Chris I need to go and meet a mate on the beach, so we head off there. Within a minute or so Tom turns up. He knows all the other local punks but he didn't know I already knew Chris. Then we sat on the beach chatting all afternoon, soaking up the sun and having a few beers.

Brinsley was on the prowl. He was in testing mode again so he got his cock out and started playing with it. He was always doing this; partly to embarrass girls and partly to advertise that he had a big cock. It never failed, though. Most of the girls would pretend they were horrified but one always came back later. We told him to put it away; we were heading up to Salisbury soon. I asked Chris if he wanted to come with us; he said "OK!" Some of the Bournemouth punks have to cry off because they can't get back after the gig. Tom heads off, he's getting a lift from some other local punks and he takes Chris with him because it's a tight squeeze in our car. So we say goodbye to the other Bournemouth punks and make our way back to our Rent-a-Wreck special. Mel sparks her up and we settle down for our journey which is about 25/30 miles. We head off in the right direction towards Salisbury, with fingers and toes crossed that we get there... everything is going great; the car whiffs a bit after Richard Head was sick down the interior. The plastic sheeting seems to be holding out OK though. We're making good time to Salisbury, so we sit back and start talking about the gig. We're getting excited about what might happen and who's coming down from London and elsewhere.

We're following all the signs to Salisbury, when the car starts spluttering. Now we're only crawling along. We're all looking concerned but none of us are mechanics. After another couple of miles the car has made its last splutter and died. Well, not died exactly - the motor is on, but we're not moving so we get out and start to push. We're pushing the car up the road towards Salisbury Tech College. We see the sign post. It's situated on a roundabout on the A36. We eventually turn into the drive and head towards the Tech. It looks like it was built in the 60s. We park the car - well, we would have to be in the car to park it so we just leave it in a parking bay. Mel was fuming. "What the fuck are we going to do about the car? Rent-a-Wreck have all my details. I'm going to have to buy a new car for them." OC shouts, "Don't be stupid; it's called Rent-a-Wreck for a reason. So why do you need to buy them a new car?" Brinsley chips in, "You might have to buy them a new wreck." Everyone laughs except Mel. We sit around for a while to catch our breath. Luckily we can still play tapes, but the rest of the car looks like something Steptoe would drive. Mel tries again with his limited knowledge to get the car to move, but the car was letting Mel know in no uncertain terms that it was now retired. "How the fuck are we going to get home?" shouts Brinsley. We all shrug our shoulders. Who knew? We sit in the car wondering what to do.

After a while we were starving so we go and find a café in the college. We feel rich after the money Rick gave us, although the money is Mel's really. Mel treats us all to a meal of our choice from the limited menu, although Brinsley takes this too far as usual and starts sticking pieces of buttered toast and jam to people's coats as they leave the café, then he slaps OC across the face with a piece. "Here you go, OC, some nice toast." Then OC starts throwing food at Brinsley. I finish my tea sharpish to go and sit outside and leave the chimps' tea party to get out of order, expecting them all to come flying out of the door any minute now, barred from the college. After a few minutes they all come out together. I don't know if they've been asked to leave and I don't care either way. We go for a walk round the college for a while but it's a bit boring with not much to see except loads of students who look down their noses at us. A group of bikers pass by but we don't think anything more of it. We go back to the car to listen to tapes until people start turning up - but at least we've found out where the gig is being held. We listen to old Ants tapes or doze; it's really relaxing.

After what seems like ages we see movement. Suddenly there are punks milling about instead of students. Our car looks so out of place. It's a wreck by name and a wreck by nature. The plastic sheeting is now flapping about and the car still stinks of sick. Finally, some of the Ants crew from Middleboro - Pete Bell, Graham Stevens and Paul Wannless start walking through the car park. We jump out to greet them and they all turn around and laugh at our transport. "Ha! Where did you get that heap from?" shouts Paul. "It got us all the way here from Bradford - well, almost. We had to push it up this road", I told them. Everyone laughed. "How did you get here then? Hitch?" "Nah, mate", Paul says. "We got a lift from someone from Boro who luckily enough was going right by this place so we got in with them. But we'll have to hitch back." We sit outside chatting for a bit and tell everyone about our skinhead friend Rick. Everyone is laughing in disbelief. Paul says, "It's a while before the gig starts. I spotted a pub round the corner called the Star. Let's go there for a drink."

As we walk to the pub we see another gang of bikers go past. "There seems to be a lot of bikers around", Paul says. "Yeah, we noticed a load as well; I think there's a bikers rally or something on somewhere round here?" says OC. We get to the pub and there are bikers in there as well. We walk past the bikers on the door and, first things first, look around and see if any of our lot are in there. There are a few familiar faces; some of the Ants crew are already in there: Joe the Collar, Huw G, Big PD, Boxhead, Robbo, Pete Vague, Tom Vague, my friend Chris from Bradford and the other local punks from Bournemouth and Southampton have all managed to get here. We have a few beers to get in the mood before the gig but there's an uneasy atmosphere so we don't stick around too long and make our way back to the college.

The gig was in a big college hall, which was also used for exams Tom Vague told me, with windows along both sides. The stage was across the far end. The bar was in the students' common room above the foyer entrance to the hall, between the Tech and Art colleges. As we walked in I saw Dunc and Popey, Johnny Aggro, Fiona C and some of the other London Ants crew are there. "Where did you lot get to?" I said. "I thought you would have come down together with Pete Vague and Joe and Huw and the others. Dunc said, "We got the train times mixed up and missed the first train." "Oh well, we're all here now." Everyone was commenting on the bikers, wondering about potential trouble, but so far so good everything seemed fine up to now. There weren't that many of us, though, so if trouble did occur we could be struggling. It's getting near gig time now. We have a laugh and a catch up with everyone. Just as we're about to go in the hall, Chris and Tom come in looking shocked. "What's wrong?" "It's all kicking off apparently. We've just seen some Bournemouth punks who have been chased by bikers. The rumour is a biker bird got stabbed in the bogs and the bikers are going mental." Tom sees a punk from Southampton and asks him what's happened. He has a different story. Some biker started on a punk and the punk knocked him out, so his biker mates started attacking punks. Whoever started it, something is happening. We shout a collective, "Shit!" "Anyway, nothing we can do now. The gig's about to start, so let's go in."

As I get through the door I bump into Longfellow, the Ants roadie. I asked him about the Belgium gig and he told me, "Frenchy turned up in Belgium with a big bag of blues, which improved the weekend considerably. My abiding memory of the weekend was of Adam on the back of the ferry opening the door to the toilets and a tidal wave of shit, piss and vomit coming out; it was a rough crossing, only those of us who were speeding didn't get seasick!" Then he walked off backstage and the Ants hit the stage with 'Plastic Surgery' almost as soon as we enter the room, so we go down the front and get involved. The Ants steam into some of their classic songs: 'Bathroom Function', 'Il Duce', 'Physical', 'Weekend Swingers', 'Song For Ruth Ellis', which they only ever played live at this gig, 'Cleopatra', 'B-Side Baby', 'Friends', 'Never Trust A Man (With Egg On His Face)', 'Catholic Day', 'Deutscher Girls' and 'Lady'.

Suddenly we hear a commotion outside near the entrance. Mark Hutchins, Mark Harding and Kev McGovern are walking into the gig. "Hi, lads, how did you get down here?" Dunc shouts. Mark says, "We came down in the old

Humber Hawk. Come to think of it, where's Kev Tredrea?" Just at that moment Kev comes through the doors and is immediately attacked from behind by some kind of unidentifiable object. Kev Staggers into the hall. Mark catches him before he hits the floor. "Shit! This gig is gonna kick off big time", says Joe the Collar. We try to look through the doorway and it looks bad even though we can't really see what's happening, but you can see bodies flying around as though there's a fight going on and lots of noise which is audible even over the Ants playing. Then there's a lull, so we get back to watching the Ants. The next thing the whole hall is invaded by bikers and straights. They stand around the periphery of the dance floor and pause. We know what's coming and the odds are not in our favour. Suddenly they start walking onto the dance floor and dragging individual people out for a kicking. We all look at each other, trying to stay together. There's only about 16 of us and about a hundred bikers and straights. I can't see Dunc. We shout "Dunc!" Then I look to my left and see a little greaser with a knife in his hand.

Dunc gets knocked to the floor but as we try and get to him a load of bikers come in our direction. We stand trying to fight them off but we are overpowered. I look again in Dunc's direction and Robbo, the Ants roadie, complete with massive clogged feet, jumps onto the dance floor and picks Dunc off the floor and carries him out to safety. Eventually the security manages to stop the trouble and clear the hall of bikers so the gig can carry on. There was a worried tone in Adam's voice. After a couple of songs the bikers were back again. This time some were armed with chains. This gig is getting out of hand now and it feels claustrophobic. There's a real sense of danger in the air. We look out of the window of the college and the area outside is now packed with bikers, wielding chains and other weapons. There's a rumour the police have been called but they're not here yet, so we have to do the best we can. The Ants finish the gig, playing 'Puerto Rican', 'Fall In' and 'It Doesn't Matter'. But it's no fun now and our usual carefree frantic dance style is a little curtailed as we need to keep our wits about us and be vigilant. We have a serious scare going on and it's the end of the gig now. We all look at each other. Joe the Collar asks where Huw is. We look around the hall and see a crumpled body behind some chairs. It's Huw. He's looking badly beaten so we help him to his feet.

Then Brinsley walks into the room. No one had even noticed he wasn't there. Mind you, when there is trouble he's usually started it before he disappears, but he's innocent this time. I shout at him, "Where you been?" "Shagging this bird round the back. Why, what's been happening?" We explained, and in Brinsley's cockiness he says, "I'll do them all, where are they?" The hall is still full of punks wondering what to do. Tom Vague goes to the door and a bouncer says, "I wouldn't go out there if I was you", pointing at some bikers armed with chains prowling about. Tom says, "Right, cheers mate", and stops in his tracks. It feels like we are all trapped in the venue. Some bikers try to gain entrance again through a side door. We spot them and go to stop them; luckily we get there first. Then we go backstage to see Adam and the band. As we walk in, the band almost in one voice shout, "Fuck! Steve McQueen, what happened to you?" That was the Ants' nickname for Huw. They look nervous as well. The mood is not good. Everyone seems pensive, playing out possible scenarios in their heads of what might lay in store. We come to the conclusion that we're going to have to fight our way out of this venue. Mel suddenly pipes up, "What about the car?" "What fucking car? It doesn't work", says Brinsley. "I'm not getting battered for a car that doesn't work; there's nothing in there except some tapes and a bit of food", says OC. "I think actually this could be our escape clause with the car", I say to Mel. "We can blame it all on the bikers and say they attacked the car, and it didn't work after that." It seemed perfectly feasible to naïve young boys that no one would check this story out thoroughly and they'd just believe us.

That sorted, we switch our attention back to 'how do we get out of this gig without getting battered?' Joe the Collar, "Let's get out of the window at the back of the group's changing rooms." Someone goes to check if it's a possibility. They open the window only to see a large gang of bikers who proceed to brick the window. Everyone ducks and someone shouts, "That option is out then." Longfellow is still on the stage with Robbo, getting ready to pack the gear into the PA van. When that is done they put the guitars into the Ants' orange VW van. With the bikers seemingly at the back of the building now, everyone makes a rush for it outside. Maf and Andy say, "Let's get as many in the vans as possible and get out of here. Maybe we can get a few in the PA van as well." We get Fiona in first; then the rest of the London Ants crew get in and the van is full. The band are going back to the Bivouac in Notting Hill in London, so it makes sense to take the London lot. Now there are just us and the Boro crew left. We have lots of money but they have fuck all. So Mel hands them some cash. "Go on, Paul, you lot go with the PA truck and here's a bit of cash to get back to Boro." There's a pause, then Mel suddenly blurts out, "I've just remembered. I'm a member of the AA; they will have to tow us back to Bradford." "That's really fantastic news, Mel", says OC. I say "Yeah, OK! Let's go stand in the car park surrounded by axe-wielding bikers. If they say anything just tell them we're only waiting for the AA to mend our broken car. I'm sure they will be sympathetic, they may even get their tool kits and come back and try mending it for us?" "Oh! Fuck off. I was only trying to help", says Mel.

It's the last call from Longfellow. "We're going now!" We tell Paul and the Boro lot to go with the PA. They follow Longfellow and Robbo to the PA truck and within seconds they are gone. Tom V and Chris B say we can stop at theirs if we get back to Bournemouth, but we don't know how we're going to get back ourselves yet. Anyway, they both pass us pieces of paper with their addresses on then they disappear also. This gig is starting to make breaking out of Hitler's bunker look like a walk in the park. Luckily the bouncers are still on the door, but I'm thinking where are the police? They were called ages ago. "Right", I said. "If we're going to try this suicidal mission of trying to get the AA to tow us back to Bradford, we need to start looking as un-punk as possible because we're going to have to stay around the car for a while." We look around this room at the end of the hall; it's like some kind of cloakroom, with hats and coats. Our hair is the most distinctive feature, as we all have dyed hair in various colours. I'm modelling the full Corona Pop colour scheme. Brinsley has gone back to his felt penned leopard skin hair, which he tried before but he had to shave all his hair off to get rid of it last time as it didn't wash out. OC is sporting the short back and abandoned look or Council Special, which is dyed red. Mel's gone for red, blue and white as Mel's the more patriotic one.

So we try these hats on and opt for these bobble hats as they seem to cover up our punk haircuts. The coats cover our punk bondage gear, although two of us are wearing bondage trousers so the zips are visible. I'm also wearing my Seditionaries Spider Man boots which always seem to attract attention; it's not every day you see peep-toed boots where webbing is supposed to shoot out. I'm stood there thinking, what a pity these boots don't come with the actual webbing. It could come in handy right now. We stand there and look in the mirror. At first glance we look like students; let's hope they don't look down at our bondage gear. We put on a brave face. "Come on, let's hope it works", says OC. Mel goes off to find a phone to ring the AA. We look through the curtain so as not to attract attention. Mel walks down the corridor, straight past a gang of bikers, and no one bats an eyelid. We all smile at each other. Then after making the phone call he walks back towards us and into the room. He says, "We have to go and stay with the car. The AA will be here within 30 minutes, they said." We look outside the hall through the windows to assess our chances. It's very bright directly outside the building because of the lights, but if we can get further away from the building undetected, it's pitch black, so we should be safe. We see some of the local punks are still trying to get out of the building, but are getting chased back inside by bikers. I can't see Tom or Chris with them. I wonder if they got out OK.

We decide to split up into twos and walk out naturally and hope no one looks at our feet. We set off walking through the building in our borrowed trench coats and bobble hats and no one even looks at us. The whole area is still full of bikers and straights. Some are walking back to the pub now, bored of waiting for the punks to come out. We see some punks lying on the ground at the other end of the car park, who look like they've been beaten up. We wonder whether to go and see if they are OK, but we are wary of attracting attention to ourselves. As soon as we get past the bikers directly outside the venue, it gets a lot darker. We get back to the car, hurriedly open the doors and jump in. Then we crouch down so we can't be seen easily. There is still a lot of tension and we can't relax. There's a howling noise as a vortex of wind gets trapped between the plastic sheets, amplifying the sound to ear-bursting levels. Mel whispers, "Someone's bound to come and look at the car just out of curiosity. It looks a right state." We're anxiously looking for the AA man as we are all hiding in the car. Brinsley jumps out of the car and gets some bricks. "If we get sussed, I'm taking the first one out." He hands us all a brick each so we can do likewise.

Mel says "You know yesterday when you said there was nothing valuable in that briefcase you nicked? Well you should have kept the bricks they would have come in handy tonight." Brinsley sniggers.

The bikers are now rowdy and drunk and in a joyous mood, after overcoming the mainly slightly underage anarchist punk gang following the Ants. There are still some bikers looking for trouble as they move backwards and forwards between the concert hall and the end of the road. Sometimes people look towards us shining torches and we just avoid eye contact, luckily they pass. This is so nerve wracking. "Where are the fucking AA?" says OC. We are so anxious by now. Brinsley is chain smoking, finishing one then immediately starting another. I'm tapping away like a demented drummer. Mel's just looking forward with fear in his eyes. OC seems to be the only one who doesn't seem affected by the situation; he's just reading the newspaper he bought this morning with the aid of the street lamp across the car park. After what seemed like a lifetime the AA van pulls up next to us and immediately Mel jumps out to talk to the guy. We stay in the car, hoping not to attract any attention. Time seems to have stood still along with our beating hearts. The AA guy is talking to Mel like it's a normal situation; oblivious, it seems, to the potential carnage that could happen if we are sussed. After about five minutes Mel comes back to the car and tells us the AA guy has sussed the position we are in, so they will tow us away to a garage down the road. That way, he can look at the car without fear of trouble. If they can't mend it they will tow us back to Bradford. The AA man hooks our car up to his van. This is starting to attract the bikers' attention again. This is the scariest part. We are so close to escaping, but could get caught at the death. Finally, we are off.

As we're leaving the car park, Brinsley leans out of the window and starts shouting abuse at the bikers as we speed off into the night. The bikers start running behind us, probably too drunk to ride their bikes after us. Suddenly the car comes to a halt with a bang. The AA van is still moving. Luckily the driver realises we're not attached and reverses towards us at speed. We all glare at Brinsley and say, "Why don't you just keep your big mouth shut?" We look out the back window through the plastic sheeting and the bikers are approaching on foot. Mel screams, "We're gonna die!" The AA man jumps out of his van and hooks us up quickly, shouting, "It wasn't fastened right!" Brinsley butts in, "That's what I say about my fly hole." The AA man jumps into his van and we're off, just as the bikers are almost upon us. We speed off into the night. Cue a big massive "Phew!"

The garage is about a mile down the road. We pull in and relax. We buy something to eat from the garage shop while the AA man looks at the car. After about 30 minutes he declares he will have to tow us back to Bradford.

He tells us, "It's going to be a long journey, so get plenty of supplies. Then we set off into the night, back to Bradders. We stop once on the way back for a piss stop and get more supplies then we hit Bradford at 8 am. We thank the AA man and park the car up at Mel's. Brinsley and OC stay at his place. I liked to sleep in my own bed, so the AA man dropped me off on his way back to the motorway. The next day I was anxious to know if everyone got home OK. First I rang Tom because I wanted to know if my old friend Chris was OK. Tom told me they had sneaked out via the kitchens and through a field which took them back into Salisbury, thus avoiding the bikers; so no casualties. Then I rang Dunc. Everyone was fine in London also; it had been a bit tight in the van, but not as tight a position as we had been in back at the gig, so all was well. Lastly I rang Paul; he had just got back to Boro. Longfellow had dropped them off at the A1 on the way back to the BANP company which was in the City at St John's Street. It was a little out of their way but they were desperate to get home. So although this was a tough trip, the toughest trip so far, we all came through OK apart from Dunc, who was a little concussed from being knocked over. Roll on the next Ants adventure.

Part 3 Music Machine 1ˢᵗ November 1978
'I'm a friend of Egon Schiele   I'm a friend of Mister Spock   I'm a friend of Doctor Kildare   I'm a friend of the Woodentops
    I'm a friend of a friend of a friend of a friend   And if I come on the night, can I get in free?'
    This gig turned out to be on a Wednesday night. It wasn't easy getting time off but I was owed some holidays so I decided to take a couple of days. I asked Paul from Middlesboro if he was going with the others, as well as Mark from Newcastle, who we'd met at the Ants gig earlier in the year. They said yes; they would be there. Boxhead and Robbo were definitely going. Mel, OC and Brinsley would be going. There would be a full crew from London and the surrounding areas no doubt, so it should be a good night celebrating the Ants' first single release on Decca. Some people got invites. Along with the invite they also received a demo copy of the single 'Young Parisians', via the record company people. These invites were for business people and family, I would guess? Dunc and some of the London Ants crew got invites and rightly so. The added bonus with this gig was the support act; the Monochrome Set.

Their lead singer Bid went to school with Andy and Lester went to Hornsey Art College with Adam, and Lester and Bid were in the first version of the Ants. So they were seen as part of the Ants family tree; although they were their own band in their own right. I really liked the Monochrome Set but they weren't a punk band, far from it. Maybe they had a punk do it yourself ethos, but musically, they were miles away. I'm not sure what you would call them really? They have their own style and plenty of it - a diversity of rhythms and soundscapes with witty, intelligent, observational lyrics.

Anyway, we were all looking forward to the gig. OC was doing a bit of dealing at the time to make money, nothing serious - a bit of speed, hash, trips, etc, but he was a rubbish dealer. He was such a nice bloke and just wanted people to have fun so he would just give all the drugs away, which could have nasty consequences for him, with the dealers he got the gear from. Once I was round his house when this big Neanderthal bloke called round for his money. OC said he would just nip out to get it and didn't come back for eight hours, leaving me with this guy. As I'm sitting there this guy looks at me and says, "Didn't you nick my car?" I said, "Nope, I can't drive." It wasn't a nice experience, sitting with this person. We had nothing in common and he didn't seem to have anything to say apart from that. Luckily the guy left after three hours, saying he would call back later, but I still had to wait for OC as he'd left me with his keys. Anyway, OC had got some speed and some hash for the gig. We all arrange to meet at mine and go down in Mel's car. On the day, Mel turns up at my place on the dot. We don't hang around as we are too excited and want to get to London as soon as possible. We get there quite early in the afternoon, park up at Brent Cross then get the tube into London. We then decide to get another tube and go down the King's Road. We always get off at Sloane Square and walk down the whole of the road for the full effect. It's about a two mile walk. There are still a lot of punks about but maybe not as many as there were down there in the 'Ted war' days of '77.

As we're walking down King's Road we get near Habitat, on the opposite side of the road to BOY where we are heading. There are a load of women looking in the shop window at something. Intrigued, we go over to see, but it's just a new flashy bed. Brinsley nudges me and says, "Watch this. I'll give them something to stare at." He calmly walks into Habitat and stands next to the big flashy bed. He puts his hands to his mouth to indicate he's tired then pro-

ceeds to take all his clothes off. He folds them up nicely, puts them next to the
bed, folds the duvet back then gets into the bed. I wish I had a camera to take
a picture of the women's faces, all open-mouthed in shock. Brinsley is all snuggled up with a smile on his face. After a minute or two he suddenly pretends
to wake up, rolls back the duvet, steps out of the bed, puts his arms in the air
and yawns, stretching as far as he can. He then lowers his arms and scratches
his bollocks.

The women are all looking admiringly at his appendage. "That's a big one",
says one lady with a snigger. Brinsley sits on the bed and gets dressed again
then he turns to the ladies and takes a bow before walking out of the shop.
The Habitat staff become suddenly aware that something is afoot and some
of them move up to the front of the shop to investigate. By the time they get
to the bed Brinsley has left the shop to be greeted by a gang of smiling, middle-aged old dears. We all look at each other and say, "You need big bollocks
to get away with some of the scams he pulls!" Brinsley says to one, "Give us
your details, darling, and I'll call you later. Then me and you can go for a whirl-
wind date on your credit card. How's about it?" She just smiled in a shy manner and turned to her friends, who were egging her on to go.

After a minute or two we looked across the road towards BOY. Mel wanted
a drink so we discuss maybe bobbing in the Chelsea Potter first, before BOY.
We decide to get a drink later, so we look in BOY for a bit and chat with Stan
Stammers and Jock Strap from the band the Straps, a well-known local punk
band who are pretty good. There's nothing in BOY of interest so we head
back down the King's Road past Robot, and all the other punk joints, until
we get to Seditionaries. We walk in the shop and look around. No Jordan
today; just Michael. I end up buying a pair of canvas bondage boots in brown
and green. Mel buys a parachute shirt and OC gets a muslin shirt with a 'Vive
Le Rock' print. Brinsley, as per usual, hasn't any money so he nicks what he
wants, unbeknown to us, of course, or the shop assistant.

When we leave he suddenly produces a full tartan bondage suit from underneath his coat, all rolled up. "How the fuck did you nick that? I was watching you." "If I told you that you'd start nicking stuff and I would be out of
business. I feel a bit guilty though, really. I don't like nicking stuff off small
shops. It's their livelihood but their clothes look fantastic… No problem nicking
off big companies though. They are greedy, self-serving bar stewards. They

only care for themselves." Then Brinsley just smiles and walks off.

We call in the Roebuck for a quick pint before walking back up the King's Road to Sloane Square. As we're walking we decide to get the tube to Mornington Crescent, via the District, Victoria and Northern Lines, which is in Camden right next to the Music Machine. The tube is the quickest and best form of transport in London. It's that packed, you could reach for something in your pocket only to find it's someone else's pocket as they walk off. It's not a pleasant journey. There's a lack of air like you're going to pass out, but it is quick. Bad point about the Northern Line through Camden is that the tube waits in the tunnel for what seems like ages, but luckily we're only going as far as Mornington Crescent; the stop before. We get off and get out as fast as possible. It's great just to breathe in the air. There's a great shop just down the road at Laurence Corner where you can buy ex army gear. Across the road are some flats where Jeremy Healy lived. Jeremy was a familiar face on the punk scene and was a friend of Brinsley's. I remember once when Jeremy lent Brinsley this beautiful Seditionaries yellow gingham muslin, with a Dickens print on. I really wanted it and nearly mugged him for it.

Anyway, we looked round the ex army shop but didn't buy anything, before we headed up to the Music Machine. There was a pub attached around the corner; the Hope and Anchor, directly opposite Mornington Crescent tube. All the Ants crew were there. Boxhead and Robbo were grinning as soon as we open the door, like a welcome party. All the various London Ants crews were there from the north, east, south and west. It was good to see them as it had been a while; obviously we saw some of them at Salisbury which had been a bit dodgy. It was nice to see Stevie Parker and Dave Holloway at the bar, along with Paul D, Popey, Dunc and Johnny Aggro. Steve Shaw was trying to impress some birds until Brinsley got in on the act. Huw and Joe the Collar were sitting down along with Bradley Hall, Terry Smith, Jerry Lamont and Krazee Kev. Paul Kirby and the east London boys Godfrey and Metin's crew were standing outside having a spliff. I looked across the pub; in the corner were Simone and the other Ant girls, all dressed up to the nines and ready to rock. Annie Dayglo's got a lovely dress on, Sandy's wearing her Seditionaries silk Anarchy muslin, Fiona's sporting a new hairstyle and Carolyn turns up with Paul Rochford, both looking dapper - and last but not least, the lovely Anna and the two Lesleys.

Everyone is having a few beers and getting in the mood. Then the door opens and the two Kevins, Tredrea and McGovern, and the two Marks, Hutchins and Harding, walk in. "Hi fellas. How did you get back from Salisbury?" I asked. Mark says, "Nightmare, mate. We thought we were lucky getting out of the car park before the bikers spotted us. We were all in a good mood, travelling down the motorway home. Then the old Humber Hawk's engine caught on fire. We shit ourselves but managed to get the car in a layby. We didn't have a clue about engines. So we walked up the motorway about half a mile each way, but there was no phone. By this point we were knackered so we ended up sleeping in the car. We didn't get back to south London 'til the day after." "Pretty eventful gig that was, mate, at least you got back", I commented as I look around the pub and think to myself everyone looks great and in a really good mood; let the party begin. The Music Machine was a good venue for punks because you could bunk in through the back of the pub and get in over the roof. We have a few beers and decide to go in. Some people have special invites to get in but as per usual there are too many of us, so some are going to have to bunk in over the roof and hope that they haven't put a bouncer there like they do sometimes.

I bump into Simone and smile. She smiles back. "How are you doing?" "I'm OK", she says. I was dying to have anther chance with her so I ask her, "Fancy meeting up after the gig?" She has that teasing smile with the eyes of a seductress. "I'm working down the club after the gig. A girl's got to earn her crust, you know. Anyway I don't know. I don't usually revisit conquests but I do like you. If I don't find someone new I may relent, but you would have to come down to the club to find out." She smiles and walks off knowing full well my eyes are burned into the back of her. It's so nice how she makes you feel so special, not, I thought. Suddenly she turns around and comes back. She tells me to close my eyes, then holds out her hand and puts a piece of paper into my hand. "Right, open your eyes." It's a ticket for tonight's gig. "Wow! Thanks for that. Where did you get it from?" "I hinted to the bouncer last week, when he came into the fetish club, that I may make it worth his while if he got me some tickets for tonight's gig. Of course he couldn't resist my womanly charms. I thought they may come in handy knowing how many of us there is and how many guest list places there usually are." "So how many did you get?" "Ten." "What you going to do when he comes for his reward?" "It will be fine; he likes the chase." "Yes, maybe; but if it goes on for ever he may get aggressive." "I'm sorted. Lal will sort him out or some other lads I know. Or maybe the Ants kids. Either way, it will get sorted." She started to walk off again towards the gig. I shouted after her, "You got any more spares left?" "Sorry!" came the reply.

I tell Mel, OC and Brinsley that I've got a ticket. I didn't say where from but I tell them to go and check the guest list; they might get lucky - but someone is going to be unlucky because Adam's bunged on a load of music exec types and friends who don't normally come to the gigs. His actress girlfriend Amanda Donohoe will be here as well. She does go to a few gigs when she's not working. I've never spoken to her but all the Ant kids say she's really friendly and a good laugh. I go into the gig with Dunc, Popey and Johnny Aggro; Chukka, Stevie P and some of the others follow. The queue for the guest list is massive - there must be about 40 of the Ants crew there. It seems most have bought tickets, knowing there would be a shortage. Brinsley also follows us, leaving OC and Mel to go over the rooftops with a few of the others. As I'm queueing to get in, I start thinking about Raffles, who went into Victorian houses over the rooftops. To get access you had to climb up onto the roof. Then up a ladder and enter via the dome. I see Brinsley push his way to the front of the guest list queue. Here it comes, I say to myself; the Brinsley spiel. Not one to do anything quietly he suddenly bursts in with, "Excuse me, young lady. I need to know if I'm on the guest list." "What's your name, sir?" "You mean you don't know who I am? I'm appalled. Wait 'til I see your boss."

By now he has embarrassed the woman with so much front; she's starting to think he may actually be someone important and she doesn't know what to do. Brinsley knows this also. It's psychological warfare and unfortunately she's fair game to him. He's behaving as badly as a toff, with his fake posh accent. No one is coming to this woman's assistance. She looks new; probably just started and feeling out of her comfort zone right now. She's anxiously looking around for assistance but none is forthcoming. Brinsley's voice is getting louder and the woman looks panicked now. Brinsley goes in for the kill. He changes tack and apologises for shouting, but before she can get her composure back he asks her to show him the guest list so that he can point his name out to her. Without thinking she shows him the list. Bingo. Job done. Brinsley and anyone next to him will get a brief view of all the names on the guest list. Not only that but some of them will nick their free promo copies of the Ants' new single as well. Brinsley has an almost photographic memory. After about 30 seconds, probably every name on that guest list will be in circulation among the Ants crew. Brinsley finds a name he likes the sound of.

"That's me", he says, "Mike Smith." Who just happens to be the head of A&R at Decca Records. The name is duly crossed off. Bugger. No free single with that name. He turns around, gutted. You can then see Brinsley go round telling people all the other names on the list. I heard a whispered "Howard Malin", who was the Ants' manager, but we didn't know him. We'd never met him. I shout across before we go in, "Where's OC and Mel?" They're going over the roof with Alvain and Roy, Grant Dell, Smiler, Malcolm and some of the others. I walk into the venue and hand my ticket over. It's finally here - the gig launch for the 'Young Parisians' single. I soak it in. The Ants have finally got a record out. Adam and the band must be buzzing. I'm talking to Dunc and Popey, "The Ants must do a proper tour now for the single." We have a chat with Mick Mercer, the editor of Panache fanzine. "You gonna plug the Ants, Mick?" "Yes, of course. The Ants need to go on tour. They've been mainly a London band for two years; people need to see what they've been missing." We agree it's the next step for the band to progress. Suddenly I can see some great new Adam and the Ants posters for the single, with the date of the gig and the venue on them. The poster was all white with a picture of Adam in leather, coming through a ripped white sheet, with the block 'Adam and the Ants' logo. The posters were identical to the ones that we've seen advertising the single - except the date and venue wasn't on the other posters. I got one of the posters off the wall before someone else nicked it, folded and stashed it.

Then I bump into Andy Warren, who appears to be on the lookout for someone. I ask about a tour and he tells me, "Yes, it's on the cards. We're just trying to get some gigs together but it might take a while", as he shoots off to find the person he was looking for. The Music Machine is a large venue with a big stage. I don't know how many it holds; a thousand maybe. We get there just in time for the Monochrome Set. They have some delightful ditties which are in contrast to the whole scene around them, but the Ants crew like them. We're singing along to 'Goodbye Joe' while waving at our own Joe the Collar. 'Puerto Rican Fence Climber' was another great song. The Ants also sang about

Puerto Ricans and the two groups also had a shared song, 'Fat Fun', played in different styles. The Monochrome Set ended their set to rapturous applause and everyone rushes to get a drink before the Ants come on. The intro tapes start. The Ants are getting ready, we are getting ready, Gary Glitter's 'Hello, Hello, I'm Back Again' is getting us ready, setting the tone - then it's straight into my favourite Ants track 'Nietzsche Baby'. It's time to do the Ant mambo. I rush down to the front. Everyone is there and ready. Let the party begin.

The band has changed. Adam is still wearing the Kabuki make up but his look has changed. He's now wearing a black shirt with a sash over his shoulder and a tie, leather trousers and a red kilt. He looks kind of smart but the kilt adds a new dimension. It seems people are getting bored with dressing like punks and are moving on. A lot of the punk bands have record deals now and maybe punk in its true form is over. The Ants are suggesting this with slogans like 'Antmusic for a Future Age'. They are becoming an entity in their own right and thinking about the future after punk.

The Ants run through a series of their classic songs. After saying this is the launch of 'Young Parisians', they didn't play the song, which was a surprise. What was more of a surprise to us was that they chose that song in the first place. It didn't represent what the Ants' sound was like. Maybe it was chosen by the record company for chart success? After the second encore, they finished with the B side of the single - and more representative of the true Ants sound - 'Lady', much to everyone's approval. After the gig I bumped into Longfellow, the Ants roadie. He said, "Did you notice the band started a different song, and then got back in sync in the chorus of the right song?" No, I hadn't. I don't think anyone had apart from him.

We ended up outside the Music Machine a bit the worse for wear. We had met some punks from Edinburgh, Dee and Doodah who were squatting round at King's Cross, just down the road from where Frenchy lived. They tell us about a friend called Wattie, who's come to visit after leaving the army, and he's going to form a punk band. Some of the others; Big Paul D, Dave H and Jo Gahan were also crashing at the squats. I suddenly thought about Simone and the club. I was too tired to walk down into the West End, with no guarantee of anything happening but a brisk handshake and maybe a hug. However much I liked Simone I opted to crash round King's Cross with the others. At least we were on the same tube line for Brent Cross in the morning.

When we get down there, there's a party in full flow. Brinsley's eyes light up. He sees opportunities, but at whose expense? There's plenty of drink, drugs and women. He's in his element. I crash out on a settee with a couple of cans. OC gets his little stash out. He brought the drugs so as to try and make some cash at the Ants gig, and forgot about them until now. OC is now open for business. People are asking, "How much for this?" and "How much for that?" OC just says, "Help yourself." I point out to OC that the dealer guy will want his money when he gets back, so he needs to try and sell some. "I can't be bothered. It will be cool; he owes me a favour anyway", said OC. Next thing, everyone is off their heads and dancing around. People are sliding off to have sex everywhere. There's this weird, 60s looking character sitting at the opposite side of the room. I go and introduce myself but I don't catch his name. I ask him, "What was the free love scene like in the 60s?" He says, "Unless you were living in Haight Ashbury or some tiny exclusive London society group, it largely didn't exist beyond people's minds. But it's happening widespread with the 70s punk movement. The 60s is recurring now, on a large scale - sex, drugs and rock'n'roll are everywhere; in this room as we speak." I reply, "Peace, man."

However much the punks like to go on about hating hippies, they are ideologically compatible. They both want positive change but they just have different ways of operating. I'm not sure if this is a good analogy but I always think that Martin Luther King was more like the hippies and Malcolm X more like the punks in the way they operated. Maybe the punks thought of the hippies as traitors for selling out and becoming part of the established elite? But yes, sex, drugs and rock'n'roll was widespread. In my limited life experience so far, until this point I didn't recall girls wanting to sleep with people on a first date, but when I got involved in the punk movement, it was widespread. People were more liberated about sex and drugs so maybe the hippie pioneer was right - maybe we were actually living the 60s now, here in the 70s? After speaking to the hippie I look around; it's carnage. Brinsley's unscrewing a door, for some reason; then he launches it outside. I'm starving, so I ask Dee if I can get some food. "Sure", she replies. I go in the kitchen to check for food. There's a dozen eggs, a bag of spuds and six slices of bread. I ask Dee if it's OK to eat it. She says yes, but I take it reluctantly, knowing full well there will be little money for food. So I give her a quid to get some more food in the morning.

I put the cooker on and start to fry eggs and chips. Suddenly everyone wants some, but there's not enough. So, off the cuff, I think of this game. I say to everyone, "Get a plate, and after I've cooked something, I'll throw it through the hatch and you have to catch it on a plate." So, as each egg gets fried, I put it onto my spatula, shout "Ready!" and throw it through the hatch. I can't see what's happening but I can hear people crashing into each other trying to catch the eggs. The kitchen is now a health hazard. There's yolk all over the walls, broken plates, people with cuts and bruises. When I get to the chips, it's even worse. Someone catches a chip in their mouth only to feel the side of a plate crash into their face. Surveying the aftermath of the food game, in retrospect, it wasn't one of my best ideas. Anyway, I manage to get myself an egg sandwich, which is my favourite. I go and find Dee to give her another quid for damaged plates. She's so off her head she can't even understand what I'm on about, but she will tomorrow. She takes the quid, smiles, and gets back to being off her head. Suddenly there's a knock at the door. I go and see who it is. I open the door to Frenchy. "Wow! Frenchy! How are you?" "I'm fine. I'm trying to fight the authorities over trying to evict us from our squats." "Nice one! How's it going?" I said. "Touch and go", he says and goes into the kitchen to look for beer.

At some stage of the evening I pass out, only to wake some hours later to the human debris around me. Bodies, clothes everywhere and someone was laid out naked with their legs up against the wall. Somebody had written all over their face in felt pen, 'Don't sleep here, it's dangerous.' There was a couple who must have just fallen asleep after sex, as the man was laid round the back of the woman with her legs wide open, with his flaccid cock resting at the entrance of his intended target. Maybe they'd been too drunk to do anything and just fallen asleep? I was feeling really ill so I went to the bog. I drank a pint of water in the hope that I would feel better. I didn't. My head was fuzzy and my stomach ached. I went into the kitchen and put the kettle on. I wasn't a big tea or coffee drinker; I could never understand the big British obsession with tea and coffee. But today I fancied one. It was cold outside and I wanted something to warm up my insides. Suddenly I hear a loud clatter and Brinsley comes falling out of a cupboard with a young lady behind him. "What the fuck", I sigh. Brinsley smiles. He has that childish grin on his face that says he has another notch on his bed post, or door handle, in this case. "You two slept in there?" "Yeah! It's quite big for a cupboard", says Brinsley. The pretty young lady grabs her clothes and runs off to the bathroom. Brinsley starts making tea. Soon Mel and OC are up. Both say at the same time, "Let's get back to Bradford." I'm OK with that, so is Brinsley. I write a note for Dee and Doodah to say thanks. Everyone else is crashed out and doesn't look like they'll be up anytime soon. I say to Brinsley, "What about your lady friend?" He shrugs. "Let's just go." "Erm… not very nice, just walking out without saying good-bye?" He just walks on down the stairwell of the flats.

We get around the corner and see a doorway with a full crate of milk sitting there. This was our staple diet on the road sometimes; along with bread or eggs. We grab a bottle of milk each and walk off. When you're skint and living on the edge, you have to take food and drink where you can find it. It's not ideal but we never took all the bottles, and usually only took from houses and flats with quite a few bottles outside. We walk down towards the tube station where all the Greasy Joe cafés were, and found one which was cheapish, for London. We filled up with food for the long journey home. We all looked knackered and were saying very little. We paid up and jumped the tube at King's Cross by climbing over the barrier like most people seemed to do. It's the normal way to travel in London. How it works best is when the guard is distracted or is on his own, because he can't leave his post to run after you. There are no ticket inspectors on the tube, so when you get to the other end you just pay from the stop before. This might sound odd, but it isn't really. Some tubes didn't have guards or ticket collectors on duty all the time, especially out in the suburbs, and they couldn't verify where you'd got on the tube at all, so it was better for them to get at least some money off you.

We jumped on the Northern Line to Brent Cross. This is a tricky line to get to, because the Northern Line splits at Camden Town into two separate lines. One goes to Edgware the other goes to High Barnet. A couple of stops before High Barnet, the tube branches off to Mill Hill. Anyway, we wanted the Edgware train. There are few things worse than a busy tube station. It's claustrophobic as hell. Those long, tight corridors weave this way and that with no end in sight, then descend into the bowels of the earth via an escalator that looks like it will devour you before you get to the bottom. There are two signs, both saying Northern Line. This is where the inexperienced get lost. If people don't know any of the places they are going to, then they'll just jump onto either, expecting them both to go to the same place. I've been to London a few times now though, so I'm getting familiar with how it works. We get down onto the platform. It feels like all the air has been sucked out of the place and it's so packed that the person stood next to you could, with a turn of their body, knock you onto the track. We stand around waiting for the train to show on the board; Mill Hill two minutes, High Barnet, six. Typical. Ours is last, Edgware, eight minutes. When it arrives we all slouch across the seats, half asleep, until we get to Brent Cross. After about 20 minutes we're coming out of Brent Cross tube station; no guards. We head straight for the car. We heave a sigh of relief and slump in our seats. I'm in the front so I pull open the glove compartment, pick a stack of various punk tapes for the journey home, then sit back and relax for the next four to five hours. I pity Mel, who has to drive feeling like shit. We set off and hardly speak to each other for the rest of the journey, we are so tired. We arrive back in Bradford five hours later. Mel drops me off and I go straight to lay on my bed and watch TV. I'm too tired to do much else. I play back in my mind some of the night's events and finally drift off to sleep.

Germany and Italy tour October 1978
The next Ants gigs were in Germany. None of our lot went. We just couldn't afford it. People don't realise how hard it was to travel about in those days; very few people of our age had a car, or had jobs that paid enough money to buy one. Hardly anyone I knew at that point in life had been abroad, except Chris. His parents loved America. It was difficult enough to get back from visiting a town or city after 9 pm, never mind going abroad. It seems Germany and Berlin in particular had a positive effect on Adam, and he came back with lots of new visual ideas for the Ants' creative output. At the time Bowie and Iggy were also in Berlin but whether Adam met them, I don't know. It was after Berlin that they reversed the 'D' and changed the 'S' in the Adam and the Ants logo. The logo was a large banner which the band had behind them on stage; it was just a square with the band name, but it looked striking and effective.

After Germany, the Ants moved on to Italy. We had a friend in Italy, Marco, who we'd met at an Ants gig earlier in the year. I had been writing to him now and again to keep him in touch with what the Ants were getting up to. He wrote back to me with a detailed report on their visit to Italy. I thought he might have had something to do with getting this gig for the Ants, but it seems that Anna Melluso, who was a friend of Jordan and Adam, had organized the tour with help from Mitzio Turchet. Mitzio had invited the Ants to open a fashion show in front of posh eccentrics in Milan at the Modanostra on the 14th of October then they added three more dates to make it worthwhile; making it two in Milan and two in Rome. Marco said nobody knew the Ants were playing this event, but he heard from some punk friends from Parma that Adam walked on stage wearing all leather, light blue ballet shoes and a leather mask with a red rose on his lapel. The gig didn't go down too well; the audience didn't even take any notice of the band so Marco's punk friends started throwing things. Adam got angry and started throwing the mic stand about and shouting abuse. Suddenly the gig was over. The Ants got a better response at the other gigs.

The Milan gigs were attended by all of the small Milanese punk elite, who were all in bands or in the process of starting one. By 9 o'clock there were about 150 people in the hall, despite the gig being well publicised with thousands of posters put up around the place. There had been a rumour of possible trouble from a radical left movement called Autonomia Operaia (working class autonomy) but it proved to be a false alarm. Marco said the Ants were brilliant. He described the gig with Adam walking onto the stage in black leather in the build up to their opening song 'Plastic Surgery'. Marco thought some of the locals were expecting a Ramones type punk band but it was nothing like the Ramones. Whenever you watch the Ants they have that atmosphere of a decadent 30s Berlin nightclub act, like in Adam's favourite films 'The Night Porter' or 'The Damned'. The Ants' song 'Dirk Wears White Sox' is a tribute to one of his favourite actors, Dirk Bogarde, in the film. You can sense the voyeur in Adam with his lyrics. A great many of Adam's lyrics seem to be about watching or looking, at isolated images or one image being copied by another, as in 'Zerox', and how that situation changes.

Marco said it didn't take the Ants long to have the Milanese punks eating out of Adam's hand. They play 'You're So Physical' and Adam starts his usual strip routine, right down to the pair of tights he wears over his upper torso - he splits the gusset so his head can come through. Adam is certainly a performer. Everything is meticulously planned. There is nothing spontaneous about the Ants performances these days; although I'd quite liked the chaos of the Marquee, I would have bet that that was all worked out as well. The Ants ended their set with some of the faster, punkier songs; 'Beat My Guest', 'Fat Fun', 'Fall In', and ended the whole thing with the fantastic tribute to the one and only Jordan: 'Send a Letter to Jordan'. After the gig Marco said he and his friends went backstage to meet the band again. The Ants' manager Howard Malin had the Italian copy of 'Young Parisians'. Adam said, "I hate that cover of the razor blade round the Eiffel Tower." Jordan's Italian friend, Anna, was also there, running to and fro. When Marco and his friends returned for the following evening's gig, news had gotten around how good the Ants were, and there were about 200 people there. Adam was wearing a grey cotton jacket, white tie, black shirt, leather trousers and baby blue ballet shoes. Whenever you mentioned Adam, you always followed with what he was wearing, because he was so stylish. The Ants started their set with 'Nietzsche Baby' then stormed through 'Puerto Rican', 'Red Scab', 'It Doesn't Matter', etc. 'Plastic Surgery' and 'Deutscher Girls' go down particularly well as the Milanese punks know them from the film 'Jubilee'. The fans are in raptures as the Ants play four encores.

After the gig, Marco said his friends Luca, Sandro and Danny went backstage to interview Adam for their fanzine 'Pogo'. Jordan's friend acted as interpreter but things didn't go too well; maybe a combination of Anna's interpreting and the hostile manner of Sandro's interviewing technique? After the interview they said they left the dressing room and bumped into Jordan. Marco's friend Luca asked Jordan what she thought of the gigs. Jordan replied, "It's been fantastic. You have just witnessed the end of Adam and the Ants; now the downfall begins." Marco said they just looked at Jordan quizzically. They didn't go to the Rome gig but Marco told me that the Ants went down well in Italy. They felt quite isolated from the European gig circuit, so they had more of an ear for underground bands than the mainstream. The Ants were a success. They did a few interviews for TV and radio while they were there. Mathew was replaced by a dummy wearing his clothes for a TV promo, because he was underage. A few weeks later Marco rang me excitedly, telling me he'd been told that the Rome show had been recorded for a famous TV show, but was never aired. He had people trying to track it down to maybe get a copy. He also told me that looking back at those Ants gigs; he shared with other

Italian Ants fans'. For them, the Ants gigs were the equivalent of the Sex Pistols gigs in Manchester in 1976. Although, Marco said the Italians didn't really like 1976-77 era punk rock very much; they much preferred the Ants' art punk. After the Ants played those gigs in Milan it inspired people to start bands or fanzines or even a radio show, and it hopefully would shape the future of Milan's music scene forever.

Part 4 Marquee 28ᵗʰ and 29ᵗʰ November 1978

'When I met you, you were just 16
Pulling the wings off flies
When an old lady got hit by a truck
I saw the wicked gleam in your eyes
Your sadistic suits my masochistic
and there's a whip in my valise
Who taught you to torture
Who taught you?'

I was really looking forward to this trip because it was my 18th birthday. It would have been better if it had been at the weekend instead of a Tuesday and Wednesday, but you can't have everything. When you're growing up your 18th birthday is the biggie. It's the gateway to adulthood. You can vote, you can drink in pubs, etc. Every teenager longs for their 18th birthday. It should be a real life affirming moment in a young man's life. Out of all the new exciting things in life on offer to an 18-year-old, I'd already moved out of home when I was 16 to live with punk friends in a bedsit in a shared house near the university. I had been drinking in pubs since I was 16, when I started going to punk gigs. My now ex-girlfriend used to stop at my place a lot as well, so there wasn't much I hadn't done by the time I was 18, apart from vote. I don't really trust politicians. As a working class kid I was expected to vote for Labour like my parents, but they seemed as useless as the Tories.

I got up at 7.30am to get ready for my coach, which left Bradford at 8.30 am. I packed a few things before giving Dunc a call, to tell him I'd see the lads when I got to London. I asked where everyone was meeting; he said to ring as soon as I got there as nothing was sorted as yet. It felt strange going on my own now after the other trips with OC, Mel and Brinsley, but they couldn't do this one. As I was walking into town I was surprised to see the doors to the Mannville Arms open, so I decided to call in and see if I could get a couple of drinks for my trip down south. I walked in and see Roy, the landlord, cleaning his pub from the night before to get it ready for opening time. I asked him if I could buy a couple of cans for my journey and announced that it was my birthday. He asked how old I was. When I told him I was 18, he said, "You've been drinking in my bar all this time under age, you cheeky bleeder! You could have lost me my licence!" Then he smiled and said, "We've all done it, ha." I set off walking into town for the coach station with a silly teenage smirk on my face. This visit would be special for me because I'd saved up enough money, along with birthday money and my wages, to treat myself and buy something nice. But it was more the fact that Adam and the Ants were playing for two nights that would be the highlight.

London, to me, wasn't just the capital of the country. It was also the capital of punk, and even though it wasn't the first time I had been there, it always felt special to be going back there, even though it was only three weeks since my last visit. Don't get me wrong; Bradford had a thriving punk scene and we were a close knit, multicultural bunch who looked out for one another. We only had three bands, the Negatives, Violation and Wrist Action, a couple of record shops and our local pub, and we were limited to where we could go in town. Even if we went out of town to Leeds, Halifax or Keighley, where there were plenty of bands playing in the surrounding areas, we were still limited. Transport was a major issue in getting back from gigs, with everything stopping at around 10.30 pm. Leeds was better because we could get the milk train at 3am. Whereas in London, there were tons of venues and shops, and most of the bands seemed to come from London or down south. Manchester was the only place up north that had a lot of punk bands, but there was only one band I was interested in seeing on this trip and that was the Ants.

I sat on the coach as it pulled out of the station, daydreaming of all the adventures I might have again in London. This happened every time I went to London; it just never lost its appeal. I had taken a book with me about the Warsaw ghetto and I got totally engrossed in it before I realised we were at Leicester Forest service station. After a short break we were off again. I got stuck into my book again. It didn't seem that long before we were heading into

London. It was time to get excited again. I couldn't wait to get to Victoria so I could disembark and commence my adventure. We came into London via Brent Cross. What a great feeling, driving through the streets of London down Edgware Road, down to Victoria… Zoom. We seemed to be flying. Before I knew it we'd turned a corner into Victoria coach station. I jumped off the coach and headed for the tube to the King's Road, stopping on the way to ring Dunc to find out our meeting place, which turned out to be a pub called the Cambridge; at 7pm. A while later I was standing outside Sloane Square station. Seditionaries was at the bottom of the King's Road at World's End, Chelsea, but instead of getting the bus down there, I wanted to walk and absorb the atmosphere of it all.

So I headed off down the road towards Seditionaries. It was great to walk again down the King's Road. I always liked call in whenever I got the chance. The clothes looked fantastic and there was too much to choose from. After checking out the clothes - and the prices - I finally bought a pair of 'Anti-Christ' boots. I'd been after a pair since I first saw them but they were expensive at around £35; which was a week's wage. People like me couldn't really afford it on a regular basis, but with it being my birthday and not knowing when I would have any money again to buy something, I thought: just buy them. I would have loved to have had enough money to go into that shop and buy one of everything, but it wasn't to be. After I left Seditionaries I headed up to Soho to the Marquee club on Wardour Street; after first dropping off my stuff in a locker. But before I did I changed into my new boots, and looked in the mirror to see how good they looked. I got there quite early. It was still broad daylight and far too early to meet up with the Ant kids, so I walked around for a bit.

Soho was where all the sex industry was housed; peep shows, book shops - they were everywhere, on every street corner. Now that place was an eye opener for a young northern punk. It seemed quite appropriate the Ants were playing there, with their heavy sexual lyrics and graphics to match.

Funny, I had never really noticed how big Soho was when I came down for the residency in January. I had quite an attentive walk around the area for a while, before bobbing into the Cambridge off Shaftesbury Avenue to meet Dunc. But I was still early, so I sat down and ended up talking to a couple of London punks who seemed very friendly. They told me what life was like for them in London, and I did likewise, telling them about living in Bradford. They seemed quite shocked that we had lots of people from different cultures who were punks in Bradford. "What are they like?" asked one of the punks. "Not much different from anyone else really."

After about 20 minutes Dunc walked in with Popey, Joe the Collar, Huw, Johnny Aggro, Spud and his best mate Kev Addison. We sat about chatting about what had been happening lately and after a couple of pints set off to the Marquee. There was a very big queue so we had to wait a while. Once inside, I went and stood in the gig area with Dunc and some of the Ant kids, chatting away for what seemed ages. Suddenly Fiona came in and told us she had been attacked by some people pretending to be Ants fans. She seemed quite shaken. We tried to comfort her and offered to go out and sort them out, but she said it didn't matter. She seemed quite subdued. Annie, Sandy, Caroline and some of the Ant ladies came in and went to the bar. I asked them where Simone was. "She seems to be keeping a low profile again right now. We hardly see her", said Caroline. "Oh, right", I said, a bit upset that Simone wasn't here. I got a drink and sat down. Simone rarely missed an Ants gig when I was in London; I wondered where she was. Then I hear a familiar voice and turn around to see Boxhead standing behind me. "Hi, yous woolly back. How yous doing?" shouts Box. "Better for seeing you, ha! It's not the birthday bash I was expecting. I feel a bit down to be honest, Simone could have cheered me up tonight, but hey ho", I replied. Pete Vague comes over and asks, "You want a drink for your birthday?" "Thanks, Pete." Then Johnny Aggro comes over to me. "You want some of this speed, you Geordie?" "Nice one Johnny boy, that might cheer me up."

Dunc and Popey and the rest of the Ants crew come back to the bar. Everyone is talking about the up and coming tour, though it's not been confirmed yet. All anyone knows is the Ants' manager and Decca are trying to arrange one. We look around to assess the crowd - would there be any trouble tonight? There aren't many skinheads in and the ones that are seem to be with punks, so it should be OK. We hung around watching the support band Local Operator before the Ants came on. The anticipation was killing me. Suddenly I hear Gary Glitter's 'Hello, Hello, I'm Back Again'. What a beautiful noise that is. It's very tribal. I can't emphasise enough how powerful that drum intro sounds when played loud in a venue. It was like a calling to arms for the Ant kids. It pounded off the wall with brutal resonance; it sounded so powerful for a basic tribal sound. That was followed by a song from the film 'If....', called 'Sanctus'. After that came a very energetic song which sounded like a musical interpretation of someone or something being chased or pursued. I stood there with eyes closed, standing tall, letting the sound engulf me.

At the end I opened my eyes. Adam was on stage in front of me, staring with those intense facial features into the crowd, wearing his green army surplus coat. Then it started - the regimented drum intro, then the booming bass of 'Nietzsche Baby'. I nudged Spud who was dancing next to me. "I love this song."

'I wore black leathers
You saw swastika
One of the chosen few
Trying so hard to ignore you
Loving is the test
Better than the rest
Love is purity
Woah-oh-oh
Frauleins in uniform
Break the heart of any storm trooper
Frauleins in uniform
(don't) Turn your back 'cos she might shoot ya.'

Then Maf's power chords kick in over the heavy sound of drum and bass. Someone once described the Ants as a heavy rock band. I hated heavy rock so I couldn't agree with that, but I would agree there is a slow, heavy sound to some of their songs. I loved the slow, restrained aggression of songs like 'Red Scab', teasing rhythmically as the song builds up verse by verse, beat by beat, getting faster and faster until it can't contain itself any longer and explodes like a climax - Adam's musical interpretation of 'Pure Sex', perhaps.

What more could a naughty schoolboy punk want? I'd been listening to an Ants tape only the other day while on a bus, and I could feel myself change instantly. I could feel the aggression building in me. I was transported back to an Ants gig. I closed my eyes and all the emotions were there. It was like a release, and I would regard myself as being temporarily not in control of myself; the music was very intense. It felt as though, in the wrong circumstances, say if someone attacked me, I could see myself beating someone badly listening to the Ants. There was nothing else that made me feel like that - a mixture of joy, pain, excitement and aggression, which sounds like an S&M experience. People say music can be similar to sex, but could Adam have created a musical equivalent of a particular sexual experience? 'That crazy beat drives you insane.' To a 16-year-old boy with very little life experience, the Ants were scary and exciting in equal measure. There didn't seem to be any other singers like Adam. When I look at the pictures of him in late 1977 leaping around the stage, he looks like a madman. Then in the next picture he looks all angelic, like the beauty and the beast. Adam wrote about a lot of taboo subjects. S&M was another subject I knew very little about - in fact I knew very little about a lot of Adam's songs' subject matter. I've always been an inquisitive soul, though, so it inspired me not to dismiss anything but to be open minded about things, make my own mind up and to look up some of these subjects. It didn't work out well for Adam though; he got slated by the music press. One journalist called him a 'Nasty Nazi puerile toilet boy.'

I'm back with the Ants again. I focus on the stage. Adam gradually stripped off his clothes as the gig progressed and the heat intensified. The craziness got crazier down the front until people were in frenzy. Most people seemed to know one another by now, or were at least aware of one another. The Ants were becoming more popular. It reminded me of the Ants badge: 'You may not like it now, but you will.' Was it blind faith on Adam's part that he knew he would be popular eventually? People are now smashing into each other and falling over each other and picking each other up. The Ant kids are still doing their own thing though, and even though no one has said anything I get the impression that they are not keen about the Ants becoming more popular. They seem to operate as an insular group, mostly sticking with the people they know already.

A few people are dressed in similar clothes to Adam, but the Ant kids are right in pole position at the front of the stage. They have their inner circle, which no one is allowed into. I think it's a subconscious but very aggressive display of power in the Ant world. Some kids inadvertently try to crash through the Ant kids' barrier only to be thrown out again, which gets them off lightly; but repeated offenders can sometimes get a quick slap to remind them of their position - or the Ant kids' position, but that reaction can also be seen as self defence. There have been a few times when skinheads or other groups have tried to cause trouble at Ants gigs, but you don't always have time to see who people are, so you just strike first and answer questions later. The Ant kids were the first Ants fans, so they are top dogs. I like and get on well with them, but sometimes think that they would really prefer it to be just themselves at Ant gigs. The Ants are a London band and we like our special relations with some people - maybe because it makes us feel a bit special? With the Ants becoming more popular it seems the band don't always have as much time for followers as they once did. But that's the nature of being in a band, I guess. You want to play to - and meet - more people.

I'm loving my Ant birthday double bonanza now. So far I've had a few drinks bought for me and I'm listening to my favourite band. Before long though the gig was over and everyone made their way out of the venue. As all the Ants crew hang about afterwards, I was curious to know what the songs had been on the intro tape that was played before they came on. Obviously I knew the Gary Glitter track and I had heard the track 'Sanctus' from the film 'If....', but I didn't know who did it. I didn't know anything about the third track at all. Popey told me, "It's a tape the band have started using when they are about to come on, so the fans would be able to get ready in time." I now loved these tracks nearly as much as I loved the Ants songs. The intro tape was a great idea and set the scene. The track I knew nothing about was called 'De Fabriken', which translates as 'The Factory'. I was hooked. It was composed by Hans Eisler, who was a German communist at the time of Hitler in the 1930s and wrote music for the communist movement. I was taught to interpret music with my mind at school in religious education classes. The teacher would play classical music and then he would tell us to close our eyes and see what visions it would conjure up in our minds, or what emotions we felt. I still tend to listen to music in this way. 'De Fabriken' was written in 1933, at the time when there was a lot of political upheaval in Germany. The song has certain energy about it; people rushing to and from situations, or being chased. There was a sinister tone overlaying the energy of the piece, like someone is trying to evade capture - a sense of urgency maybe. Adam certainly was influenced by that turbulent part of German history. There were numerous subjects I was inspired to find out about because of my love affair with the Ants.

We're all outside, buzzing and chatting about the gig. Dunc asks me where I'm staying, which I hadn't thought about, and Spud offers to let me stay at his in Edgware. Pete Vague also says I can stop at his place in Kilburn. I say thanks to both of them, but opt for Edgware with Spud after he tells me he has some weed. I wasn't a big weed smoker, but because someone gave me some speed earlier for my birthday, and with the tons of beer I'd had, I thought the weed might make sleeping easier. I would have to sleep in Pete's mum's living room if I stopped at his, so I took Spud up on his offer instead and we shoot off to try and catch the last tube at Tottenham Court Road to get the Northern Line to Edgware. Edgware was right at the end of the line in the suburbs of leafy north London. Spud's house was just off the high street. It was situated on the end of a row of semi-detached houses, with a decent garden. The house looked quite big from the outside and Spud had to sneak me inside. He went in first to see if the coast was clear, then I ran upstairs quickly so no one saw me. I waited at the top of the stairs for Spud to follow. His room was the second left at the end of the landing. Once inside the room, it was quite compact. We lay down on the floor then Spud said, "Fancy a spliff?" "Yes, of course. You got a lot of weed then?" I asked him. "Not really. Just my own home grown plant which is quite big - really this needs to be dried out properly but I can grill it." "OK", I said. So Spud took some leaves off his plant and went downstairs. Then he came back. "You hungry?" he said. "A little", I said. Then he was gone again.

About ten minutes later he came back with some tea and snacks, plus the dried out home grown. We sat about listening to Ants tapes and talking about the gig. He duly skinned up the dry leaves from his plant, and we laid back and smoked but it wasn't very strong and kind of left us both feeling a little frustrated. Spud says, "I'm gonna dry some more leaves out. Wait here." So off he goes again downstairs. I lay on the bed looking at his Ants stuff and other punk mementos. After another ten minutes he's back. He sits down and rolls another spliff. It goes too quickly and we still feel frustrated, so we lie there for a while then Spud goes, "Fuck it. I'm doing the whole plant." So off he goes yet again downstairs to dry the weed under the grill. I just lie there listening to an old Ants tape. After a while Spud comes back in with a handful of dry leaves. He says, "Look what I found!" and from behind his back he brings out a small bottle of spirits. So we polish that off and carry on smoking. The weed has a powerful smell and we are rolling one joint after another. When I go to the toilet you can smell it on the landing. Shit", says Spud, "I'll have to open a window." Then we hear a noise from the other room. "I hope that's not my mum coming", says Spud. Nothing happens. So we just relax. Spud gives me a blanket to sleep on and after a while we're both out for the count.

In the morning I hear Spud's mum shout up. "Daniel, your breakfast is ready." I'm thinking who is Daniel? Then it dawned on me. Spud wasn't christened Spud. It must be his real name, or a brother's. Well, actually, Spud wasn't christened anyway. Spud was Jewish; not as though it mattered. I nudged him, "I think your mum's shouting for you?" No response. Spud just rolled over, groaning. After a while his mum comes and knocks on the door. "Daniel, get up." Still no reply. So she walks in then, sees me, and I can tell immediately from the look on her face that she doesn't like me. She comes over and nudges Spud, while giving me the eyes. Spud wakes up. "What's he doing here?" she says to him, like I can't answer for myself, "Get up now." Spud gets out of bed and smiles at his mum as she leaves the room. "Your mum's straight talking and straight to the point", I said. "Oh, don't mind her. She's like that with all my friends, particularly the punk ones."

We get up and go downstairs. Spud's mum gives me the daggers. She looks like she hates me. "Do you want something to eat before you go?" Spud asks me. "Yes, as long as it's OK with your mum?" I'm trying to be friendly and reassure her I'm OK, despite my appearance, which is obviously not to her liking. I'm dressed in a mixture of punk clothes with a studded nose and dyed hair. She looks round in a startled fashion, maybe it's my accent that alerts her, I don't know? Spud says, "Go in the kitchen and make some toast while I just nip upstairs", then he dashes off. I go into the kitchen followed by Spud's mum. "I'm not going to nick anything", I say. "I trust you as far as I can throw you", she says, just as Spud walks back in. He starts laughing again. "Oh, mum, stop it", he giggles. I'm sure he knew this was going to happen. I have some tea and toast and decide to leave. I've never met such a rude person but I would rather she be up front with me than pretend to like me. Spud sees me to the door and says, "I'll see you tonight at the Ants." I say "Bye" to his mum. "Don't come back again," she says. Spud laughs, "Don't worry, you can stay tonight.

She will have calmed down by then." "Do you think so? I suppose she will have made me supper as well?" I turn and walk out the door, then go down the street to catch a tube or a bus into central London. Spud's mum follows me to the door with a face that could haunt Halloween and stands there until I'm out of sight before she slams the door shut.

I find a shop for some pop and a sandwich as I'm still hungry. On the walk to the tube station I try ringing Dunc but there's no reply. I could ring Penny but it's been a while since I spoke to her. I think about it a little while longer because I'm already going through Camden, so I could get off and go to see her. I decide to ring her instead but there's no reply. I try another couple of people but there are still no replies, so I catch the train into central London and walk round Soho looking in record shops. I'm still quite tired, so I look for somewhere where I can get some sleep. I nod off for an hour on a patch of grass just off Shaftesbury Avenue, before another walk round the Soho shops. It's only early afternoon still so I make a few more phone calls but most people are still out. I'm wondering what to do with myself - maybe the King's Road or Camden, or maybe Portobello Road? I've been down the King's Road loads of times and it's the other side of London, so it's one of the others. On Portobello I can pop into Rough Trade and maybe find some bootlegs on the market.

Then it came to me. I could surprise Clapham Sarah; she works at Better Badges on Portobello. That's my afternoon sorted. I met Sarah at an Ants gigs earlier in the year and we hit it off immediately. I get off the tube at Notting Hill Gate. As you come out of the tube heading towards Shepherd's Bush, there's a road that brings you out at the top of Portobello Road. At the top end it's all antique dealers; in the middle there is a fruit and veg market. Rough Trade is about halfway down on the left hand side. I spend a while in there looking at all the new punk records on offer. It was nice to see the Ants single on the wall, along with loads of others. They had some great posters too but when I enquired if any were for sale I was told "No!" So I moved on to look at the fanzines. I could spend all day in here. It wasn't that big a shop but there was so much stuff to look at. The wall in front as you walked in was full of singles, with racks of records below. The counter was at the front and to the right. I spent a while in there but I didn't buy anything, because I didn't want to carry anything. If I bought a bootleg, it would have to be pretty special for me to carry it. I could give it to Sarah and she could post it to me, I suppose.

I left Rough Trade and walked to the end of the road, took a left under the bridge past another part of the market until I got to 286 - Better Badges. I ring the buzzer and ask for Sarah. "Hang on", says a voice. A minute later I hear Sarah's voice. "Who is it?" "It's me." Sarah recognises my northern accent. "Oh, hi! I've got a tea break in ten minutes. Can you hang on?" "Yes, I'll be in the bootleg shop across the road." "OK, I'll come and find you." I go to look at the bootlegs; there are lots, but nothing out of the ordinary. There are a few Ants cassettes but none on vinyl. I asked the shop guy why not. "There are no great recordings of the Ants, that's why. Vinyl is for quality recordings only. It's not worth doing them otherwise." I have all the Ants tapes so I don't buy any. Suddenly Sarah appears. We hug and she suggests going for a walk.

There's a park nearby beside the Westway, so we grab coffees and something to eat, and talk in there for a while. We discuss the Ants gig last night and tonight's. I really like Sarah. She sends me letters and generally keeps me in touch with what's going on. After about 30 minutes she has to go back to work, so we hug and I tell her I'll see her tonight. I head back up to Notting Hill Gate for the tube back to Oxford Street via the Central Line, and head down Regent Street, onto Carnaby Street and into Soho via Berwick Street then slowly through Wardour Street, checking out the shops on the way, as well as the scenery.

I bob into a food place to grab a bite to eat, and it's there I see Simone. "Oi, stranger!" I shout. Simone seems startled as she looks around to see who is shouting. "Oh! It's you, silly bleeder", she says. "Where were you last night at the Ants? I missed you", I said. "Oh! Thanks. I couldn't make it. Well, I could have, but I would have missed something special, and because the Ants are playing tonight as well, I just went to the other event." "But it was my birthday. I wanted you to be there", I said. Simone replied with her seductress eyes, "Well, you can have another birthday tonight and maybe I may give you a special present." Teasing again, I thought. I smiled and said "What you up to now?" "I'm running an errand for my boss. Then I've got to get changed for the gig, so I will see you later", she said. She picked up whatever it was she'd come for and squeezed past me, giving me a kiss on the cheek as she went on her way. Oh bugger, I thought, why do I like her so much? As she wanders off up the street, I watch her go off into the distance.

Next minute, Jock Strap, Irish Tom, Stan S and the Brixton punks walk in. "Hi, lads, you going to the Ants gig tonight?" I say. "Not sure yet, might go up to the Music Machine. You can bunk in over the roof there", says Tom, who is standing there wearing a pair of swimming goggles on his head. Jock gives me a gig flyer for his band, the Straps. I tell them I'll bob in if I'm around. I use the phone in the café and try calling people again to see where they are. But no one is in again, so I assume they are all on their way. I head over to the Intrepid Fox, which is situated just down the road from the Marquee on the corner of Brewer Street, and within spitting distance of the famous Soho burlesque bar Madam JoJo's.

I get talking to this skinhead outside the pub. He's telling me he's off to get a tattoo on his face of a Maori symbol. He pulls out a picture of a Maori chief with his face fully covered by a tattoo. The skinhead's pointing at the face, saying "I'm getting that bit there tattooed on my face." He tries to point to one aspect of the full face design. "OK, mate. Good luck," I say. "I've got the appointment in five minutes", he tells me. Then he says, "You're northern. Whereabouts you from?" "Bradford", I tell him. "That's full of Pakis! They're horrible bastards", he says. "No, they're not. There's good and bad in every race", I say. "I bet you can't prove it", says the skinhead. So I stand there and think about this. Can I think of any way of showing a positive light on this? Then I say, "We have Muslim punks in Bradford." "No way!" the skinhead replies, "I bet they're called punk-a-wallahs, ha ha. Do they have turbans with Sex Pistols badges on? I bet they don't wear Sham 69 badges, ha ha."

Suddenly I remember Joe, who is a Muslim but drinks alcohol and eats sneaky sausage sandwiches when no one is looking. I decide to tell the skinhead a story about Joe which I hope will make him think differently: Joe meets a young white college student and gives her his number in case she gets into any trouble. Later that day she rings Joe because she met some other young Asians who turned out to be not so nice. So Joe tells her to stay where she is until he gets there.

When he arrives he bangs on the door and the young girl comes out. These young Asian kids confront Joe. He says to them, "Meet me here tomorrow, if you want to fight." Then Joe takes the girl to safety. The next day Joe turns up with about a hundred other Asian mates and the youth didn't want to know.

In his glue haze, the skinhead says, "He doesn't sound a bad lad. Why aren't they all like him?" I'm not sure it was such a good example though, because Joe was more western in his approach to life than traditional Muslim.

Then I try the funny story about Joe in Queensbury. "All right", I say to the skinhead. "Listen to this story. We have a pool team back home which Joe plays for, and sometimes I help out when they are short. We had to go and play in this place called Queensbury, which is one of those places where if you're not a local, you're going to get trouble, whoever you are. Anyway, their local MP was National Front. A few people drop out so I offer to help. Joe's saying he's not going, but we all tell him if there's any trouble we'll back him up. So reluctantly, he says yes. We get a taxi to this pub called the Ring O' Bells and walk in. As soon as we walk through the door everyone stops doing what they're doing and stares. One guy runs out the door and you know he's going to get someone, which could spell danger. We go and get a drink and sit down. Joe prefers to stand in the doorway so he has an escape exit. Everyone is still staring at us. Then one of the locals comes over and says, "You better get out of here. They've gone for the NF." I say, "We've come to play a pool match." The local looks at Joe and says, "He does know that cue's not for swinging around?" I look him in the face and say, "Yes. He's familiar with the rules of the game and is actually our best player." The local looks shocked at this.

Suddenly the doors open with a loud bang and in walks this lad with a deathly stare. The locals' eyes start to gleam with excitement and one of them says, "Your friend might need that pool cue now to defend himself, ha ha." There's a moment's silence, like a freeze frame. Everyone waiting to see what will happen. Then this NF guy looks at Joe and says, "All right, Joe! How you doing?" Joe replies, 'Hi, matey, how's you?' The locals' faces are a picture, mouths wide open in disbelief. I smile at the first local and say, "Well, that wasn't the reaction you were looking for, ha ha!" Joe then asks the NF guy why he is here. The NF guy says, "Someone just told me there's a Paki in here." Joe says, "Really? Where?" And they both look around the room together. The rest of the team are looking on in disbelief. It's like a mad comedy; you have Joe helping the NF guy look for Joe. You couldn't make it up. I shout "Joe! He's looking for you, you daft bugger." Joe replies, "What's he looking for me for?" "Derr! I give up", I said. "Eventually everyone realised how funny it was, everyone relaxed and we had a great night. The locals loved Joe. They were inviting him round for tea and all sorts. It was one of those great nights where you learn something about people. It transpired that Joe had saved this NF guy from a kicking when he lived near Joe. But he can't have been a proper racist if he accepts Joe." The skinhead is now putting his glue bag in his pocket and getting ready for the tattooist appointment. He says, "I like your mate Joe now, and I've never met him. He sounds a right laugh." Then he says, "Right, my northern friend. Catch you later."

I watch him as he staggers down the road. I'm just sitting here waiting for someone to turn up. I go to the bar and get another drink. I'm bored now. I wait about another hour before someone appears. First through the door are Sandy and Caroline; we sit down and have a chat until others start turning up - Big PD, Joe the Collar, Godfrey, Metin, his brother Cetin, Malcolm, Lesley, Anna, Terry Bradley, the Harding brothers, Jerry. Everyone is here. Suddenly it feels like it's going to be a good night again. No Simone, though. Everyone's getting sorted for the gig. People are flashing pills about, doing lines of speed in the toilets and getting ready for the greatest punk rock show in the world - Adam and the Ants, live, across the road at the Marquee. Drinks are flying down - maybe something to do with the speed. Then the door opens. I'm expecting Simone, but Clapham Sarah walks in with her friend, Scrubber. I give Sarah a hug and say hi to Scrubber then I ask Sarah if I can stay at hers tonight. "Fine", she says. "But we're off to an all-night party after the gig."

I go outside for some fresh air. It's too packed in this pub; the smoke is so thick I can hardly breathe. I notice the skinhead I was speaking to earlier is back. "OK, mate, how you doing?" He looks up and goes, "Alright, mate." I look at his face and he appears to have half of it tattooed in that Maori design he showed me earlier. "What happened to your face? You said you were just getting one little part done." The skinhead replies, "I'm not really sure. I gave the picture to the tattooist and said I want that bit tattooed on my face. I gave him a wad of money then passed out in the chair, and when I woke up I had half my face tattooed." "Oops! Nowt you can do now", I say. "Nope", the skinhead replies. "I might have to get the other half done now." "You might be able to join the local Maori group. I have a friend Tony who is a Maori. He might be able to point you to the local London clan." The skinhead isn't impressed. "I don't like darkies of any kind." I tell him, "You almost look like two people now. You could be an advert for schizophrenia or you could be an advert for the multicultural man, two cultures living in perfect harmony in one body." "Fuck 'em! I'm English and proud. No one can take my birth right from me, tattooed face or not", he says. I didn't see the point in carrying on this discussion, so I said, "Bye."

Back in the pub I see the sight I'm looking for: Simone. She's just coming in through the other door. I dash over to her but try not to look too desperate to see her. "Oh, you made it, then." "Yes, of course. I said I would and I always keep my word", Simone replies. "Fancy a drink?" "No, it's OK. My friend is at the bar getting me one", she replies. "OK. Anything happening after the gig tonight?" I ask. "Might be", she says. "Like what?" "Not sure yet", she says. Simone seems to be acting a bit strange. She's avoiding eye contact and just not acting like her usual self. I usually get a bit of banter or flirting but nothing tonight. Her friend comes over, looking very glamorous. "Here you go, doll", says the friend. "Thanks, babe", replies Simone. She introduces me to the friend but then says to her, "Let's go sit over there", and they just walk off. There's nothing I can do. Simone is a free agent. So I just go over and talk to Dunc and the rest of the Ants crew. The other Ant ladies come over and ask what's happening with Simone, as she hasn't been in contact with them either. "I don't know and I don't care anymore", I reply. "She's too temperamental. She's fine one minute and doesn't want to know the next."

So we focus on getting in the mood for the Ants gig. I notice people are getting off their heads on whatever their preferred tipple is. There are a few skinheads outside the Marquee but they don't appear to be causing any trouble; probably just tapping 10ps or sniffing glue. There's a bit of a queue but it's not long before we are in the club. We go straight to the bar and order more drinks. Suddenly there's a bit of a disturbance outside the loos. Paul Kirby's fallen on top of a skinhead and nearly flattened him, while Steve Shaw seems to be having a row with another skinhead. Everyone gets ready to steam over, then we see Steve land a killer punch and it's over. Kirby and Steve return to the bar. Everyone is in good spirits and ready for the gig now. Not long after, the intro tape starts and we make our way in to the concert room through the narrow passage that links the two areas. The Ants kick into a classic set: 'Nietzsche Baby', 'Bathroom Function', 'Il Duce', 'You're So Physical', 'Kick', 'Cleopatra', 'Catholic Day', 'Boil in the Bagman', 'The Day I Met God',

'Never Trust A Man', 'Press Darlings', 'Fall In', 'Red Scab', 'Lady', 'Puerto Rican', 'It Doesn't Matter', 'Beat My Guest'. The Ants were pretty much like the night before: excellent.

As I'm walking out of the venue, Simone suddenly walks past me. She doesn't look at me or say anything but grabs my hand and squeezes; then in a blink of an eye she's gone. I'm too tired to wonder what all that's about so I just dismiss it for now, knowing full well it will be on my mind and come up again at some point. Right now I'm wet with sweat, tired and hungry and I'm wishing I could just beam up into my bed at home. Oh well, Spud had said I could stay with him at Edgware again, which I wasn't really looking forward to, with his mum. She made me feel uncomfortable, although Spud laughed it off, but she'd made it clear I wasn't welcome. Sarah had said I could stop at their squat, but they were going on to a party somewhere, and after two nights I'm knackered. I asked Pete Vague when he came out, but he said he was full; Tom Vague and Boxhead were stopping there. Most of the other Ant kids still lived at home so it was difficult to stay with any of them. So that was it then. I decided I would tempt fate with Spud's mum and hope for a friendlier outcome. Spud was chatting to a few people outside the venue. I shouted over to let him know I'd be back in a minute. I'm not 100% certain he heard me but he looked deep in conversation and I'd only be a couple of minutes finding something to eat, so I go off on my own and when I get back everyone has gone. There's not one person there I know. I hang around for a while to see if Spud is coming back but he doesn't, and thinking about it, he would have probably have had to rush off to get the last tube.

"Shit!" I sat on a bench for a while, wondering what to do. I decided to go down to Victoria Station. At least I'd be near to the coach station for the following morning. When I got there I sat on the benches, just watching people on their way home and wishing that was me. Then some guy came over and sat down next to me, asking me where I was from and where I was going. He looked well dodgy. He was dressed like John Travolta but was about 20 years older, and with greasy hair and puss filled boils on his face that look about to burst. Maybe they got the idea for the follow up film from this guy? Mind you, he certainly didn't look like 'Greased Lightning' to me. So when he offered me somewhere to stay, I declined. I wasn't keen on 'Saturday Night Fever' so I wasn't hanging around to wait for 'Sunday Morning Nightmare'. Anyway, I wasn't in the mood for this crap so I just told the guy to "fuck off." He took the hint. I looked around me. The place was full of drunks and perverts on the lookout for young lads or lasses with nowhere to stay. I decided to head up to the car park next to the coach station. As I was walking, I started to think about all the times I'd been hanging round train stations in London, realising what a well dodgy place it was to be, for a young punk.

I remembered one Ants' trip. It was later on, in Victoria station, when Scotland were playing in London. All these Scots were off their heads, attacking anyone in sight who didn't look Scottish. They saw me and headed straight for me. I thought my tartan Seditionaries bondage trousers might save me but no. Maybe the Scots were affronted by the zips and a strap attached to the tartan? There wasn't a lot this young whippersnapper could do against those odds so I ran into the guard's office. I was getting the impression Scotland had lost. The guard told me to get out. "No way", I said. As he tried to force me out, all these drunken Scots started hammering on the door. "Come out, ye English bastards." The guard bolted the door and rang the police, and we hid behind his desk until the police arrived. We had to hide for about an hour before they turned up. When the guard asked the police what took them so long, they told us, "It's kicking off all over the city tonight." Ah, those were the days, I thought. When I got to the car park next to the coach station, I just lay down in a corner. I was so tired I fell asleep, despite the cold. The next day I had never wanted a coach to turn up so much. I had a wash in the toilets, and just enough money for something to eat. As soon as the coach came I dived onto the back seat, dreaming of 'Home Sweet Home'. When I finally did get home, I was still so tired that I just carried on sleeping.

Next Ants gig for us was the Rainbow on December 20. I travelled down to London with OC, Mel and Brinsley in Mel's car, but it never happened. We got there and the gig was cancelled, so we hung around for a bit. Then Jock McDonald, the promoter, started a protest march. No one had even explained why the gig had been cancelled. It was a total washout. Adam marched with the punks as well. We marched for a while too but then got bored. We ended up with some of the Ants crew and just went for a few beers. We bumped into some punks from Middlesboro who I'd first met in 1977 in Leeds when they were following 999 on tour. They now lived in Herne Hill near Brixton and they let us crash at their house. The day after, feeling really hungover, we just headed straight back to Bradford.

My friend Chris came back to Bradford from Bournemouth for Christmas, so I went round to his house to see him. It was great that he was back. We sat around with his mum and dad and watched films and chatted. I had known Chris and his family for years. When we were younger we used to go down the market where Chris's dad Albert had a unit. As kids we could earn £5, which was a lot of money for a Saturday morning's work; which was basically just riding around in the lorries. They had a good lifestyle. His dad owned a plane at one point. His dad was a character. He was obsessed with the American west; most of their holidays were spent there. His dad would get dressed up like John Wayne in full cowboy gear, complete with guns in holsters and a rifle over his shoulder - just to go to his local pub, the Black Bull, at the top of Canterbury Avenue. His dad belonged to some Wild West appreciation society. Anyway, after watching a film and having tea, we were bored and had nothing to do, so Albert suggested we go with him to the King's Arms on Halifax Road for his local gathering of western freaks. So we did.

We got to the pub. Everything was western themed. The bands played country and everyone was dressed up as cowboys, except for one guy who was dressed up as an Indian. We were dressed in our usual punk gear. The entire pub just stared at us and sniggered. It didn't bother Chris and me, we were used to it. Albert, Chris's dad, seemed to enjoy the comments. After a few beers this one guy dressed as an Indian came over and asked sarcastically, "What tribe are you?" and looked around for approval from his cowboy mates. I said, "When are you going to stop doing the white man's work for him?" He just stood there with a bemused look on his face. These guys were all friends with Albert and we're starting to take the piss a bit. One of them says to us, "Look at the state of you two. You look a right pair of idiots." Followed by a group snigger. I could be a right cocky bleeder at times so I replied, "We're 18 years old and we're acting our age. But we're clearly more mature than you lot because we grew out of cowboys and Indians at ten years old, so what's your excuse?" This didn't go down well at all. The atmosphere changed dramatically. Albert wasn't pleased either. It seemed they didn't like us young folk answering back and things started to get a little heated. There were now about ten of these head honchos gathered around, staring at me and Chris. Suddenly I said to them, "How comes there's only one Indian, are you all racist?" which didn't help the situation. We didn't really want to cause any problems, especially for Albert, so Chris and I decided to get a taxi into town to see what was happening there and leave the cowboys and Indian to have fun.

With it being Christmas, and so few gigs on tonight, we end up in the Mannville for a few beers, being entertained by the regular eccentrics; Granville, who is touting to clean drains for a couple of pints of cider, and the old guy in the corner whose party trick was to strike matches and put them in his mouth, then when you'd forgotten about them, he would pull them back out of his mouth again. Pissed-up Pete is well pissed up. He's lying half asleep in his seat, dressed in his grey army coat, with his puppy dog sticking out of the top of the coat. The dog appears to be munching on something attached to Pete's beard, which looks alive, with all the stuff clinging to it. Anyway it was pretty quiet tonight. The Mannville was our spiritual home and Roy, the landlord, let us put our own songs on the jukebox, so we banged a few coins in and listened to some punk rock classics from the Pistols, the Damned, the Clash City Rotters and some of the more obscure punk records; the Rings 'I Wanna Be', the Snivelling Shits 'Terminal Stupid', Alberto Y Lost Trios Paranoias 'Snuff Rock' EP, X-Ray Spex 'Oh Bondage Up Yours', Penetration 'Don't Dictate'.

Suddenly I look towards the pub's bow window in front of us. You could see pairs of eyes looking in. There were always a lot of underage punks hanging around outside, trying to get a piece of the action. It was OK in the summer because we would always be outside, but in winter when it was cold we preferred to be tucked up in the warmth inside. After a couple more beers we eventually got a taxi home and crashed out. I can't wait for the New Year. The Ants recently announced the dates for their first UK tour starting in Leeds on January 11; then the next day our home city of Bradford. We were all looking forward to going to as many dates as possible. It was nice to see the Ants were playing York Pop Club as they'd played there just recently and I couldn't go, which was typical - first gig near us and I hadn't been able to make it. Mel, Brinsley and OC had gone and said it was a good night. Some of the London lot came up and the Boro crew came down.

END OF PART ONE

Part one is the dark beginnings of Adam and the Ants where the band slowly built up a decent size following among punk rocks Street urchins. Where Adam can formulate his ideas. See what works and what doesn't. Also it gives him time and space to see see what he canget away with lyrically.

Throughout this time the band slowly build up a loyal band of dedicated followers from among the punk rocking street urchins. These kids would follow the band whether ever they played.
In these early days it was mainly the dodgy pubs and clubs of London town .However they were never far from danger of marauding skinheads of other groups of young teenagers out to have a pop at them However No one going to stop them follow the band.
All the time The band are steadily getting themselves ready to reveal them selves to the world. Meet Jordan the band, Johnny Rotten and a host of other punk rock stars.

Part 2 of the book (coming soon) Adam and the Ants are now ready to bring Antmusic for a future age and unleash it on the UK
Is the world ready for Antmusic?
Follow the Ants and their merry band of dedicated followers around the towns and cities of the UK and see what mischief they get up too, Who will be waiting for the band and their followers in these towns and cities around Britain's many hamlets. You've heard of Sex, Drugs and Rock N Roll well here it all is live on tour coming to a venue near you. Meet The beautiful Ant Ladies and their leather clad soldier Ants along with Adam and his band.
As they party and fight their way across the UK pursued by Rampaging Skinheads, Teds, Bikers and a whole host of other teenage groups out to stop them following the band they love.
Put your life in their hands and follow the Ants on the Ants invasion of the UK